£9.50 £12.50

OXFORD MEDIEVAL TEXTS

General Editors

V. H. GALBRAITH R. A. B. MYNORS

C. N. L. BROOKE

THE CHRONICLE OF
THE ELECTION OF HUGH

ABBOT OF BURY ST. EDMUNDS
AND LATER BISHOP OF ELY

St. Edmund in Glory
Pierpont Morgan Library MS. 736 f. 22^v
(See below, pp. xvii, xlii–xliv, 4 n. 2, 123 n. 4.)

THE CHRONICLE OF
THE ELECTION OF HUGH
ABBOT OF BURY ST. EDMUNDS
AND LATER BISHOP OF ELY

EDITED AND TRANSLATED

BY

R. M. THOMSON

OXFORD
AT THE CLARENDON PRESS
1974

Oxford University Press, Ely House, London W. 1

GLASGOW NEW YORK TORONTO MELBOURNE WELLINGTON
CAPE TOWN IBADAN NAIROBI DAR ES SALAAM LUSAKA ADDIS ABABA
DELHI BOMBAY CALCUTTA MADRAS KARACHI LAHORE DACCA
KUALA LUMPUR SINGAPORE HONG KONG TOKYO

*Printed in Great Britain
at the University Press, Oxford
by Vivian Ridler
Printer to the University*

TO
MARION GIBBS

PREFACE

THE present work grew from an M.A. thesis, University of Melbourne, consisting of a translation and introductory study only. It was Miss Marion Gibbs, sometime Reader in History of that University, who suggested the project, partly because she felt that the chronicle had been unduly neglected. To Miss Gibbs therefore I owe the original inspiration behind this book and much wise guidance since. Thanks are also due to my former colleagues in the Department of History, Sydney University, especially Dr. J. O. Ward, for stimulating criticism and helpful suggestions. Professor C. N. L. Brooke kindly accepted my early drafts as the basis for publication, and is responsible for countless corrections and improvements. If ever I thought the task of general editor a light one, he has disabused my mind. To my wife I owe gratitude for many stylistic improvements and invaluable help in the onerous tasks of proof-reading and indexing.

RODNEY THOMSON

Melbourne, 1973

CONTENTS

ABBREVIATED REFERENCES

Bury Chronicle	*The Chronicle of Bury St. Edmunds, 1212–1301*, ed. and trans. A. Gransden (Nelson's Medieval Texts, London, 1964).
Cheney, *Letters*	*The Letters of Pope Innocent III (1198–1216) concerning England and Wales*, ed. C. R. and Mary G. Cheney (Oxford, 1967).
Corpus Iuris Canonici	*Corpus Iuris Canonici*, ed. E. L. Richter and E. A. Friedberg, 2 vols. (Leipzig, 1878–81).
Councils	*Councils and Synods, II, i, 1205–1265*, ed. F. M. Powicke and C. R. Cheney (Oxford, 1964).
Curia Regis Rolls	*Curia Regis Rolls* (Temp. Ric. I–1230), Public Record Office Texts and Calendars, 13 vols., 1922–59 (in progress).
Ducange	*Glossarium Mediae et Infimae Latinitatis*, ed. C. du F. Ducange, 8 vols. (Paris, 1840).
EHR	*English Historical Review*.
Gibbs, *Bishops*	M. Gibbs and J. Lang, *Bishops and Reform, 1215–1272* (London, 1934).
Itinerary	See below, under *Rot. Litt. Pat.*
James, *On the Abbey*	M. R. James, *On the Abbey of St. Edmund at Bury*, Cambridge Antiqu. Soc., Octavo publs., xxviii (1895).
JB	*The Chronicle of Jocelin of Brakelond*, ed. and trans. H. E. Butler (Nelson's Medieval Texts, London, 1949).
Kalendar	*The Kalendar of Abbot Samson*, ed. R. H. C. Davis, Camden third ser., lxxxiv (1954).
Lanfranc, *Constitutions*	*The Monastic Constitutions of Lanfranc*, ed. and trans. D. Knowles (Nelson's Medieval Texts, London, 1951).
Latham, *Word-List*	R. E. Latham, *Revised Medieval Latin Word-List* (London, 1965).
Magna Carta	J. C. Holt, *Magna Carta* (Cambridge, 1965).
Major, *Acta*	*Acta Stephani Langton*, ed. K. Major, Canterbury and York Soc., 50 (1950).
Mem. i–iii	*Memorials of St. Edmunds Abbey*, ed. T. Arnold, Rolls Series, 3 vols. (London, 1890–96).

MGH	*Monumenta Germaniae Historica.*
MO	D. Knowles, *The Monastic Order in England* (Cambridge, 2nd edn., 1963).
Monasticon	*Monasticon Anglicanum,* W. Dugdale, ed. J. Caley, H. Ellis and B. Bandinel, 8 vols. (London, 1817–30).
Painter	S. Painter, *The Reign of John* (Baltimore, 1949).
PL	*Patrologiae Cursus Completus, Series Latina,* ed. J. P. Migne, 221 vols. (Paris, 1844–64).
PRS	*Pipe Roll Society.*
PUE	*Papsturkunden in England,* ed. W. Holtzmann, 3 vols. (Berlin and Göttingen, 1930–52).
Reg. Ben.	*Regula S. Benedicti.*
RHS	*Royal Historical Society.*
Rot. Litt. Claus.	*Rotuli Litterarum Clausarum . . . ,* ed. T. D. Hardy, 2 vols. (Record Commission, London, 1833–4), i.
Rot. Litt. Pat.	*Rotuli Litterarum Patentium . . . ,* ed. T. D. Hardy (Record Commission, London, 1835), I, i. (Also contains the *Itinerary* of King John, unpaginated.)
RS	*Rolls Series.*
Sayers, *Judges Delegate*	J. E. Sayers, *Papal Judges Delegate in the Province of Canterbury, 1198–1254* (Oxford, 1971).
VCH	*Victoria History of the Counties of England.*
Walther	*Lateinischen Sprichwörter und Sentenzen des Mittelalters,* ed. H. Walther, 6 vols. (Göttingen, 1963–70).
Whileblood	S. Whileblood, 'Anglo-Papal Relations, 1213–16', unpubl. M.A. diss., Manchester University (1947).
Whittingham	A. B. Whittingham, 'Bury St. Edmunds Abbey; the Plan, Design and Development of the Church and Monastic Buildings', *Archaeological Journal,* cviii (1951), 168–87.

INTRODUCTION

When Roger Wendover, in the late 1220s, inaugurated the historiographical tradition which was to distinguish St. Albans among English abbeys for the next three hundred years, the Benedictine house at Bury St. Edmunds, Suffolk, was already without peer in this field. Leaving out of consideration locally produced hagiographical works such as Hermann's *De Miraculis S. Edmundi* (written *c.* 1100), in which copious historical material is included, by the end of the twelfth century Bury could boast a fine set of Annals from Creation (probably compiled after 1215),[1] a copy of 'Florence' of Worcester interpolated with local and other notices (*c.* 1135),[2] and Jocelin's well-known biography of Abbot Samson, worked up during the period 1182–1203, with further additions.[3] The *Relatio de Pace Veneta*, a vivid eyewitness account of the 1177 negotiations between Frederick Barbarossa and Pope Alexander III, copied into a locally written book in an early-thirteenth-century hand, is doubtless the work of a Bury monk, although this has not hitherto been recognized.[4] Even the chronicle

---

[1] Hermann's work is edited in *Mem.* i. 26–103, and by F. Liebermann, *Ungedruckte Anglo-Normannische Geschichtsquellen* (Strassburg, 1879), pp. 203–81; the Annals in *Mem.* ii. 1–28 and Liebermann, pp. 97–155. The entry recording Abbot Hugh's profession as a Bury monk in 1202 (*Mem.* ii. 10) indicates that the Annals continued into his reign, although they end imperfectly in the year 1212 in the only surviving MS.

[2] Oxford Bodleian Library MS. Bodl. 297, from which Arnold printed the interpolations relating to local events, in *Mem.* i. 340–56. These, however, are not the only locally made interpolations; the whole MS. deserves careful study.

[3] 1203 is the latest date in *JB*; my own researches into its text suggest that Jocelin wrote it in several stages over the period mentioned above, every now and then revising and polishing the whole. An appendix was added by William of Diss (*JB*, pp. 138–9), and the story of Henry of Essex, which has no stylistic affinity with the rest of the work, is undoubtedly another interpolation, *pace* Davis (*Kalendar*, p. liv).

[4] B. M. MS. Royal 6 C. ii, f. 188 ᵣ⁻ᵛ; edited by W. Arndt (*MGH, Scriptores*, xix. 461–3) and (much better) by U. Balzani, in *Bullettino dell'Istituto storico italiano*, x (1890), 7–16. The MS. was written in the Bury scriptorium *c.* 1100, and was still there in the late fourteenth century; the addition of the *Relatio*, in an early thirteenth-century hand, was therefore certainly made locally, and the text is either the author's autograph or very near it.

found at St. Neots by the sixteenth century was a product of the
Bury scriptorium in the first quarter of the twelfth, and was in use
there for a time.[1] No twelfth-century St. Albans chronicle survives;
the only evidence for historical writing there at so early a period is
provided by extracts from two *rotuli* preserved in Matthew Paris's
Gesta Abbatum, one by Adam the cellarer (*fl. c.* 1150), the other
anonymous.[2] True, by 1300 the score was different; St. Albans
now far surpassed its nearest rival in the sheer volume and con-
tinuity of its historiography, which embraced impressively large
tracts of domestic and general history. The composite chronicle
produced at Bury during the thirteenth century, although valuable,
was designed as a continuation of the *Annales*, not as a connected
narrative with the amplitude of Paris's major works.[3] The Bury
historians, however, ventured into a field upon which St. Albans
offered no challenge, and in which they achieved a lasting notoriety
unapproached, perhaps, by any other English house. This domain
was the short monograph devoted to the study of one particular
figure or event, as exemplified by the *Relatio*, by Jocelin's famous
Chronicle and its successor, the narrative of the election of Abbot
Hugh II (1215–29), known as the *Electio Hugonis*.

The *Electio* covers the years 1212 to 1215, that is, from the
death of Abbot Samson until the final installation of his successor,
after a lengthy dispute whose course and character form the
writer's principal interest.[4] It is important on several counts:
firstly, as the earliest substantially documented description of an
English monastic election dispute, dating from the time when such

[1] W. H. Stevenson, *Asser's Life of King Alfred* (new edn., revised by D.
Whitelock, Oxford, 1959), pp. cxli n. 3, 101.
[2] R. Vaughan, *Matthew Paris* (Cambridge, 1958), pp. 182–5; but see p. 23
for a possible 'St. Albans Compilation' used by Wendover.
[3] *Bury Chronicle*, pp. xviii–xxix.
[4] Perhaps due in part to Thomas Arnold's disparaging remarks in the introduction to his edition, the *Electio* has received only superficial scholarly attention.
It has either been briefly cited as a typical example of such an election dispute,
or mined for facts and figures of only incidental relevance to its main theme.
Miss Gibbs (Gibbs, *Bishops*, pp. 9–10) used it for an assessment of Hugh of
Northwold prior to his election as bishop of Ely, with which period of his life
she is mainly concerned. D. Knowles refers to it in passing in *MO*, pp. 400,
469, 713, and at more length, although still only hinting at its interest, in his
article 'Abbatial Elections', *Downside Review*, xlix (1931), 271–2. J. C. Holt, in
several of his Magna Carta studies, most recently in *Magna Carta*, pp. 138,
154–5, has drawn on it for information about events immediately preceding
Runnymede. Dr. A. Gransden, in her forthcoming book on English medieval
chronicles, will discuss the *Electio* in the context of Bury historiography.

conflicts are of maximum interest for the historian. Secondly, King John's refusal to confirm the election, which had been made without reference to his wishes, divided the Bury monks into two factions, one advocating the maintenance, the other the abandonment of the election as made. From the details of the parties' composition supplied by the chronicler, an analysis of the monks' motives can be made which is of more than local interest. This is because the St. Edmunds dispute impinged upon the larger conflicts of King John with the pope and later with his barons, similarly over the issue of liberties. From the first of these larger disputes resulted the decree permitting 'free' ecclesiastical elections, accepted by the king only a few days after his fruitless attempt to overawe Hugh's supporters. The second culminated in Magna Carta, the drafting of which followed hard on John's reconciliation with the abbot elect of St. Edmunds upon the field of Runnymede.

1. *Date and Authorship*

A reading of the *Electio* leaves no doubt that the writer was a Bury monk and a participant in the affairs of 1213–15. Four times in the course of his work he touches on his own involvement in the dispute,[1] and in spite of the large number of documents which he quotes, most of his account seems based on direct, personal observation.[2] Twice he mentions the purpose of his work, which was to instruct later generations of monks to avoid the position adopted by Hugh's opponents.[3] This means that the tract can have been conceived only after July 1215, when the victory of Hugh and his party was assured by the granting of the royal assent. Equally, it cannot have been written after June 1229, when Hugh was consecrated bishop of Ely, for it concludes with a prayer that the abbot may continue to favour those who had supported his election, by promoting them to obedientiary positions—'for the labourer is worthy of his hire'.[4] The author's intention, and the

[1] See below, pp. 47, 49, 61, 173.

[2] J. C. Holt (*The Northerners*, Oxford, 1961, pp. 102, 103 n. 9) seems to suggest that while the *Electio* is based on a contemporary account, it was first written down in its present form about the middle of the century. He gives no evidence for this; as demonstrated below, the earlier and only complete MS. (H) is clearly a copy, perhaps at one or more removes from the autograph.

[3] See below, pp. 55, 57.   [4] Below, p. 173.

heated tone and circumstantial detail of his work suggest a date
early in this period. Although his frank condemnation of those who
opposed the election must have embarrassed and annoyed the
monks who had adopted that stance, the author would naturally
have enjoyed the protection of the new abbot. However, the two
principal leaders of the opposition to Hugh, Robert of Graveley
the sacrist, and Richard the precentor, are so vilified by the writer
that he must surely have composed his chronicle after they had
left the abbey. Robert became abbot of Thorney late in 1217,[1]
while Richard, if, as seems certain, he is Richard de L'isle,[2] was
made abbot of Burton in 1222.[3] There are several other pointers
towards a date about this time or shortly after for the composition
of the work. By then many of the senior men who had opposed the
election would be dead. Moreover, in 1220 Richard of Newport
was promoted from the subsacristy to the sacristy.[4] The fact that
the writer refers to him at one point as being *tunc subsacrista*
suggests that he was writing after this date.[5] An error in the text
points in the same direction: 'R.' earl of Winchester refers to
Roger de Quency in error for his father, Saer, who died in 1222.[6]
This seems more likely to have been a slip of the author's memory
rather than a scribal mistake, and it becomes understandable if the
writer was working, say, a few years after 1222. Whatever preparations he made, therefore, between 1215 and 1222, we may assign
most of the author's work on the *Electio* to the years 1222-9.

Who was the author? Not only can it be stated with conviction
that he was a Bury monk and a participant in the dispute which he
chronicled, but he was very clearly a supporter of Hugh's election.
Since a complete list of the St. Edmunds monks, divided according
to their stand on the election issue, can be constructed from the
Electio, the field of inquiry is narrowed to some 36 individuals.[7]
R. H. C. Davis, in the introduction to his edition of Abbot
Samson's *Kalendar*, suggested his identification with Jocelin of
Brakelond, author of the famous *Cronica de Rebus Gestis Samsonis
Abbatis*,[8] John Bale having stated this categorically long before.[9]

[1] *Rot. Litt. Claus.*, p. 347.   [2] See Appendix III, p. 185.
[3] *Annales Monastici, RS*, i. 225.   [4] *Bury Chronicle*, p. 4.
[5] See below, p. 90.   [6] Below, p. 82.
[7] See Appendix III, pp. 186-8.
[8] *Kalendar*, p. lvii.
[9] J. Bale, *Illustrium Majoris Britanniae Scriptorum Summarium* (Basel, 1559),
pp. 259-60.

Two men named Jocelin figure in the 1213–15 election dispute; one, the almoner, supported the sacrist; the other, Jocelin of the Altar, *quondam celerarius*,[1] was a prominent member of Hugh's defence. Davis was able to show, using Abbot Samson's charters, that Jocelin of Brakelond was cellarer 1198–*c*. 1200, and that he is consequently to be identified with Jocelin of the Altar, supporter of Hugh.[2] However, although Jocelin of Brakelond was a defender of Hugh's election, he was not the author of the *Electio*; so much is plainly demonstrated by a stylistic comparison of the *Electio* with Jocelin's *Cronica*. The differences in vocabulary and construction are obvious, and need not be laboured here; a comparison of the range and method of quotation and adaptation in the two works will serve to illustrate the wider differences. Thus Jocelin quotes from classical *auctores* some 26 times, including two repetitions. All of them, with the exception of one or two school-texts such as Seneca and Cato Minor, are well-known *Sprichwörter*, suggesting wholesale employment of a *florilegium*.[3] The Bible is quoted 73 times, and Gratian's *Decretum* mentioned twice. Of this last Jocelin might have had first-hand knowledge, since there was a copy in the abbey library at the time.[4]

The author of the *Electio* commands only half a dozen classical tags (they can hardly be dignified with the title of quotation), but he quotes the Bible more than 100 times, drawing on most of the books of the Old and New Testaments, as well as the Apocrypha. He refers several times to the Rule of St. Benedict, to the Code of Justinian at least once, and seems acquainted with works of Peter the Chanter, Hildegard of Bingen, and others. There is much in his latinity, apart from the occasional direct quotation, which suggests close familiarity with local hagiography, represented by the works of Abbo of Fleury, Hermann, and the anonymous author of a 'Life of St. Edmund' in N.Y. Pierpont Morgan MS. 736. Just as sharply differentiated are the actual methods of quotation adopted in each chronicle. Jocelin's citations are accurate and can mostly be set between quotation marks. The author of the *Electio*, on the contrary, often misquotes, and usually adapts his source somewhat, probably relying more on memory than Jocelin.

[1] See below, p. 8.
[2] *Kalendar*, pp. li–vii; cf. *Mem.* ii. xi–xii.
[3] They are nearly all found in Walther.
[4] James, *On the Abbey*, p. 30, item 171. I notice that D. Knowles (*MO*, p. 507 n. 2) thinks the *Electio* 'certainly not written by Jocelin', without elaborating.

Extension of this comparative method to other stylistic features of
the two works yields essentially the same results, indicating the
workings of two quite distinct personalities.

The process of elimination may be carried further; Hugh of
Northwold can hardly have been the author, and William of Diss
was responsible for an addition to Jocelin's Chronicle which has
little in common, stylistically, with the *Electio*.[1] When, on some
members of the convent undertaking a journey, the writer describes
in detail, not their travels, but events at the house during their
absence, it can surely be inferred that he himself did not accompany
them. This would eliminate John of Lavenham, Master Thomas
of Walsingham, Simon of Walsingham, and Richard of Hingham.[2]
Again, as the author would be unlikely to record anything which
reflected unfavourably on himself, some more of Hugh's supporters
may be struck from the list: Robert the chamberlain, Richard of
Saxham, and Peter the cellarer, all the recipients of implied
criticism at the writer's hand.[3] Finally, the writer clearly dissociates
himself from Hugh of Thetford.[4] The field is now narrowed to
twenty-six.

But there is positive evidence as well. The *Electio*, like Jocelin's
Chronicle, shows a special interest in affairs involving the cellary.
Up to a point this is not surprising since, as will be shown later,
Hugh's defenders included many office-holders in that department.
However, the account of Richard of Saxham's deposition from the
position of subcellarer, the details of Hugh's reorganization of the
cellary manors in 1215, and other remarks made in passing, have
no special relevance to the author's main theme.[5] Their presence is
best explained by assuming that the writer himself held office in
the cellary at some stage of his career. We must therefore pay
particular attention to members of Hugh's party with this
qualification.

The author of the *Electio* often derides the leaders of the opposing faction for their lack of education, particularly in the fields of
law and theology.[6] Thus Richard the precentor is ridiculed for
seeming to say 'I have not been to Babylon [instead of Bologna],

[1] *JB*, pp. 138–9.   [2] See below, pp. 15, 37.
[3] Below, pp. 5, 65, 73.   [4] Below, p. 61.
[5] Below, pp. 29, 51–3, 63–5, 71–3, 165–7.
[6] Below, pp. 29, 57–9, 81. In contrast to Jocelin, who, also a member of the
educated party in the cloister, defines his position in terms of 'literate' as opposed
to 'illiterate', with special reference to the study of dialectic (*JB*, pp. 11–14).

and I am no expert in civil law',[1] and the sacrist is put on record as
having been corrected by the prior of Dunstable, a learned jurist,
for saying *canone* instead of *iure*, that is, for referring to a set of
specific canon law articles instead of law in general.[2] Noteworthy
also is the quotation from the *Digest*, especially as the writer could
just as easily have quoted canon law on the point in question.[3]

His trenchant criticism of the sacrist's Easter sermon reveals
the writer's interest in and knowledge of theology. Three errors
are singled out for ridicule. The first involved a simple ignorance
of the Bible; the sacrist said that Christ raised the centurion's
servant from the dead, when in fact He only healed his sickness.[4]
The second error, that Christ took His title from His anointing
(chrism), is, in fact, backed by good patristic authority, and was
taught by the Lombard.[5] The writer's position, on the other hand,
that 'chrism', like 'Christian', takes its name from 'Christ', since
the creature is named after the Creator, not vice versa, seems to
have no such authority. Perhaps the author is wrong, but since
he develops this doctrine at length, and with some cogency, it may
be that it was discussed in the Schools at the time. The final error
made by the sacrist, that Lazarus stank because he had died in
mortal sin, was a gross confusion of the literal and spiritual senses
of the story as interpreted by the Fathers and contemporary
exegetes.[6] The writer's contrasting of *ratio* and *voluntas*,[7] his
statement that 'contraries are often opposed for greater efficacy',[8]
his large number of biblical references, and his acquaintance
with various continental theologians (as well as patristic writers),
all suggest a special interest in preaching, and contact with
academic theology and biblical exegesis.

The chances are, therefore, that the writer had pursued higher
education on the Continent, most likely at Paris, perhaps even at
Bologna, and that he was one of the *magistri* in the cloister. All six
of the *magistri* mentioned in the *Electio* were supporters of Hugh's
election. Master Thomas of Walsingham has already been ruled
out, and the field can be narrowed still further. There are five
occasions in the *Electio* when events outside the house are recorded in such detail that we can confidently suppose the author to
have been present. These are the appeal before the archbishop;

[1] See below, p. 29.   [2] Below, p. 81.   [3] Below, p. 46.
[4] Below, p. 57.   [5] Below, pp. 57-9.   [6] Below, p. 59.
[7] Below, p. 24 n. 3.   [8] Below, p. 57.

the meeting between Hugh and the king outside London; the one sitting of the inquiry at a place other than Bury, in describing which the writer is not merely quoting the records; and, finally and most convincingly, in the king's presence at Nottingham, Oxford, and Runnymede.[1]

There was, in fact, one monk present on all these occasions who satisfies the other criteria for authorship as well—Master Nicholas of Dunstable. Master Nicholas first appears as a Bury monk in a charter of Abbot Samson dated by Davis to 1200–11, most probably towards the end of that period.[2] For a time during 1213 he was prior's chaplain, between 1215 and 1220 he was infirmarer and before 1220 cellarer.[3] He may also have been abbot's chaplain for an indeterminate period after 1222, but this is unlikely.[4] Evidently a forceful personality, he was a persistent opponent of the sacrist's candidature, the spearhead of Hugh's defence, the advocate of the abbot-elect's party before the legate, and their leading proctor in the inquiry of the judges delegate.[5] Furthermore, there is some evidence that he had received formal legal training. While the legate was at Bury,

> Master Nicholas stood up and described ... in most eloquent language how they had carried out the election and appeal, and he proved that the precentor had no more right than anyone else to first voice on any matter or in any place except within the church. [Then] the precentor rose in their midst and said: 'Lord legate, I have not been to Bologna, and I am no expert in civil law.'[6]

The precentor's petulant outburst is surely unaccountable unless Master Nicholas had actually been to Bologna. Master Nicholas's speeches, moreover, which are quoted more frequently, extensively, and approvingly than anyone else's, are nearly all based to some extent on juristic arguments.[7] As an educated man, therefore, trained in law, a relative newcomer to the abbey, probably not past his prime, as the leader of Hugh's defence and an office-holder in the cellary, he seems the most likely choice as writer of the *Electio*. The personal enmity between Master Nicholas and

[1] Below, pp. 93–9, 163, 165, 169–73.
[2] *Kalendar*, p. 154, no. 135. A comparison with the witness-lists of those other charters dated by Davis 1200–11 suggests that this one must be at least post-1206.   [3] See below, pp. 13, 141, and Appendix III, p. 187.
[4] Appendix III, p. 187.
[5] See below, pp. 7–9, 29, 43–5, 49, 91, 99–100, 135–7 143–5.
[6] Below, p. 29.   [7] Below, pp. 29, 43–5, 49, 93, 135–7, 143–5.

Robert of Graveley which the chronicle illustrates time and again, and the role of master-villain cast for the sacrist by its author, point to the same conclusion.[1] Finally, after his promotion to the office of cellarer (no doubt as a reward for his earlier support of Hugh's election) Nicholas was in an excellent position to write the *Electio* unhindered, firstly because of the close association with the abbot which he would now enjoy, and secondly because he now outranked the rest of the convent except for the prior and sacrist. At all events, the fact that the abbey at this period was not dependent on Jocelin alone for its literary output, however modest, is evidence of its standing as a community capable of attracting men of culture and higher education.

II. *Purpose and Accuracy of the Account*

Both the *Electio* and Jocelin's *Cronica* are related to a genre of quasi-historical literature common among English religious communities from the eleventh century on: the literature of precedent and privilege. It owed its origin to the necessity of defending the rights and privileges originally conferred by the kings and now being augmented by the papacy, against the royal and baronial powers, aided by the creative, humanistic urge towards historical writing which was a feature of the 'twelfth century renaissance'. Its source was the charters and documents bestowing or confirming grants of privilege or possession, and its purpose was both legal and propagandist; to record for posterity established rights so as to prevent their erosion and loss, and to create precedents, often in the face of opposition, for the exercise of new ones.[2] Election-literature as a subdivision of this class appears at the beginning of the thirteenth century, as a result of the increasingly sophisticated deployment of canon law in the struggle between the royal and sacerdotal powers for control of ecclesiastical elections. Specifically, the 1215 Lateran Council's decree on elections may be seen as an important stimulus to the writing of such literature, of which Bury furnishes, besides the *Electio*, two later examples.[3] On the other

---

[1] Below, pp. 7–9, 101
[2] For an earlier example of this motive at work, cf. Eadmer, *Historia Novorum*, *RS*, pp. 1–2.
[3] The *Electio Symonis* (1257) and *Electio Thomae* (1302); see Appendix II pp. 182–3.

hand, the combined evidence of the *Electio* manuscripts, considered below, suggests that election-documents were being carefully filed before that date. In embryo, an election-tract was no more than a collection of such records, like the one covering the accession of Richard de L'isle, Hugh's successor.[1] The next step was to intersperse the documents with brief segments of narrative, sufficient to establish their chronological sequence and causal relationship. If the election had proceeded smoothly, as with the two later Bury examples, then the tract remained at this level, its modest purpose being solely to exemplify the legality of the procedure. The *raison d'être* of the *Electio* is rather different, largely because of the dispute involved. Thus it is unusually long and detailed, fully meriting the title of 'chronicle', since narrative, including such informal devices as direct speech, preponderates over documentation. In contrast to the two later Bury tracts, not all of the documents in the case are quoted. Instead they are carefully selected from a pre-existing collection to illustrate the writer's point of view. For the *Electio* is not merely a legal exemplification; it is an *ex parte*, moralistic statement justifying and commending Hugh and his party and denigrating his opponents.

Jocelin's *Cronica* is not an election-tract, and is only at points related to the wider class of records exemplifying and polemics defending monastic privilege. It does contain a very full, although undocumented account of Abbot Samson's election,[2] and much material relating to the rights and customs of the abbey and its offices, especially the cellary.[3] Primarily, however, it is devoted to a masterly portrayal of a remarkable abbot over nearly twenty years of his life, and the choice of material for inclusion in it was largely determined by its relevance to this theme. In the *Electio* the reverse is true. Hugh of Northwold and Robert of Graveley never come alive because they are only seen as embodiments of abstract principles, the abbot of those conventional virtues traditionally associated with the defender of the Church's liberties, his opponent of the unrighteousness of the oath-breaker, and assailant of monastic privilege. In a word, Jocelin's *Cronica* is biography, the *Electio Hugonis* apologia.[4]

---

[1] B.M. MS. Royal 7 C. iv, f. 2, previously a blank leaf; there are four letters in all, unprinted.

[2] *JB*, pp. 16–25.   [3] Ibid., pp. 118–20, 132–7, etc.

[4] Other monastic chronicles of the time contain election accounts as well as

It would be surprising if Jocelin and his *Cronica* had not had some impact on the form and style of the *Electio*, even though this is not susceptible of proof. Nicholas, although displaying greater learning, does not compare with Jocelin as a writer of lucid, colloquial prose. None the less, in occasional, untypical moments of racy narrative and colourful direct speech he forcibly recalls two outstanding features of the *Cronica*.[1] Both writers seize with enthusiasm upon the memorable, aphoristic utterance.[2] Both works show a particular interest in the office of the cellary, and Nicholas's account of Richard of Saxham's demotion from the subcellary (an incident only distantly relevant to his main theme) bears an obvious resemblance to Jocelin's autobiographical description of 'Jocellus's' dismissal from the same office.[3]

By reason of its purpose the *Electio*'s purview is extremely narrow. Nothing is included which is not strictly relevant to the election issue and the accompanying cloistral quarrels. King John's relations with the monks of St. Edmund and his attitude to their election are, of course, treated in detail, but his quarrel with the pope and then with his barons is sketched in very lightly and unevenly. The year's vacancy between the death of Samson and Hugh's election is dismissed in a sentence although, as other abbey chronicles and the public records show, it was by no means an uneventful time for the house.[4] Even a great fire, which on 3 June 1215 destroyed a large part of the vill, passes unmentioned.[5]

Where the author's statements can be checked against an independent authority his accuracy, especially respecting his dates, is generally vindicated. His accounts of the trial conducted by the judges delegate, and of the convent's relations with the king are buttressed by documentary evidence and must be accepted as substantially correct. It is in his treatment of affairs within the

material relating to the rights and privileges of the house. Cf. the account of Abbot Odo's election in *Chronicon Monasterii de Bello*, ed. J. Brewer (London, 1846), pp. 145–62, and the famous 'Evesham case', narrated in the *Cronicon Abbatiae de Evesham*, RS, pp. 100–253, and discussed in *MO*, ch. xix.

[1] Cf. *JB*, pp. 30–2, 34–6, 48–50, etc., and below, pp. 81–91, 119–27.

[2] Cf. *JB*, pp. 4–5, 23, 58, 97, and below, pp. 13–15, 29, 51, 65–7, 73, 119–21. This is very much a traditional topos, at least among twelfth-century English chronicles. Cf., for instance, Eadmer's use of the memorable, apposite statement in his *Historia Novorum*, commented on by C. N. L. Brooke, 'Historical Writing in England between 850 and 1150', *Settimane di Studio*, xvii (Spoleto, 1970), i. 244–7.

[3] *JB*, pp. 122–3; see below, pp. 71–3.

[4] See below, p. 6 n. 2.   [5] Below, p. 169 n. 5.

monastery that he is open to suspicion for here he is emotionally involved, and his account largely unsubstantiated. His discussion of the election issue is manifestly biased inasmuch as the opposing party is represented as guided solely by impious and selfish motives, those of his own faction being, of course, correspondingly pure and noble. Of Robert the sacrist, for instance, special object of the writer's malice, the earlier part of the *Gesta Sacristarum* (written shortly before 1280) has this to say:[1]

> After [William of Diss, the previous sacrist] came Robert of Graveley, who bought the vineyard and enclosed it with stone walls, for the comfort of the infirm and those who had been bled. He furnished the nave with new rafters and made a canopy over St. Edmund, adorning it with a great variety of pictures. . . . To speak the truth, this Robert, the dispute [between him and Hugh] continuing for a long time, so it is related, met the expenses of both parties adequately.

In other words, far from being a 'dilapidator of his house',[2] he was an efficient and imaginative man, if not untainted by ambition, worthy of his later election as abbot of Thorney. This bias of the *Electio*, however, is so ingenuous as to be readily detectable whenever it is operating, and the real truth of the matter is only thinly veiled by it. On the other hand it must not be exaggerated; the writer does not hesitate to record the discomfiture of his own party when, for instance, one hot-headed member accused the opposition of seeking Hugh's death, and his fellows tried, dishonestly and vainly, as the writer admits, to mitigate this scandalous suggestion.[3] In his treatment of conventual affairs, then, the author offers a partisan interpretation of character and motive; did he try to support it by tampering with the facts? The *Gesta Sacristarum* states that 'on the death of Abbot Samson, Robert [the sacrist] was elected abbot by some of the convent, Hugh of Northwold by others'.[4] This directly contradicts the *Electio*, which maintains, not that Robert was elected in opposition to Hugh, but that he was ruled ineligible before such a possibility could arise.[5] The *Gesta* may be drawing on written evidence, but the earlier account, which is supported by the *Bury Chronicle*[6] and consistent with the verdict of the papal justices delegate, is to be preferred. Nevertheless, the doubt is raised, and cannot be quite allayed.

---

[1] *Mem.* ii. 293. [2] See below, p. 9. [3] Below, p. 65.
[4] *Mem.* ii. 293. [5] See below, pp. 7–9. [6] *Bury Chronicle*, p. 1.

III. *The Value of the Work*

The *Electio Hugonis* is the most detailed eyewitness account of an English monastic election dispute extant.[1] Whereas in most instances our knowledge of such conflicts is founded upon official, formal, and impersonal documents, designed to publicize the ostensible motives of the protagonists, in this chronicle we gain an insight into the feelings and motives, both real and assumed, of the rank and file in a monastic community. Moreover the *Electio* possesses a merit which must be almost unique among medieval chronicles: sufficient statistical data to confer on this insight a certain degree of precision. This in turn makes possible a fresh look at the tension between *regnum* and *sacerdotium* in England at this period, as it operated at the grass-roots.

A reading of the *Electio* raises two main questions: why was Hugh elected in the way that he was? And what issues divided the two parties in the cloister?

In being made independently of the royal will Hugh's election marked a departure from both Bury tradition and royal custom. As Professor Knowles has shown, nearly all known English monastic elections during the late eleventh and twelfth centuries were subject to some degree of control by the kings.[2] This control bore particularly heavily upon Bury, as a royal foundation of great wealth and strategic importance. The appointments of nine of the ten abbots before Hugh were subject to some measure of royal manipulation, ranging from direct imposition of a favourite, as in the case of Robert I (1100–2), to peaceful negotiation, as in the case of Samson (1182–1211).[3] Only two of the ten had been Bury monks before their elevation. There were three election disputes between the abbey and the crown prior to Hugh's. In 1100 the monks repudiated the candidate thrust on them by the king,

---

[1] Knowles, 'Abbatial Elections', p. 271.

[2] Ibid., pp. 262 ff.

[3] The first abbot, Uvius (1020–44), was presumably Cnut's appointment (*Mem.* i. 47–8); on Leofstan (1044–65) see A. J. Robertson, *Anglo-Saxon Charters* (Cambridge, 1939), p. 193; for Baldwin (1065–97), *Mem.* i. 56–8; for Robert I, Robert II and Albold (1100–19), *Mem.* i. 353–6; on Anselm (1121–48), R. H. C. Davis, 'The Monks of St. Edmund, 1021–1148', *History*, new ser., xl (1955), 237; nothing is known of the appointments of Ording (1138, 1148–56) or Hugh I (1157–80); Ording had apparently been a monk of the house for most of his life (*Mem.* i. 93, 95), but Hugh had been prior of Westminster before his abbacy, and so was probably not the monks' first choice. On Samson, *JB*, pp. 16–24.

Robert of Chester, and in 1102 he was deposed by Archbishop Anselm.[1] The convent then elected their own choice, also named Robert, who because of royal opposition could not be consecrated until 1107, although exercising full abbatial powers during that time.[2] The final clash occurred at the next vacancy, 1107–14, when the monks wished to elect their own prior, Baldwin, but encountered royal opposition.[3] The eventual appointment of Albold, prior of St. Nicaise, Meulan, probably represented some sort of compromise solution. These breaches in the good relations between crown and abbey, occurring within a few years of each other, were probably rather exceptional; in the first case the royal candidate was particularly obnoxious, and in all three instances the urging of Archbishop Anselm seems to lie behind the monks' obdurate stand. In fact, the relationship between king and convent was far from one-sided; the royal and patriotic character of its patron saint and the benefits conferred by the monarchs stimulated within the cloister a policy of loyal support for the royal house. By 1066 the abbey owed to the kings not only its very foundation as a Benedictine community, but its position of wealth and independence, conferred by Edward the Confessor in a series of important grants.[4] The Norman kings respected these privileges and assets, and tended to favour them in time of dispute, while never adding to them materially.[5] The Conqueror is described as 'a friend of father Baldwin',[6] then abbot of Bury, persuading him to begin construction of the great Romanesque abbey church, and apparently donating towards the project.[6] He even had thoughts of creating Baldwin bishop of Bury.[7] Three times Bury and other chronicles record the abbey's support of the royal house at times when it faced difficulties. It was on Stephen's side in the civil war,[8] stood by Henry II during his sons' rebellion,[9] and supported the

[1] *Mem.* i. 353, 355.
[2] Ibid., pp. 355–6.
[3] B.M. MS. Harl. 1005 (H), f. 217ᵛ.
[4] H. W. C. Davis, 'The Liberties of Bury St. Edmunds', *EHR*, xxiv (1909), 417–31; F. E. Harmer, *Anglo-Saxon Writs* (Manchester, 1952), pp. 138–66.
[5] H. W. C. Davis, pp. 420–1.
[6] *Mem.* i. 85.
[7] V. H. Galbraith, 'The East Anglian See and the Abbey of Bury St. Edmunds', *EHR*, xl (1925), 227.
[8] Lord F. Hervey, *Pinchbeck Register* (Oxford, 1925), ii. 297–9; *Mem.* iii. 6.
[9] Jordan de Fantosme, *Chronique*, in *Chronicles of the Reigns of Stephen, Henry II, and Richard I, RS*, iii. 287–95.

absent King Richard when John made his bid for the throne.[1]
This support was no mere lip-service, but positive and practical,
as Jocelin's account demonstrates:[2]

When news reached London of the capture of King Richard and his
imprisonment in Germany, and the barons had met to take counsel . . .
Abbot [Samson] sprang forth before them all, saying that he was ready,
secretly or otherwise, to seek his lord the king until he found and had
sure knowledge of him; from which saying he won much praise.

And, during John's rebellion:[3]

. . . the abbot, with the whole convent, solemnly excommunicated all
makers of war and disturbers of the peace, fearing not Earl John, the
king's brother, nor any other; for which men called the abbot a man of
high spirit. And . . . he went to the siege of Windsor, at which, with
certain other abbots of England, he carried arms having his own
standard and leading a number of knights at great expense. . . .

This attitude of respect towards the crown can be seen in the
Electio itself, whose moderate, even favourable view of John has
often been remarked. Particularly significant is the way in which,
by incorporation into the abbey's hagiographical tradition, this
attitude of loyalty was elevated to the status of ideology. Thus the
death of Prince Eustace in 1153 was attributed to St. Edmund's
vengeance for his treachery to his father,[4] and during the war
between the older and younger Henry, the defeat of the Flemings
who had been invited into East Anglia by the rebel earls of
Leicester and Norfolk in 1173, was ascribed to St. Edmund.[5] On
this occasion St. Edmund's banner was borne before the king's
army, and their war-cry was 'God and St. Edmund'.[6] Both
Eustace and the Flemings are simultaneously condemned for their
designs upon the abbey lands, thus demonstrating how closely the
causes of king and abbey were identified in the minds of the local
hagiographers.

Hugh's election, therefore, broke not only with royal custom,
but with the local tradition which identified the interests of crown
and convent. The suddenness and seriousness of the break may be
gauged by comparing Hugh's election with that of his predecessor,
Samson, as detailed in Jocelin's *Cronica*.[7] On this occasion a small

[1] *JB*, pp. 54–5, 65–8, 85–7.   [2] Ibid., p. 54.   [3] Ibid., p. 55.
[4] *Mem.* iii. 6; C. Horstman, *Nova Legenda Anglie* (Oxford, 1901), ii. 636.
[5] Fantosme, op. cit.
[6] Hoveden, *RS*, ii. 55; Fantosme, p. 291.   [7] *JB*, pp. 16–25.

minority of monks were in favour of electing a candidate at the
house and presenting him to the king for confirmation, as was
done in Hugh's case; but the majority quickly quashed this move
as offensive to the royal dignity. At least a choice of several
candidates ought to be presented him. Initially, no one seems to
have defended the king's dignity at Hugh's election. Ostensibly,
the Bury monks now embraced the contrary principles propagated
by the papacy. The reason for the change can be provisionally
located in the increasing unsatisfactoriness of the royal alliance in
terms of benefits accruing to the house, and the growing realization
that stronger links with the papal power might provide a more
reliable alternative.

Especially from the time of Abbot Ording on (d. 1156) there are
signs of strain in the relationship between Bury and the English
kings. In fact it was becoming lop-sided; the kings no longer gave
generously, while taking ever more rapaciously. Henry II only
visited the abbey once during Samson's reign, Richard not at all,
and John, although he made a pilgrimage to the shrine immediately
after his coronation, 'led thither by devotion and a vow, . . . offered
nothing save a single silken cloth which his servants had borrowed
from our sacrist—and they have not yet paid the price'.[1] And
although, according to the *Annales*, when John laid the English
churches under contribution during the interdict, he made an
exception in favour of the land of St. Edmund, 'out of reverence
for the saint',[2] four years later the same record has the king
demanding a heavy aid from the house, totalling, according to the
Electio, 4,000 marks.[3] Perhaps most revealing of all are the accounts
in Jocelin of the alienating of the convent's church plate and
precious ornament to pay for Richard's wars and ransom.[4]
Naturally there was a reaction, reluctant at first, but gathering to
a climax with Hugh's election. Thus, some letters of John of
Salisbury to Abbot Hugh I (1157–80) indicate that the convent
was sympathetic to him and his master, Thomas Becket, in their
exile.[5] Samson, in spite of his native loyalty, quarrelled with
Richard over a benefice which he refused one of the king's clerks,
so that the monarch threatened 'that he would be avenged on this
proud abbot . . . save that he refrained out of reverence for St.

---

[1] *JB*, pp. 116–17.   [2] *Mem.* ii. 16.
[3] Ibid., p. 25, and *Mem.* iii. 9. See below, p. 143.
[4] *JB*, pp. 46–7, 96–7.   [5] *PL*, cxcix, *Epp.* cl, clxxxvi, cclxxiii.

Edmund, whom he feared'.[1] But the most fruitful reaction was not
to rebel, and so incur the charge of treason, but to build an
alternative alliance—an alliance with the Holy See.

As Professor Knowles has said, Bury was one of a small group
of important English houses which owed their foundation and
earlier privileges to the crown, and the later augmentations of their
liberties to the papacy.[2] It was in the 1070s that the abbey first
began to think in terms of a protector other than the reigning
monarch, when the Norman Herfast, bishop of East Anglia with
his seat at Thetford, attempted to transfer it to Bury.[3] Initially he
had the royal support, but Abbot Baldwin opposed him, and the
suit was eventually carried to Rome, where the verdict was given in
Bury's favour. While in Rome Baldwin obtained from Alexander II
a papal privilege confirming the liberties granted to St. Edmunds
by the English kings—thus proclaiming the insufficiency of a royal
confirmation *per se*—and its exemption from episcopal authority.[4]
The formula of exemption employed in this charter was the most
elaborate then current, and lifted the abbey into the most privileged
class of those religious houses which were directly dependent on
the Holy See.[5] Each successive abbot of Bury petitioned, and each
new pope supplied confirmation of this original grant.[6] By the
reign of Anselm (1121–48) the papacy was being asked to sanction
and confirm grants and exchanges of abbatial property.[7] Abbot
Hugh I deliberately accelerated this process, by which a whole
series of new privileges was obtained. In 1162 Alexander III
pronounced that future abbots of Bury were to be freely elected
and might appeal to the Holy See on any important matter[8]—a
decisive step in the formation of this 'alternative alliance'. The
abbot was congratulated on certain reform measures, and invited
to still closer dependence upon Rome. This invitation was quickly
taken up. In 1172 the abbot of Bury gained the use of the dalmatic
and tunicle, and the right of profession to the pope alone. No one
except the pope and his legate could excommunicate, suspend, or
interdict the monastery, and no bishop, archbishop, or their

[1] *JB*, p. 98.   [2] *MO*, p. 591.
[3] *Mem.* i. 345–7.   [4] *PUE*, iii, no. 8.
[5] *MO*, p. 581.
[6] *PUE*, iii, nos. 44, 64, 121, 140, 187, 347, 382, 383, 442.
[7] Ibid., nos. 64, 98.
[8] Ibid., no. 140. Cf. Z. N. Brooke, *The English Church and the Papacy*
(Cambridge, 1931), pp. 212–14.

officials could enter its banlieu without the abbot's permission.[1]
Mass could be celebrated, *sub voce*, during an interdict, and only
the abbot had the right to constitute officials of the abbey lands.[2]
Only a year later Alexander granted the abbot the temporalities
of those clerks in his churches who did not pay a fixed rent, the
right to impose and dissolve penance in the vill and to tonsure its
clerics, and the use of the episcopal sandals.[3] Two years later the
same pope, at Hugh's request, granted the house exemption from
the legatine powers, except in the case of a *legatus a latere*.[4]

Samson lost no time in building upon the foundations laid by
his predecessor. In 1187 he gained the right to give the episcopal
blessing within the banlieu 'first among all abbots of England'.[5]
Early in the 1180s he was first appointed a papal judge delegate,
and in this capacity assisted in the adjudication of numerous
disputes, some of considerable importance. More letters of
Innocent III survive addressed to him than to any other English
abbot.[6] In 1189 he was given the authority to judge cases concerning matrimony on his lands.[7] Jocelin's story of the attempted
visitation of the house by Archbishop Hubert Walter in 1198,
frustrated by an appeal to Rome, illustrates the effectiveness of the
papal alliance for the Bury monks' defence of their liberties, and
their quest for ever more comprehensive privileges.[8] It also helps
answer the objection that most of the privileges listed above were
designed to defend the abbey against the episcopal, not the royal
power. For Hubert Walter was the king's justiciar at the time of
his attempted visitation, and claimed to be visiting Bury in that
capacity.[9] Conversely, Abbot Samson was able to argue that he
was visiting as legate, and so infringing the abbey's privileges;
either way, the result was the same; a royal justiciar was barred
from entering the chapter-house of Bury. This is not to imply that
the papal privileges sought by Bury were directed against the
episcopal clergy solely in their capacity as royal officials; but it
does suggest that their campaign for freedom from episcopal
control had wider ramifications, that it was, in fact, but a stage in
a long-term campaign for freedom from all outside interference,
whether lay (including royal) or clerical.

[1] *PUE*, iii, nos. 186–7.   [2] Ibid., no. 187.   [3] Ibid., nos. 195, 197.
[4] Ibid., no. 217.   [5] Ibid., no. 399; *JB*, p. 56.
[6] Ibid., p. 33; Cheney, *Letters*, index under 'Samson'. There survive thirty-
nine letters in all.
[7] *PUE*, iii, no. 416.   [8] *JB*, pp. 81–3.   [9] Ibid., p. 84.

By the end of the twelfth century the abbey of Bury was in the papal confidence. A letter of Innocent III, dated *c.* 1200, directs Abbot Samson, together with the bishops of Durham and Ely, to meet the exempt abbots of England at London in general chapter, to preside over it in order to promote reform, and thereafter to meet annually.[1] The alliance with the papacy was now surely supplementing, if it had not actually replaced, the traditional *détente* with the monarchy in the esteem of the Bury monks. It seems arguable that the election of Hugh of Northwold, without reference to the king, was the logical outcome of this development. There is nothing surprising in this; Charles Duggan and others have seen the move for free elections by religious houses in the reign of John as due to papal influence, in the shape of increased definition of canon law over the late twelfth century in the papacy's interest, and in the work and personality of Innocent III.[2] However, two alternative views must be examined before proceeding on this assumption. A contemporary writer states that if the ordinary custom of royal appointment or veto had been followed by the ten houses vacant in 1213, elections could have been easily held, but the bishops of the papal party stood out for a fully canonical election.[3] The suggestion is that the decision to hold 'free' elections was imposed from outside the monasteries themselves, namely by the episcopate. On the other hand, David Knowles at one time suggested 'the monks' struggle for liberty was for exemption against the bishops, not for election against the king', although later he appeared to agree with Duggan by labelling the parties in the Bury dispute 'royalist' and 'papalist'.[4] On the evidence of the *Electio* both alternative views must be modified. The Bury monks did seek the advice of the papalist bishops over the method of election to be followed, and they certainly looked for and received support from them after the king had announced his opposition. But this advice was sought by the monks, not imposed on them, and they carefully selected their episcopal advisers—termed by the *Electio* 'those bishops who feared God and defended the liberties of Holy Church'.[5] Had the

[1] Cheney, *Letters*, no. 463.
[2] C. Duggan in C. H. Lawrence (ed.), *The English Church and the Papacy in the Middle Ages* (London, 1965), pp. 86–97, 105–7, 108–13, etc.; cf. C. R. Cheney, *From Becket to Langton* (Manchester, 1956), chs. i, iii, and *passim*; Z. N. Brooke, op. cit., pp. 215–28.   [3] *Chron. Barnwell*, in Walter of Coventry, *RS*, ii. 213.
[4] Knowles, 'Abbatial Elections', p. 276; cf. *MO*, p. 400.
[5] See below, p. 7.

convent been merely obeying instructions from the bishops, moreover, Hugh's supporters would not have been so steadfast in their resistance to the threats of King John and his barons. The *Electio* makes it abundantly clear that Hugh's friends really believed in the cause for which they fought. Nor is there the slightest hint that the monks felt themselves to be battling for exemption from the episcopal power. This fight had already been won under Hugh I and Samson, and relations between convent and episcopate as revealed in the *Electio* are very cordial. We have a prima facie case, then, for explaining Hugh's election in terms of an increasingly close and beneficial alliance of the abbey with the papacy. We may now proceed to examine more closely the meaning of this alliance for the Bury monks: Why did they espouse it? What benefits did it bring? In other words, what significance have the terms 'royalist' and 'papalist' as applied to the opponents and defenders of Hugh's election within the cloister? An analysis of the issues dividing the two parties will serve to define more precisely both these terms and the nature of the papal alliance as conceived by the Bury monks.

Firstly we may examine the issues as expressed verbally by the two factions. In the case of the anti-election party this is particularly difficult, since they tended to alter their ground, depending on the circumstances. Before the king and lords, they maintained that they were serving the royal liberties, which Hugh and his friends were betraying.[1] Within the confines of the cloister, they insisted that the house would be brought to ruin by opposition to the royal wishes.[2] This was the burden of the sacrist's sermon, in which he provided *exempla* of opposers of the state authority who were ruined as a result of their attitude.[3] Before the ecclesiastical authorities, on the other hand, this party argued that the election was uncanonical. At first they tried to prove that the procedure had been incorrect,[4] but so many precautions against this had been taken that it proved impossible to substantiate. The charter of ratification which they had approved was a decisive piece of evidence against them, of which the opposing party was quick to make use.[5] They then sought to prove that Hugh was not a fit candidate,[6] a proposition equally impossible to maintain, since he so evidently was. From their verbal arguments (admittedly as

---

[1] Below, pp. 87, 123–9.   [2] p. 15.   [3] p. 59.   [4] p. 19.
[5] p. 51, 125.   [6] p. 149.

represented by an enemy) it is plainly impossible to draw any certain conclusion as to their real motives.

Hugh's supporters were less equivocal. Before the legate and judges delegate they had merely to protest the election canonical, which indeed it was.[1] Faced with the king and his lords they made the same claim, adding that the convent's liberties, conferred by Edward the Confessor and confirmed by John himself and his ancestors, included the right of free election.[2] The king did not dispute this, but simply pointed out that 'free election' had never been interpreted in this way before.[3] This particular argument of the defending party is at one and the same time directed against the traditional custom of England, and yet derived from it. It does not demonstrate this party to be 'papalist'. Why did they not argue from pro-papal, canonistic principles? Perhaps for diplomatic reasons, such as influenced the actions of the legate Nicholas in the dispute?[4] But the defending party were brave enough to take their stand openly before the king in person, when no reasoning of any kind would have availed to assuage the royal wrath. Two of them even dared to reproach John on this occasion with 'sharp words'.[5]

If Hugh's supporters were papalists at heart, we should expect them to support the reforming decrees of Pope Innocent. One of Cardinal Nicholas's duties, as revealed in the *Electio*, was to suppress corrupt and luxurious customs within conventual houses, such as excessive pittances and the practice of private meals.[6] Bury St. Edmunds, in spite of Abbot Samson's honoured place in Innocent's reform programme for English houses, stood open to censure in this regard. Although it apparently cut down on pittances at the legate's command, the convent appears to have ignored his orders regarding private meals, and the writer records that after a time only half a dozen monks dined in the refectory.[7] One of Hugh's party, Richard of Saxham, the subcellarer, certainly seems to have been a supporter of reform, for he refused to dispense the convent ale by a larger measure than the king's, when pressed to do so by the sacrist.[8] The latter alleged the support of the rest of the monks, and, although the author of the *Electio* plays this down, it may well have been true. Finally, the sacrist, hoping—says the writer—to bring on the opposing party the imputation of

---

[1] pp. 33–5, 95–7, 157.   [2] pp. 89, 121–5.   [3] p. 125.   [4] p. 35.
[5] p. 125.   [6] pp. 28–9.   [7] pp. 63–5.   [8] pp. 71–3.

xxxiv INTRODUCTION

laxity and misrule, suggested that the convent should disobey the restrictions of the interdict by celebrating mass more often than the pope had prescribed.[1] There is some doubt as to Innocent's exact intention in this regard,[2] and the sacrist may have been trading on the abbey's papal privileges which gave it special rights in time of interdict.[3] Although the writer speaks vaguely of opposition from the election party, the fact remains that the whole convent appears to have acquiesced in what may have been an abuse of privilege, and was certainly not a strict observance of the papal decree. Although the spokesmen of the pro-election party obtained a letter from Innocent urging correction of lax customs within the house,[4] there is much to suggest that this was a tactic designed to impress the pope with their own faithfulness to his ideals, in comparison with the opposing faction; it carries much the same weight as the protestations of disinterested loyalty made before the king by the sacrist's party. In general, the attempt by the *Electio*'s author to equate support of Hugh's election with obedience to the papal reform decrees is most unconvincing. In order to illuminate the real motivation behind the two parties, it is necessary to get behind their own quasi-official statements and those of the writer about them, and attempt to ascertain what sort of men constituted their membership.

Immediately upon learning of King John's anger at their action, a count was made in the convent of those who wished to continue in Hugh's support, to the number of forty,[5] leaving about thirty in opposition. A year later the figures were even, with thirty-five on each side, and although there were some marginal changes of allegiance at various points in the dispute, this number seems to have remained surprisingly constant. It is fortunate that the *Electio* provides a list of the members of each party, from which some facts about their composition can be worked out.

Firstly, a count of all those on both sides who held obedientiary positions either before, during, or after the dispute, reveals equal numbers holding equally important offices; but it also clearly demonstrates that the king's party was a party of the sacristy, while their opponents were associated with the cellary.[6] Of the

---

[1] p. 45. [2] p. 44 n. 1. [3] *PUE*, iii, no. 187.
[4] See below, p. 79. [5] Below, p. 17.
[6] Arnold saw as one of the most significant differences between the parties the fact that the major obedientiaries nearly all came out in opposition to the election, suggesting an alignment of experienced administrators against younger

former, their leader Robert of Graveley was currently sacrist, Richard of Newport subsacrist and later sacrist, Richard the precentor was later to hold the same office, as was his deputy, Gregory, and Walter Gale was subsacrist during 1214–15. None of the opposing faction is known to have held a position in this department at any time.[1] Of their number, Peter of Worstead was cellarer during the dispute and Nicholas later, Hugh of Northwold was subcellarer before and Richard of Saxham after his election, and Jocelin of the Altar and Peter of Lynn had both held office as cellarer earlier. John of Lavenham held a position (*firmarius*) which seems to have been a sub-department of the cellary. Significantly, on one occasion the sacrist's party held that tidings of the election's confirmation by the pope had been concocted in the monks' cellar.[2]

Jealousy between these, the two most important departments in the abbey, can be traced back at least as far as Samson's reign. At Bury the sacristy, because of its long association with the impressive building programme, had accumulated far more glamour and prestige than the cellary, so that by the late twelfth century an active member of that department stood a good chance of promotion to the abbacy.[3] Samson himself had been subsacrist before his election, and under him building, repair-work, and interior decorating were vigorously prosecuted.[4] That he favoured the sacristy, often at the cellary's expense, is alleged by Jocelin, himself demoted for a time from the office of cellarer for supposed mismanagement.[5] His sense of grievance was particularly sharpened by the erosion of the cellarer's rights in the vill, where nominally both departments exercised shared powers.[6] In 1213, therefore, when Robert of Graveley, the able sacrist, expected to obtain the abbacy as a matter of course,[7] he found himself excluded by a strong movement for the rehabilitation of the cellary,

or less capable men (*Mem.* i, xii). This is simply not in accordance with the facts; see Appendix III.

[1] An unimportant exception is William of Diss, sacrist for four days only, before Robert of Graveley (*Mem.* ii. 293).

[2] See below, p. 67.

[3] *Mem.* ii. 289–93; Davis, 'The Monks of St. Edmund', p. 231.

[4] *Mem.* ii. 291–3; *JB*, pp. 9–10, 28, 72, 96–7, 111–12, 116, etc.

[5] *JB*, pp. 79–81, 87–91, 122–3.

[6] Ibid., pp. 99–105.

[7] This seems to be what the *Electio* means by saying that the sacrist feared Hugh, the 'successor', 'more heredis'; see below, p. 71.

which his own department had for so long overshadowed. Here, then, is a motive of purely local origin and significance, bearing no relation to 'papalist' or 'royalist' ideals.

Another obvious difference between the parties is in respect of education. Of the party opposing the election, Prior Herbert is known to have been unlearned,[1] Richard the precentor was at the very least no lawyer,[2] and if Robert of Graveley made the gaucheries in his sermon attributed to him by the writer, then he must have been grossly ignorant of Scripture and shaky on its traditional exegesis.[3]

The other side included all the convent *magistri*. Master Nicholas of Dunstable was their spokesman, seconded by Master Thomas of Walsingham, and Master Thomas of Beccles the third prior. Other, less articulate, members were Master Alan of Walsingham and Master Henry of Ely. Another of their number, Simon of Walsingham, is known to have been literate, since he wrote an extant Anglo-Norman poem on St. Faith.[4] Wido (or Guy), an insignificant member of the same party, is probably the same man who became precentor later in the century, and had two extant books written for the abbey library.[5] Similarly, William of Diss, a member of this faction, although he does not appear in the 1214 lists, ordered the writing of two extant library-books.[6] Lastly, but by no means least, must be mentioned Jocelin of the Altar, *alias* of Brakelond, who needs no introduction as a cultured man and talented writer.

This division also had a history among the monks of St. Edmund. Jocelin records the speculation during the vacancy in 1180, as to what sort of man made a good abbot.[7] Some placed a high priority

---

[1] *JB*, pp. 127–8. [2] See below, p. 29.
[3] Below, pp. 57–9.
[4] D. Legge, *Anglo-Norman in the Cloister* (Edinburgh, 1950), p. 11.
[5] Both books are inscribed accordingly. They are Cambridge Pembroke College MS. 94, containing Origen *super Vet. Test.*, Innocent, *De Officio Missae*, and John Damascene, *Sententiae*; B.M. MS. Royal 2 E. ix, containing John of Abbeville's sermons.
[6] Both inscribed accordingly. They are Cambridge Pembroke College MS. 27, containing Peter Comestor's sermons, Richard of St. Victor's *Allegoriae*, and Ralph Niger, *De Re Militari*; B.M. MS. Royal 7 C. iv, containing a collection of the diverse senses of scriptural words and phrases, and another of *proprietates rerum*. As, unlike Guy, William was apparently never precentor, he may have been armarius (*JB*, p. 36). He was also responsible for a short addendum to Jocelin's chronicle (see above, p. xiii n. 3).
[7] *JB*, pp. 11–15.

on learning, others preferred a man virtuous and practical. Samson's election was a compromise initially satisfactory to both parties, since he had been a Master in the Schools, specializing in dialectic and medicine,[1] but was latterly more interested in administration and practical pursuits than in meditative scholarship.[2] In the long run his appointment brought little joy to the literate monks. In 1200, when the priorate fell vacant, these men, 'few, it is true, in numbers, but more praiseworthy in counsel',[3] sought the promotion of a mature and well-educated man. The rest, however, including Samson himself, wished for the appointment of the young and simple Herbert. To his election the literate monks objected, lest 'literate clerks should for the future disdain to take the religious habit among us, if it should so fall out that a dumb image were set up in our midst and a log of wood given preferment in such a convent as ours'.[4] But the abbot had his way. The next day, in chapter, he nominated three candidates, including Herbert, 'all of them young men, . . . possessed of but a modicum of learning. . . . These then the abbot named, putting them above the subprior and many others who were older, superior, and more mature, men, too, who were literate and had of old been Masters of the Schools.'[5] Eventually Herbert was chosen, but put his supporters to confusion by admitting his inability to preach the necessary sermons.

But the abbot, for his consolation and (as it would seem) to the prejudice of the literate, replied at length, saying that he could easily commit to memory the sermons of others and inwardly digest them as others did; and he condemned rhetorical ornament and verbal embellishments and elaborate general reflections in a sermon, saying that in many churches sermons are preached . . . for the edification of morals and not for the display of learning.[6]

By the time of Hugh's election Bury had not had an abbot who encouraged learning for some sixty-five years.[7] The literate monks had a long-standing grievance, therefore, and the prospect of a

---

[1] *JB*, pp. 33, 44; *Mem.* iii. 7.   [2] *JB*, pp. 33–5, 40–1, 128.
[3] Ibid., p. 125.   [4] Ibid., p. 126.   [5] Ibid., p. 127.
[6] Ibid., p. 128; cf. p. 130, where the illiterate monks take up the abbot's words, and use them to mock the others.
[7] i.e. since the time of Anselm (1121–48), a great patron of art and letters. Ording was remembered as unlearned (*JB*, p. 11), and what little is known of Hugh I does not indicate that he was a man of learning. This division between learned and unlearned over Hugh's election was noticed long ago by B. Smalley, 'A Collection of Paris Lectures', *Cambridge Historical Journal*, vi (1938–40), 106.

new abbot gave them a fresh chance to get their own way. Now Hugh was not a Master, and it must be admitted that next to nothing is known of his attitude to learning. Certain details suggest that he was at least sympathetic; he is recorded as having presented the convent during his abbacy with *primam partem Biblie preciosissimam*,[1] and as bishop of Ely, it has recently been revealed, he may have exercised some influence on the definition of the earliest statutes of Cambridge University,[2] besides arranging facilities for the monks of Ely priory to study there.[3] He has some claim, therefore, to be called a patron of scholarship, although not a conspicuously learned man himself.

But I do not think that Hugh's own interests fully explain his support by the Bury *magistri*. There was a principle involved. Jocelin names five Masters in the *Cronica*, none of whom appears in the *Electio*, and conversely, none of the Masters in the *Electio* figures in Jocelin's account. The inference is that the *magistri* who took part in Hugh's election were fairly recent entrants into the cloister. Master Nicholas and Master Thomas of Walsingham alone of their number can be identified as Bury monks prior to the period covered by the *Electio*'s record. They appear as witnesses to a charter of Abbot Samson, dated 1206–11, and presumably professed as Bury monks not many years earlier.[4] They and the other *magistri* who were members of the house in 1213–15, then, would have been pursuing their secular studies during the last two decades of the twelfth century. Since at that time the Schools, activated by the influence of Innocent III, were prime vehicles for the dissemination of strict, pro-papal canonistic doctrine,[5] this, as well as the traditional friction between literate and uneducated in the Bury cloister, might explain their united defence of Hugh's election.

Age and date of profession are, indeed, other possible differences between the parties. Of the faction opposing the election, Prior Herbert, a Bury monk since 1186, was elderly, dying in

[1] James, *On the Abbey*, p. 181; see Appendix V, p. 194 n. 10.
[2] M. B. Hackett, *The Original Statutes of Cambridge University* (Cambridge, 1970), pp. 38–40.
[3] J. Bentham, *The History and Antiquities of the Conventual and Cathedral Church of Ely* (2nd edn., Norwich, 1812), i. 147.
[4] *Kalendar*, no. 135. See above, p. xx n. 2, and below, p. 103 n. 9.
[5] W. Ullmann, *A History of Political Thought: the Middle Ages* (Harmondsworth, 1965), pp. 118–20.

1220.[1] Jocelin, almoner since 1206–9 at least, and probably earlier, must have been ageing, and Henry Rufus is described as such by the author.[2] John of Diss, a fully fledged monk before 1198, must have been at least middle-aged, and Adam the infirmarer seems to have been an obedientiary before 1186, as was Richard the precentor. Subprior Albinus seems to have died before c. 1217–20, during which period he was succeeded in office by Adam. On the other hand, Robert of Graveley, Richard of Newport, Richard the precentor, and his deputy Gregory, had long careers ahead of them, and Philip and Richard of Stortford must have been either young or newly professed, the former because he was only put forward for ordination in 1214, the other because the seniors thought him too young for a minor obedientiary post in 1215.[3]

As to the other side, Hugh of Northwold himself, who entered the cloister in 1202 and died in 1254, was exceptionally young. Thomas of Walsingham was ready for ordination in 1213, and therefore probably made his profession in 1206.[4] He and Richard of Saxham are found as wardens of St. Saviour's hospital between c. 1217 and c. 1220. Robert, who appears as chamberlain in a charter of Abbot Samson c. 1211, was still holding office after 1222, apparently not continuously, since Thomas of Walsingham was chamberlain between 1220 and 1222, and a certain Richard a little earlier. Within this same time Hugh of Thetford appears as abbot's chaplain. Master Nicholas was certainly infirmarer and cellarer between 1217 and 1220 and, as we have seen, perhaps abbot's chaplain and certainly active after 1222. The seniors thought Master Alan too young for an obedientiary position in 1215,[5] and there are three monks, Peter of Lynn, Maurice, and William of Stanhoe, who are called iuuenes. The remaining magistri, on the evidence considered above, were probably recent entrants to the cloister, not beyond their prime, and Guy, if he is the same man who was precentor after 1234, would have been very young. On the other hand, Jocelin of the Altar, a monk since 1173, was ageing, and Simon of Walsingham, if he is the Simon pictor who painted the abbot's seat in the 1180s

---

[1] For these and all subsequent dates and calculations, see Appendix III.
[2] See below, p. 125.
[3] Below, pp. 139, 161.
[4] Ordination usually took place seven years after profession; D. Knowles, The Religious Orders in England, ii (Cambridge, 1955), pp. 232–3.
[5] See below, p. 161.

(which is however highly doubtful), must have been at least middle-aged.[1] At all events he was still active after 1215, since he appears as pittancer during Hugh's reign. Thomas the third prior was out of office, presumably dead, by 1217–20. Finally, William of Diss, a monk before 1198, and brief holder of a major obedientiary office towards the end of Samson's reign, would have been of at least mature years. But he too was still alive and active after 1215.

The foolish old monk, Henry Rufus, told the king on his visit to the abbey that he had been defending the royal rights in the face of opposition from 'certain novices',[2] a contemptuous characterization of those supporting the election. Hugh's party on their own account, asking Richard Marsh for time to seek legal advice over the granting of the release, urged as their excuse that the sacrist's party had spread it abroad that they were immature and inexperienced; if this were true, then they ought to have time to consult expert opinion.[3] Significantly, at one point the author refers to his party as 'the wiser members of the convent, although not the maturer in years'.[4] The evidence is fragmentary, but seems to suggest that on the average Hugh's was the slightly younger party, and that more of its members were newly professed. Thus far the evidence indicates nothing certain about the monks' motives, but it is beginning to look as though different groups of them chose sides for varying reasons.

There is a final difference to be considered before a satisfactory conclusion can be drawn. Of the thirty-five members of the party opposing the election, fourteen bear surnames denoting their place of birth, and the birthplaces of a further four or five can be surmised from external evidence.[5] Five or six of them came from Norfolk, one to six from Suffolk, one or two from Essex, four from Cambridgeshire, Hertfordshire, or Berkshire, and one each from Ely, Wales, and perhaps Scotland. Of the thirty-six members of the other party, twenty-seven bear surnames denoting place of origin, fourteen from Norfolk, eight from Suffolk, one perhaps from Italy, and one each from Bedfordshire, Ely, London, and Oxford. Even allowing for the incompleteness of the figures, it seems that Hugh's party contained a higher percentage of men

---

[1] See Appendix III, p. 188 n. 2.   [2] See below, p. 125.
[3] Below, p. 137.   [4] Below, p. 19.
[5] Evidence for these figures is given in Appendix III.

from Norfolk and Suffolk than the other. The difference is particularly marked as regards the leading lights. Robert of Graveley, Richard of Newport, Richard the precentor, and Richard of Stortford came from Cambridgeshire, Essex, and Ely. Of their opponents' leaders, John of Lavenham, Master Thomas of Walsingham, Hugh of Northwold himself, Peter of Worstead, and Richard of Saxham all came from either Norfolk or Suffolk. Master Nicholas, of Dunstable in Bedfordshire, was not really an exception, as will be shown.

The difference between the parties in respect of birth is not simply one of men born near the abbey as against those born at a distance. Some of the Norfolk members of the abbot elect's party were born further from the abbey than those of the sacrist's following who hailed from Essex or Hertfordshire. The difference is rather between monks born within or outside the area of East Anglia. This is not surprising. As D. C. Douglas has shown,

the amalgamation of Norfolk and Suffolk into one district is no mere matter of propinquity, but the result of the earlier history of both counties. . . . The individual character of East Anglia is made clear from the seventh century onwards. In later days the unity between the two shires is . . . symbolized by their subjection to a common bishop and a common earl, both of which have their origin in pre-Conquest arrangements of an early date. In the eleventh century . . . writs were often addressed to the magnates of Norfolk and Suffolk jointly, and it seems probable that in the twelfth century the two shire courts often met together. . . . Of more importance, however, than these administrative arrangements, is the broad line of cleavage which marks off the district from the neighbouring shires.[1]

Why, then, did the East Anglians defend Hugh's election? Partly, no doubt, because Hugh was one of them, whereas Robert of Graveley was a 'foreigner'. This dichotomy also may have had a history at St. Edmunds. In the course of the discussion over who made a good abbot, during the vacancy of 1180-2, one of the monks exclaimed: 'From all good clerks, O Lord deliver us; that it may please Thee to preserve us from all Norfolk barrators, we beseech Thee to hear us.'[2] This may have had direct reference to Samson, who was both a Norfolk man, and a 'good clerk'. However,

---

[1] D. C. Douglas, *The Social Structure of Medieval East Anglia, Oxford Studies in Social and Legal History*, ed. Sir P. Vinogradoff, ix (Oxford, 1927), pp. 2-3, 205-19.   [2] *JB*, p. 12.

two other possible reasons for Hugh's strong East Anglian vote merit attention.

East Anglia, and Norfolk especially, was the heartland of the cult of St. Edmund. According to legend current by the twelfth century it was at Hunstanton that he had first landed in England, and at nearby Maidenbure he had performed a notable miracle.[1] His court was at Attleborough, his last great battle against the Danes at Thetford. In Lord Hervey's (certainly incomplete) list of English churches dedicated to St. Edmund before modern times, Norfolk comes easily first with seventeen, Yorkshire well behind with seven, followed by Suffolk with five. Most other counties had at least one.[2]

What relevance has the cult of St. Edmund for the election of Hugh of Northwold? As R. H. C. Davis has pointed out, St. Edmund was pre-eminently the protector of his men against tyrants.[3] His most famous and characteristic miracles are of this type; thirteen of them are recorded between the date of his martyrdom and the end of the thirteenth century.[4] Two of these, the saint's vengeance on Swein of Denmark in 1014 and Prince Eustace in 1153, are quoted by John of Salisbury in the *Policraticus* to illustrate the 'end of tyrants'.[5] All of the thirteen are directed against men of rank and position, nobles, bishops, and kings, because they are exercising their authority tyrannically. The idea that their saint could protect his men against the tyranny even of a king was kept constantly before the monks by the liturgy. The *lectiones* for the Vigil of St. Edmund's feast-day, selected from Hermann's *De Miraculis* between c. 1100 and c. 1124, tell of Swein's attempt to exact tribute from the men of St. Edmund, and the saint's subsequent revenge.[6] Even more pointedly, the almost programmatic versicle and response which followed the second of these *lectiones* were eventually elevated to become the first processional of the Vigil Office: '*R*. Felix Edmundus suorum misertus uerba cum minis regi Swein mittit dicens, In meos quid

---

[1] *Mem.* i. 99–100.

[2] Lord F. Hervey, *The History of King Eadmund the Martyr* (Oxford, 1929), pp. 21–2.

[3] Davis, 'The Monks of St. Edmund', pp. 227–9.

[4] *Mem.* i. 30–2, 35–8, 54–6, 58–9, 62–4, 147–8, 148–51, 353–5; Horstman, op. cit. ii. 636–7, 667–9.

[5] Ed. C. C. J. Webb (Oxford, 1909), ii. 393–4.

[6] New York Pierpont Morgan Library MS. 736, pp. 171–5.

INTRODUCTION   xliii

furis? Quid tributarios facis? Cessa, cessa tributum exigere quod
nullo dederunt sub rege. *V.* Prope namque cognoscas quod Deo
michique displices.'[1] The saint's power was taken seriously. In
1198, after many of the church's ornaments had already been sold
to held pay King Richard's ransom, the Exchequer barons began
to think of stripping St. Edmund's feretory. Samson, who was
present, dared them. 'And each of the judges replied with an oath,
"I will not, nor will I. For the fury of St. Edmund can reach those
who are absent and far away; much more will it strike those who
are present and desire to strip his shirt from off him." '[2] In 1232,
after his fall from office, it was to St. Edmunds that the great
Hubert de Burgh fled for sanctuary.[3]

As Lord Hervey says, 'It is essential to realize . . . that to the
minds not only of kings and clergy and nobles, but also of the
people, the saint was a living and active presence and force, in his
own kingdom and far beyond its limits.'[4] If kings and neighbouring
barons took St. Edmund's power seriously, much more did those
who lived within the area of his old kingdom and were steeped in
his legends from childhood. What practical effect this could have
is illustrated by the story which Abbot Samson, himself a native
of Tottington in Norfolk, told Jocelin of his childhood.[5] When he
was nine years old, he had a dream in which St. Edmund saved
him from the devil who tried to catch him outside the abbey
gates, although he had never seen the abbey, and only recognized
it as the church of his dream when his mother took him there
soon after. According to the abbot's own interpretation of the
dream, the devil which he had seen was the pleasure of this world
which sought to entice him, 'but St. Edmund embraced him
because he desired him to become a monk of his Church'.

The influence of the cult partly explains the strong East
Anglian support for Hugh's election. In maintaining their right of
free election these men were defending St. Edmund's liberties,
under his protection. This was their claim when faced with the

[1] Norwich Record Office MS. St. Peter Hungate Museum 158.926.4g(4), f.
111ᵛ. This MS., a Processional from the abbey, dates from the second half of
the fifteenth century, but the Use which it contains is probably much older.
[2] *JB*, pp. 96–7.
[3] Wendover, *RS*, iv. 245–8. According to a Bury source, however, it was his
wife who sought shelter there (*Bury Chronicle*, p. 8).
[4] *History of King Eadmund*, p. 17.
[5] *JB*, p. 37.

king and his lords.[1] The *Electio* states that they were ready to contend for the saint's rights even to the shedding of their blood.[2] In other words, for these men the power of St. Edmund was more real, more comprehensible than that of the king. The party opposing the election, whose leaders came from further afield, had a greater appreciation of the royal power and authority. It may be added that Master Nicholas, from Dunstable in Bedfordshire, is not necessarily an exception among the leaders of Hugh's party, for Dunstable priory possessed the relics of St. Fremund, Edmund's brother, whose cult was intimately related to that of Bury's patron.

Yet a third and final reason for the East Anglian membership of Hugh's party may be mentioned. As is well known, this area was one of the two main centres of the baronial rebellion against King John. Could it be that the defence of Hugh's election bears some relation to the baronial cause? This is not easy to answer, for the writer of the *Electio*, probably to discountenance any suggestion of disloyalty on the part of Hugh and his followers, is extremely coy about relations between the abbot elect and rebel barons. Yet there are enough scattered hints to build up a case for such a connection.

On 5 November 1214, when the king was at Bury, the sacrist said to him, in front of Hugh, 'My lord king, this man assisting you and conducting himself as abbot elect, is working with might and main to deprive you of your royal crown. And unless he is quickly persuaded by the royal provision to abandon this wicked idea, it is to be feared that within a short time he will accomplish what he has already set in motion against the royal dignity.'[3] Hugh, of course, denied this, but it could be that he had exchanged correspondence with Langton and the barons concerning their proposed meeting at St. Edmunds, arranged probably for 20 November.[4] After the rebellion had broken out, it was to the barons in London that Hugh sent Richard of Saxham to seek their advice as to whether it was worth while continuing to entreat the king's favour.[5] A little later, when Hugh was before him at Runnymede, messengers had to be sent to and fro between John and the barons before final settlement could be reached.[6] This suggests some kind of bargaining, comprehensible only if Hugh

---

[1] See below, pp. 89, 121.   [2] Below, p. 121.   [3] p. 129.
[4] See Appendix IV.   [5] See below, p. 169.   [6] Below, p. 171.

had struck up an alliance with the magnates of the baronial party. Relations between John and the abbey after Hugh's confirmation, and Bury's stand in the civil war, are equivocal.[1] Three members of Hugh's party, however, Hugh of Hastings, Roger FitzDrew, and Richard de Flamvill, bear the surnames of local knightly families, of which one was certainly and one probably involved in the rebellion.[2] None of the opposing party seems to have had similar connections, and in a letter dated March 1216, the king refers to the sacrist as *fidelis noster*.[3] Finally, there is evidence from Hugh's later career that he was sympathetic with the aims of the baronial party. His name heads the list of English abbots who witnessed the third Great Charter of Henry III, 1224–5, and in the year before his death, at a Parliament held at London, he witnessed the Sentence of the bishops against all breakers of charters, his name following those of the archbishop of Canterbury and bishop of London.[4] At the conclusion of the 1248 Parliament, at which the king had sought a subsidy and been refused, he called Hugh to him, and entreated him, as one who had proved himself a capable royal servant, to help him. But Hugh replied sharply: 'My lord, if I have at any time done you service, I am much pleased; but your majesty knows that . . . if we prelates yielded to your un-restrained will, the Church would be impoverished, and, to the injury of your pledge and oath, would be subject to perpetual tribute and slavery.'[5] In 1252 another incident shows that Hugh was never a mere royal yes-man. William de Valence, the king's half-brother, after hunting without permission in the bishop's park at Hatfield, broke into the lodge there, and held a drunken orgy.

[1] John sent only one letter to Hugh after his confirmation (*Rot. Litt. Pat.*, p. 142). Otherwise, when he wrote to the abbey he addressed the prior and sacrist (ibid., p. 161), suggesting that he had only given his consent to the election under duress. Late in 1215 John ordered the prior and sacrist to throw down the defensive wall which they had erected around the vill, and to expel thence the enemies of his majesty (ibid.). Perhaps this order was disobeyed, for early in the following year Savary de Mauleon and the earl of Salisbury drove a large number of 'soldiers and noble ladies' from Bury, compelling them to fly to the protection of the isle of Ely (Coggeshall, *RS*, p. 177). On the other hand, the abbot was granted the forfeited lands of the rebel William of Hastings which were in his gift (*Rot. Litt. Claus.*, p. 265).

[2] William of Hastings certainly; see *Rot. Litt. Pat.*, p. 194, and *Rot. Litt. Claus.*, pp. 260, 265, 279, 281–2. Walter FitzDrew was an outlaw in 1202 for breach of the king's peace (*Rot. Litt. Pat.*, p. 20).

[3] Ibid., p. 172.

[4] Mathew Paris, *Chron. Maj.*, RS, v. 373–5.

[5] Ibid., pp. 330–2.

Hugh took the news quietly, but said: 'It is a cursed thing that there should be so many kings in one kingdom, and all tyrants.'[1]

There is some evidence, therefore, for sympathy, perhaps for a more substantial alliance, between Hugh's and the baronial party—not surprisingly, given the similarity of their causes. To what extent, on the other hand, did the opposing faction constitute a 'king's party'? Although the sacrist was always ready to protest his loyalty, there is no doubt that he and his followers were not above manipulating the royal power in their interests. Twice he bribed courtiers to blacken Hugh's character before the king, when it looked as though he was about to confirm the election.[2] It must also be noted that, apparently, none of those who eventually joined this party protested against the method of Hugh's election until after the king's opposition was known. One can take it, therefore, that the sacrist himself was motivated by personal ambition, and that he played on the fear of the royal power which many of the monks genuinely felt. His following can only be called a 'king's party' in the sense that they opted for political reality as they saw it when the issue came to a head; they were not really concerned about the infringement of the royal rights *per se*.

We may now sum up the unexpectedly complex motives which caused the monks of Bury to take sides for or against Hugh's election. His defenders included the younger and better-educated monks. They were a party of the cellary, mostly East Anglians, drawn from a distinct and homogeneous community to which the cult of St. Edmund contributed a particular ethos. They hoped for a young abbot, sympathetic to learning, favourable to the cellary, an East Anglian; they were aware of the more recent currents in canon law which encouraged the extension of papal power in the making of ecclesiastical elections, and they were prepared to identify papal policy on elections with their liberty, the liberty of St. Edmund, by whose power they would defend it against a tyrannical monarch who shook his 'traditional custom' at them. Their opponents, older, less educated, many of them connected at some time with the sacristy, opted for the tried and tested path of accepting the realities of royal power. Yet one central aim was common to them both. Each wanted to maintain, perhaps enlarge, the privileged, independent status of the abbey; only their methods differed. That adopted by Hugh's party was

---

[1] Ibid., pp. 343–4.   [2] See below, pp. 37, 107.

new, radical, yet not so surprising in view of the abbey's past history. The saint's power had been invoked against barons, great churchmen, two princes of the royal house—why not against the king himself, if he was tyrannically overreaching the Church's liberties? And it was the method of the moment, for the pope and many of the English barons, as it were, backed it.

In a word, the struggle within the Bury cloister provoked by Hugh's election must be seen in terms of a long, incessant drive by the community for more independence of outside authority, whether baronial, episcopal, or royal—in other words, a 'communal movement'. All the monks were agreed on the method of Hugh's election which, if successfully carried through, would be an important new precedent for the exercise of yet more liberty. It was only when tough opposition developed that half of them lost faith in the new alliance and retreated to the shelter of the old. The final question is, of course, to what extent these findings can be applied to the whole movement for free elections in and before the reign of John. Professor Barraclough has recently warned historians that 'one swallow does not make a summer'.[1] Lacking comparable documentation for any of the other contemporary election disputes, the question must be left open for the present. Nevertheless, it is well worth raising.

iv. *The Manuscripts*

The text of the chronicle is extant in Brit. Mus. Harl. 1005 (H), and an extract from it is found in Cambridge, Univ. Libr. Add. 850 (C). Both volumes were produced in the abbey scriptorium and kept in the library there. Each contains a large number of pieces of varying character and date.

H: *B.M. Harl. 1005*[2]

The *Electio* is found at ff. 171–192ᵛ (modern foliation), written

---

[1] G. Barraclough, 'What is to be done about Medieval History?', *The New York Review of Books*, xiv (1970), i. 55. The proverb is from Aristotle, *Nic. Eth.* 1098ᵃ18: 'one swallow does not make a spring'.

[2] The 'Liber Albus' from the abbey library, bearing the late 14th century press-mark (C.68) inscribed by Henry de Kirkestede, who has also provided foliation. It is an octavo volume of 282 parchment folios, mostly in two similar small, neat, cursive hands of *c.* 1270, containing local customs and chronicles, treatises on estate-management, and miscellaneous information on the history and administration of the abbey; it was doubtless made for the use of some

in a single book-hand of the second half of the thirteenth century, almost certainly before 1280.[1] The text is in double columns, 47 lines to a page, with some spaces for headings and initials, filled in informally later by other hands. It bears all the marks of a bad copy made by a hasty and ignorant scribe, abounding in dittographies and haplographies, misread words and case-endings, and with more than usually haphazard punctuation. Corrections are in four hands: the scribe himself, infrequently; a smaller, contemporary book-hand (Hand A), occurring quite frequently and employing another text, possibly the exemplar, to fill in lengthy scribal omissions; a nearly contemporary cursive responsible for many other annotations and entire texts in the same and other Bury MSS. (Hand B), and a second large, rough cursive which has annotated or copied other items in the MS., including charters of 1401–3 (Hand C). The title to the work and one correction near the beginning are in the hand of Henry de Kirkestede, prior of Bury in the late fourteenth century.[2]

C: C.U.L. Add. 850[3]

The anonymous local chronicle, dubbed by Thomas Arnold *Cronica Buriensis*, occupies ff. 25ᵛ–48ᵛ (modern foliation), and is written in single columns, 41 lines to a page, in two similar neat cursives of c. 1400, found in other Bury MSS. of the time. According to Dr. Gransden, this version is a copy of which the original, written during the fourteenth century, must have been a composite work by an indeterminate number of authors. It is almost entirely

obedientiary, probably either a sacrist or cellarer, and later annotations indicate that its useful life extended into the early fifteenth century. The texts of the *Electio* and Jocelin's *Cronica* (ff. 127–170ᵛ) which it contains, however, are in two similar book-hands, and may have existed independently of, and earlier than the rest of the MS.

[1] It has been annotated by one of the two cursive hands (Hand B). This hand was responsible for the *Gesta Sacristarum* (ff. 120ᵛ–122) up to c. 1270–80, when it breaks off, and another hand continues.

[2] R. H. Rouse, '*Bostonus Buriensis* and the Author of the *Catalogus Scriptorum Ecclesie*', *Speculum*, xli (1966), 481–2.

[3] An octavo volume of fifty-five parchment folios, in four similar cursives, with red or blue filigree initials. It was originally bound with Cambridge Univ. Libr. MSS. Oo.6.110, ff. 84–90, and Oo.7.48, ff. 16–26, all three of which together form only a small remnant of the original book. C contains a metrical Life of St. Edmund, preceded by two hymns; the *Cronica Buriensis*, ending imperfectly, due to the loss of a quire of 8 leaves; a copy of a letter of Edward III to Pope Benedict XII, and a Provinciale. The Bury section of Oo.6.110 contains two treatises on prosody, and that of Oo.7.48 the Penitential of Thomas de Chabham.

conflated from texts, mostly extant but some lost, the choice of
subject-matter being to some extent determined by the availability
of this documentary material.[1] It is for this reason that Hugh's
election achieves such prominence in it.

The chronicler begins the account of the election dispute in his
own words, although often recalling the vocabulary and construction of the *Electio*, a text of which he evidently had before him.
In three respects, however, his account supplements the H text.
Firstly, Hugh of Northwold is named as one of the seven electors;[2]
this could have been deduced—with a good deal of perspicacity—
from H, but it is more likely that another source is being used.
Secondly, the scrutiny carried out by the seven electors is described
in greater detail than in the *Electio*, partly, no doubt, drawing on
the writer's personal knowledge of such procedure, with the
intention of clarifying the rather vague account given in the
Electio.[3] The precise information on the length of time occupied
by this examination, however, if not simply invented, must derive
from a written source. Finally, the texts of two letters and of the
convent's charter of ratification are supplied,[4] none of which
appears in the *Electio*. The text of a third letter, found also in the
Electio, is given here more completely.[5] The inference is that the
writer had before him not only the *Electio* itself, but a collection
of documents relating to the dispute, not all of which were used by
the author of the election chronicle.

Following his own account of the election procedure, the writer
of the *Cronica Buriensis* supplies an extract from the *Electio*,
beginning with Pope Innocent's admonitory letter to the judges
delegate,[6] and ending a few lines from the conclusion. There are a
good many variations between this extract and the H text; some
are merely orthographical (this applies especially to the place-
names); many represent scribal errors in C or its exemplar; a few
are corrections made in C to errors in H, and there remain a few
variations in which either version could be right. A few of the
variations suggest, without however proving decisively, that the C

---

[1] A. Gransden, 'The *Cronica Buriensis* and the Abbey of St. Benet of Hulme',
Bulletin of the Institute of Historical Research, xxxvi (1963), 77–82. Arnold
printed the *Cronica* in *Mem.* iii. 1–73, following the old foliation.

[2] *Mem.* iii. 12.   [3] Ibid., pp. 12–13.

[4] Ibid., pp. 14–16.

[5] See below, p. 12.

[6] Below, p. 154.

extract is independent of H. A *stemma* will best indicate their relationship as I see it:

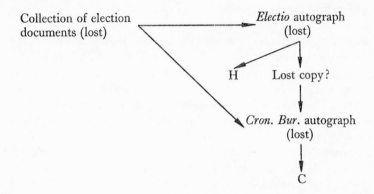

v. *The Editions*

The *Electio* was edited by Thomas Arnold in the second volume of his collection *Memorials of St. Edmunds Abbey* (pp. 29–130), from H alone. His version, an indifferently accurate transcription of the MS., suffers from an inadequate and haphazard critical apparatus. He did make a number of corrections to the rather corrupt H text, sometimes unnecessarily, but failed to eliminate the extensive dittographies which obscure its meaning at various points. He did not distinguish between the hands of the medieval correctors, sometimes ignoring their alterations, sometimes incorporating them into his own version with or without comment. When he came to print the *Cronica Buriensis*, in the third volume of the *Memorials* (pp. 1–73), Arnold did give the variations between the *Electio* extract in it and H, but so inaccurately as to render his service valueless. One is grateful, nonetheless, for his provision of a workable text, and of the textual annotations to the present edition, Arnold supplies upwards of half.

This edition is based on H, collated with C where they overlap. The C text is, on the whole, no better than H, but it does occasionally correct and clarify some of the more obvious blunders. Only those variants which are not merely orthographical are noted. The orthography of H is rigorously followed, but not its chaotic punctuation. As it has no divisions, Arnold's paragraphing has in

most cases been followed. Given the state of the text, emendations are necessarily frequent and sometimes conjectural, but have never been made silently. As far as possible, corrections by the scribe and the various other hands have been distinguished. Biblical references are to the Vulgate.

CRONICA DE ELECTIONE
HUGONIS ABBATIS

CRONICA DE ELECTIONE HUGONIS ABBATIS POSTEA EPISCOPI ELIENSIS[a]

ANNO ab Incarnacione Domini MCCXI,[b] nocte proxima instanti post festum[c] beati Thome martiris,[1] hora quasi xiiii., inter lupum et canem,[2] uenerabilis memorie Abbas Samson de hoc mundo migrans ad Illum qui terminos hominum posuit,[3] quos inpossibile est aliquem preterire, pro temporalibus celestia, pro labore requiem, pro merore et tristitia gaudium et consolacionem, pro perituris eterna commutans,[4] ouesque suas morsibus luporum deputatas, non tamen sine graui dolore a tanto pastore desolatas,[5] licet mercenariorum tutele ⟨eos⟩ reliquisset, eius[d] recessum deffleren-t⟨es⟩ irremediabilem, ⟨et⟩ de subtractione eiusdem tractare non differentes, communi omnium superiorum inferiorumque consilio, pulsata tabula,[6] omnes simul hora eadem in locutorium minu-torum[7] conuenire. Et licet ad presens de pastore prefitiendo sine regio assensu et gratia eius super electione libera perquisita, plene non possent tractare et sufficienter, ad maiorem tamen cautelam et domus sue securitatem, omnium uoto pariter et assensu, senten-tiam excommunicationis cum stolis et candelis accensis a domino priore prolatam, et ab aliis omnibus respondentibus 'amen' deinde confirmatam, inferre non distulerunt, uidelicet ne quis, uacante pastore, propriam procuraret[e] ad abbatiam perquirendam promo-cionem, seu bona ecclesie ob causam abbatie perquirende, per se uel per alium, siue pro se siue pro alio, inconsulto conuentu alienaret.[8]

---

[a] *Written across the head of the leaf by Henry de Kirkestede; Hand C has added* mortuo abbate Sampsone, *no doubt as a memorandum referring to the account of the election dispute in the late thirteenth century* Gesta Sacristarum, H *f. 121* (*Mem. ii. 293*), *which begins* Mortuo autem abbate Sampsone
[b] XI *added over erasure by Henry de Kirkestede* [c] *Added in marg. by Hand B* [d] eiusque H [e] H *adds* qui

[1] 30 December. So also the *Annales Sancti Edmundi* (*Mem.* ii. 19).
[2] A common expression for the time of dusk or twilight. See Ducange, s.v. *canis.*
[3] Ps. 104: 9.

CHRONICLE OF THE
ELECTION OF HUGH, ABBOT OF ST. EDMUNDS
AND LATER BISHOP OF ELY

ON the night after the feast of the blessed martyr Thomas,[1] at about nine o'clock, the time when wolf cannot be distinguished from dog,[2] in the year of our Lord 1211, Abbot Samson of respected memory passed from this world to be with the Ordainer of each man's inescapable end,[3] exchanging earthly for heavenly things, for labour rest, for sorrow and sadness joy and consolation, and for that which perishes, things eternal.[4] His flock, left to the care of hirelings and given over to the ravening wolves, were greatly distressed at losing so great a shepherd.[5] Nevertheless, to mourn his irremediable departure, and to begin discussion of the situation arising from his death, the whole community, both young and old, met together that very same hour in the parlour,[7] summoned by the gong.[6] At that time they were unable to proceed fully and sufficiently to appoint a pastor, since they had not sought the king's assent and favour for a free election. Even so, for greater safety and for the security of their house, and by unanimous wish and agreement, then and there they pronounced sentence of excommunication, with stoles and lighted candles; that is, the prior recited and all the rest confirmed with their 'amen' the following: that during the vacancy no one should attempt to buy his promotion to the abbacy, or alienate the church's goods for this purpose unknown to the convent, through or for himself or another.[8]

---

[4] Ioh. 6: 27.

[5] Ioh. 10: 12–13.

[6] The *tabula* was a wooden board beaten to summon the monks to a special meeting, especially on the occasion of a death in the community. See Ducange, s.v., and Lanfranc, *Constitutions*, pp. 122–4.

[7] The room where those who had been bled were permitted conversation, situated between the northern wall of the north-east transept and the chapter-house. A. B. Whittingham, 'Bury St. Edmunds Abbey; the plan, design and development of the church and monastic buildings', *Archaeological Journal*, cviii (1951, publ. 1952), 176 and pl. xxi.

[8] Doubtless based on the actual words of the sentence.

Quo facto, Robertus sacrista, Robertus camerarius et magister Thomas de Walsingham, communi consilio conuentus illa nocte uersus curiam properantes, dominumque regem, nisi fallar, apud Fresomantel inuenientes,[a1] humili premissa ex parte conuentus salutacione, causam rei euentus prosequuntur,[2] et ad gratiam ipsius regis facilius perquirendam ornamenta et suppellectilia prefati pastoris in auro et argento secum deferentes ipsi protenderent. Sed (licet non absurde, utpote diuina pocius ammonicione quam terrore mundiali) ob reuerentiam prefati sanctitatis uiri, manum suam ad oblata nulla uoluit posse extendere; quinimmo, ut qui eidem regi in uita sua non destinauit, nec post decessum temere attrectare presumebat. Quo uiso, sacrista monachique secum comitantes, magis terreno se preferentes amori quam diuino, ad captandam[b] regis beniuolentiam[3] inpremeditanter dissimulata ueritate responderunt: 'Non audiuimus ex ore eius, adhuc eo uiuente, quod eo defuncto ista domino suo regi nostro precepit deferri.' Hiis ita auditis, et nimis credulus eorum uerbis,[4] dominus rex, utpote qui et monachi et sacerdotes fuerunt, uerum et qui a uia ueritatis nullo timore seu amore terreno debuerant declinare, oblata gratanter suscipiens,[5] eorum electionem, a predecessoribus suis et ab eodem scriptis diuersis confirmatam et concessam, coram presentibus liberam esse fatebatur.[6] Sicque a curia discedentes, custodiamque abbatie per consilium sacriste sub nomine prioris suscipientes, inconsulto conuentu et sepius contradicente, pre diuersis periculis, uidelicet utriusque partis commixtione, priori reportabant.[7]

^a inueniendo H   ^b cartandam H

---

[1] The *Itinerary* is a blank from 26 December to 20 January. On 18 December the king was at Fremantle, on 25 at Windsor.

[2] Cf. *lectio iii* for the office of the vigil of St. Edmund in New York Pierpont Morgan Library MS. 736, p. 11: 'Ingressusque ad regem ex parte sancti Eadmundi humili praemissa salutatione legationis causam prosequitur. . . .' This MS. is a liturgical *libellus uitae* made at Bury *c.* 1124.

[3] The *captatio beneuolentiae*, originally a term in classical rhetoric, was a common dictaminal device employed in medieval letters.   [4] Gen. 39: 19.

[5] *Curia Regis Rolls*, vi (1932), p. 189 (Hilary term, 1212): 'Monachi de Sancto Edmundo uenerunt ad curiam et duxerunt domino palefridos abbatis qui obiit et iocalia tulerunt, que ipse domino regi legauit.'

[6] It must have been on this visit to court that the bargain was struck between the prior and King John in which the prior was granted custody of the abbot's estates during the vacancy for a payment of 400 marks, to be paid in instalments over a year (*Pipe Roll 13 John, PRS*, new ser. xxviii, 1951–2, p. 6). By 1214, however, £145 was still owing, and there is no record of its ever being paid (*Pipe Roll 16 John, PRS*, new ser. xxxv, 1959, p. 173).

[7] i.e. the two parts of the abbey lands, assigned respectively to the abbot and convent since early in the twelfth century (*JB*, p. xxv). Under this system the

Then Robert the sacrist, Robert the chamberlain, and Master Thomas of Walsingham, with the advice of the whole convent, hurried that very night to the court, finding the king, if I am not mistaken, at Fremantle.[1] After presenting their humble greetings on the convent's behalf, they announced the reason for their coming,[2] and in order to gain the king's favour more easily, offered him gold and silver ornaments and utensils, their late pastor's property, which they had brought with them. But the king in his wisdom, prompted by the divine admonition rather than by worldly fears, and by reverence for the abbot's sanctity, would not touch any of their gifts. For he did not rashly presume to appropriate after the abbot's death what the abbot had not intended for him while he was alive. Perceiving this, the sacrist and the monks with him, preferring worldly to the divine love, fabricated a lie on the spur of the moment in order to gain the royal favour,[3] saying: 'We heard from his lips, while he still lived, that after his death these goods were to be presented to our lord king.' Hearing this, and giving it too much credit,[4] since after all they were monks and priests, who ought not to have forsaken the truth either from fear or love of this world, the king gratefully accepted their gifts.[5] And before those present he acknowledged their right of free election, conceded and confirmed by his predecessors and by himself in various charters.[6] Then they left the court, receiving the custody of the abbey, by the sacrist's advice, on behalf of the prior, to whom they now made their report. In this action the convent was not consulted, and often spoke against it, because of the many dangers which would arise from the mixing of the two parts.[7]

king was supposed to administer only the abbot's portion during a vacancy. As indicated above, the abbey had on this occasion bought the right to administer both portions themselves. This confounding of the two parts, although perhaps of immediate financial benefit, evidently worried some of the monks as setting a dangerous precedent (cf. *JB*, pp. 81, 89–90). In fact by May 1214 John had decided that this bargain was not profitable enough to the crown, and moreover wished to put pressure on those monks who were still maintaining the validity of Hugh's election. He therefore took the abbey lands into his own custody (see below, pp. 81–3). It is not clear whether he included the conventual as well as abbatial lands in this. In any case there had always been limitations on the degree to which John permitted the monks custody of their lands. The patent rolls show clearly that from the first the king reserved the right to present to vacant churches both on the abbot's and the convent's lands: *Rot. Litt. Pat.*, pp. 92 (May 1212), 97b (April 1213), 102b (July 1213), 107b (January 1214), 114 (April 1214), 114b (May 1214), 122b (October 1214), 124b (November 1214).

Sed cum in eadem custodia plane annum et quantum restat amplius, a Natali usque ad kalendas Augusti, gauderent, necdum aliquid de pastore prefitiendo tractassent, seu tractare permisissent,[1] concepit dominus rex in animo domibus terre sue uniuersis pastore uacantibus[a] consulere; proposuit enim tunc transfretare.[2] Mandauitque litteris suis domibus uacantibus,[a] quatinus secundum consuetudinem antiquitus usitatam de pastoris electione preuisis ⟨litteris⟩ curiam adissent. Hoc quidem mandatum speciale per litteras domini regis suscepti conuentus die sancti Oswaldi regis et martiris[3] in hec uerba:

I(ohannes) Dei gratia rex Anglie, dux Normannie, comes Andegauie et ⟨dux⟩ Aquitanie, priori et conuentui sancti Aedmundi salutem.

f. 171ᵛ   Mandamus uobis quod sine dilatione et occasione mittatis ad nos de discrecioribus uiris conuentus uestri | quot uideritis expedire, cum litteris de rato, paratos et bene[b] instructos ad eligendum uobis abbatem secundum consuetudinem Anglie, et si forte in Angliam nos[c] non inuenerint, nos sequantur, et custum quod posuerunt in ueniendo ad nos uobis computabitur ad scakarium.

Teste meipso apud Corfe, xxv.[d] die Iulii, anno regni nostri[e] xv.[4]

Misimus propter ⟨hoc⟩ priorem et sacristam.[5] Consilio tandem domini Cantuariensis[6] episcoporumque Deum timentium[7] ⟨at⟩que libertates sancte ecclesie fouentium super forma et modo electionis secundum Deum et canones, ut in unica persona eligenda unanimiter consentientes, corpus Domini et reliquias deferri in capitulo iubebant. Quibus allatis erexit se magister Nicholaus, et multiplici ratione contra sacristam suffitienter premissa et ostensa,

---

[a] uagantibus (bis) H   [b] plene Rot. Litt. Claus.   [c] et si forte nos in
Angliam Rot. Litt. Claus.   [d] xv. Rot. Litt. Claus.   [e] regni nostri
om., Rot. Litt. Claus.

[1] This is unfair of the writer, since all abbatial elections were suspended during the interdict.

[2] John had summoned the host to muster at Portsmouth in late July for his intended continental expedition (Wendover, RS, ii. 82); his actual departure did not take place until February 1214. It is a pity that the writer is not more informative about events at Bury during the vacancy. In 1212 the monks bore heavily on the burghers of the vill to help pay the 4,000 marks ablata extorted from them by the king. The townsmen pleaded against the abbey in the royal court, but lost the case. The reason why is seen in Pipe Roll 14 John (PRS, new ser. xxx, 1954), p. 181, which reveals that the monks paid 100 marks, the burghers 400 for the royal judgement. The king obviously had everything to gain

But when they had enjoyed the custody of their house for one full year and from Christmas to 1 August of the next, and had not done or permitted anything to be done about appointing a pastor,[1] the king decided to consult all the vacant houses of his realm, for at that time he intended to go overseas.[2] And he wrote to the vacant houses, that on receipt of his letter, according to the traditional custom when electing a pastor, they should come to court. The convent received their particular mandate from the king on the feast of St. Oswald king and martyr[3] as follows:

> John by the grace of God king of England, duke of Normandy and Aquitaine and count of Anjou, to the prior and convent of St. Edmunds, greeting.
>
> We order you to send to us without delay or hesitation as many of the wiser men of your convent as you think necessary, with letters of authorization, well prepared and instructed to choose an abbot for you according to English custom; and if by chance they do not find us in England, they are to follow us, and the money which they spend in so doing will be made up to you at the Exchequer.
>
> Witness myself at Corfe, 25 July, in the fifteenth year of our reign.[4]

So we sent the prior and sacrist.[5] After taking the advice of the archbishop of Canterbury[6] and of those bishops who feared God[7] and defended the liberties of Holy Church over what form and mode of election was to be adopted according to God and the canons (that is, in which unanimous consent is given to the election of a single person), they ordered the host and relics to be carried into the chapter-house. Then Master Nicholas rose and brought many charges against the sacrist, which he supported

by protecting the monks from whom he was mulcting such an enormous sum, while making further profit from the townsmen.
  [3] 5 August 1213. In June the king was absolved and letters were sent to ten vacant abbeys, asking them to proceed to elections as above. *Chron. Barnwell* in Walter of Coventry, *RS*, ii. 213.
  [4] The text of this letter is also given in *Rot. Litt. Claus.*, p. 147.
  [5] But not to court, according to what follows. Some words may be missing here.
  [6] Stephen Langton, archbishop of Canterbury 1206/7–1228. For his career see F. M. Powicke, *Stephen Langton* (Oxford, 1928). The others would have been the 'papalist' bishops, Eustace of Ely and William of London, according to later statements of the writer (see below, pp. 25, 37).   [7] *Reg. Ben.*, c. 65.

tum quia immitis et immisericors, tum quia fratrum derisor et contemptor, tum quia ambiciosus, tum quia domus sue dilapidator, tum aliis quam pluribus ad digitum rationibus ostensis, appellauit ne idem sacrista eligens fieret neque electus. Exurgensque R(icardus) de Saxam, postquam magister Nicholaus loqui cessauit, aliaque contra eandem personam consimilia proponens, eandem repetiit appellacionem. Auditis tamen appellationibus in pleno capitulo, presente sacrista, et eisdem appellationibus cedentibus in negocio, uolentes procedere elegerunt communi consilio tres sub nomine Trinitatis, qui prestito sacramento ⟨iurauerunt⟩ super corpus Domini et super reliquias ibidem presentes, quod non dimitterent pro prece uel precio, odio uel amore, nec pro morte nec pro uita, seu pro aliquo temporali emolumento, quin secundum conscientiam suam eligerent de toto conuentu septem de fidelioribus et melioribus et discrecioribus ad faciendam electionem,[1] qui non essent suspecti quod magis essent familiares unis quam aliis, nisi propter Deum et uite meritum.[2] Electis uero tribus, uidelicet A(lbino) suppriore, I(ocelino) elemosinario et R(icardo) precentore, prestito super corpus Domini sacramento, sicut superius habetur, exierunt foras, conuentu tamen in capitulo remanente, et conferentes ad inuicem de singulis, moresque omnium et fidelitatem reuoluentes, elegerunt Robertum sacristam, magistrum Henricum de Ely, Ioscelinum de Altari quondam celerarium,[3] Iohannem de Laneham firmarium,[4] Hugonem subcelerarium,[5] magistrum Thomam tercium priorem et magistrum T(homam) de Walsingham, ut essent electores. Sed mox ut sacrista inter alios fuisset nominatus priori, N(icholaus) et R(icardus) appellationem renouauerunt contra eundem. Vnde communi conuentus consilio, eodemque consentiente, ut tamen in rem procederent, deletus fuit sacrista, appositusque fuit per conuentum camerarius in loco sacriste.[6] Quibus electis, iurauerunt super corpus Domini quod fideliter scrutatis singulorum conscienciis et examinatis, tam ipsorum septem quam et tocius conuentus, unum de misericordioribus et benignioribus et discrecioribus ad abbatiam regendam

---

[1] Probably the exact words of the oath, which would be taken according to a written formula (see below, p. 183).

[2] *Reg. Ben.*, c. 2.

[3] This is Jocelin of Brakelond. *Kalendar*, pp. liv–lvii.

[4] *Firmarius*, according to Latham, *Word-List*, is 'infirmarer', but later in the chronicle (p. 70) John and Richard of Saxham both appear as *firmarii* while

with abundant evidence, namely, that he was severe and unfeeling, a scoffer and slighter of the brothers, ambitious, a dilapidator of his house and much else, moving that he be ineligible either as an elector or for election. When he had finished, Richard of Saxham rose and seconded his motion, stating other, similar charges against the same man. These appeals were heard by the full chapter in the sacrist's presence, but were laid aside because they wanted to proceed with more pressing business. They then chose three men by unanimous vote, according to the number of the Trinity. These men swore on the host and relics that they would not turn aside for gift or entreaty, love or hate, neither for life or death nor for any temporal emolument, but that they would choose, according to the dictates of their consciences, seven of the more trustworthy, virtuous, and discreet members of the convent to conduct the election;[1] men who were not suspected of more familiarity with one brother than with the rest unless because of his godly and virtuous life.[2] And they chose these three: Albinus the subprior, Jocelin the almoner, and Richard the precentor. After taking oath on the host as mentioned, they went outside, leaving the rest of the convent in the chapter-house, and discussing each man's faith and way of life in turn, they chose as electors Robert the sacrist, Master Henry of Ely, Jocelin of the Altar, one time cellarer,[3] John of Lavenham the victualler,[4] Hugh the sub-cellarer,[5] Master Thomas the third prior, and Master Thomas of Walsingham. But as soon as the prior had named the sacrist among the others, Nicholas and Richard renewed their appeal against him. The convent, therefore, consulted together and consented to it, so that they could get on with the business. The sacrist was struck from the list and the convent replaced him with the chamberlain.[6] The chosen men now swore on the host that, after they had fairly scrutinized and weighed the actions of each man, both of their own number and of the rest of the convent, they would choose,

Adam simultaneously holds office as *infirmarius*. One of their duties was the supervision of the convent's ale-supply, so that their office was probably a sub-department of the cellary.

[5] *Cronica Buriensis* (*Mem.* iii. 14) states that this was Hugh of Northwold.

[6] The late-thirteenth-century *Gesta Sacristarum* (*Mem.* ii. 293) states that the sacrist was actually elected by one part of the convent. But the account given above is supported by the decision of the judges delegate, by the *Cronica Buriensis* (*Mem.* iii. 12–16), whose author had access to records not included in the H text of the *Electio*, and by the *Bury Chronicle*, p. 1. The last two accounts, which are very similar, are probably based on the lost portion of the *Annales*.

et pastorale officium, secundum regulam sancti Benedicti, siue de seipsis siue de toto conuentu, salua tamen conscientia eligerent.[1] Peracto quidem a septem tali modo sacramento, totus conuentus iurauit uersa uice, priore incipiente, aliis omnibus singillatim sequentibus, quod quemcunque de conuentu prefati septem eligerent, pro electo sine contradicto haberent. Quo facto, finitum est capitulum.

Et conuenientes septem in capellam sancti Sabe,[2] ceperunt illo die officium examinacionis iniunctum prosequi; duo tamen ex illis septem singulorum examen et nomina in scriptum redigentes. Examinatis quidem omnibus, moribusque singulorum et conuersacionibus uirtutibusque inter se collatis et ponderatis, adquieuerunt in unam personam.[3] Qui mox ingressi capitulum petierunt litteras de rato ad confirmandum sacramentum a conuentu factum, scilicet quod quem septem presentarent pro electo haberent. Quod quidem assensu omnium et uoto concessum est.[4] Exeuntibus de capitulo cum litteris de rato, mo|dicoque facto interuallo, regressi nominauerunt uoce iocunda fratrem Hugonem de Norwolde, uirum honeste conuersacionis et bene morigeratum, uirum in utroque Testamento suffitienter edoctum, uirum gratia et misericordia repletum, benignum, omnique amaritudine destitutum, sobrium et castum, modestum, pium, quietum, et in exterioribus agendis prudentem et probatum.[5] Quo electo et nominato, et pro cuius electione causa canonice facta, omnes singillatim in osculum pacis irruentes benedicebant Deum.[6] Eumque in sinistra parte chori in loco eminenciori iuxta priorem collocantes, appellauerunt ne quid fraudis uel doli instinctu maligno seu machinacione alicuius contra eandem electionem fieret. Conpleta sunt ista tali modo in crastino Transfiguracionis Domini[a] in capitulo sancti Aedmundi.[7]

f. 172

a H *adds* in capella uel, *canc.*

[1] Probably a close paraphrase of the text. The form of election adopted at Bury on this occasion was that known as the *uia compromissi*, described by Gervase of Canterbury (*RS*, ii. 125–6).

[2] The north-eastern apsidal chapel in the presbytery of the conventual church, dedicated in the reign of Abbot Anselm (1121–48).

[3] The account in the *Cronica Buriensis* (*Mem.* iii. 13) is clearer and more detailed. The seven were chosen to symbolize the sevenfold grace of the Holy Spirit, and the examination continued until about 9 a.m. the next day. It was conducted by the whole convent filing past the examiners, who wrote down each man's nomination with his reasons for it.

according to the *Rule* of St. Benedict, one of the more tolerant, good-natured, and sensible, either from among themselves or the rest of the convent, saving their consciences, to rule in the pastoral office as abbot.[1] When the seven electors had taken this oath, the rest of the convent one after the other, beginning with the prior, swore that they would accept as elected, without opposition, whomsoever the seven chose from their community. After this the chapter ended.

The seven, meeting in the chapel of St. Sabas,[2] began the process of examination that very day, two of them taking down in writing each man's opinion and nomination. After examining everyone, and considering and weighing the habits, behaviour, and virtues of each individual, they finally settled on one person.[3] Next, entering the chapter-house, they asked for letters of ratification confirming the oath taken by the convent, namely that they would accept whomsoever the seven presented as abbot-elect. This was carried unanimously.[4] Then, after retiring from the chapter-house with the letters of ratification and remaining outside for a short time, they returned and joyfully nominated brother Hugh of Northwold, a man good-humoured and upright, learned enough in the Old and New Testaments, full of grace and compassion, pleasant, absolutely devoid of moroseness, sober and chaste, modest and devout, calm, and reliable and prudent in his actions.[5] When he had been chosen and nominated, and the election process fulfilled canonically, everyone, giving thanks to God, rushed forward one after another to give him the kiss of peace.[6] Seating him in the raised seat next to the prior's on the left side of the choir, they appealed against anyone who should devise fraud, malice-inspired trickery or any machinations whatsoever against his election. All this was done in the chapter-house of St. Edmunds on the day after the Lord's Transfiguration.[7]

---

[4] *Cronica Buriensis* (*Mem.* iii. 14) supplies the text not of this *carta*, but of that confirming the election specifically of Hugh. See Appendix I.

[5] Cf. Matthew Paris's eulogy of Hugh (*Chron. Maj., RS*, ii. 582–3), and similar lists of virtues in *Reg. Ben.*, c. 64: 'sobrius, castus, misericors; in utro Testamento . . . edoctum', and Tit. 2: 5: 'prudentes, castas, sobrias, domus curam habentes, benignas . . .' The author's description is in fact a typical hagiographical *Tugendkatalog*, offering little real appreciation of Hugh's individual characteristics. See B. de Gaiffier, 'Hagiographie et historiographie', *Settimane di Studio*, xvii (Spoleto, 1970), i. 157–63. For Hugh's character and career see Appendix V.

[6] Lanfranc, *Constitutions*, p. 72.   [7] 7 August.

Electo itaque uenerabili fratre H(ugone) in crastino Transfiguracionis, quod est vii. idus Augusti, summo mane iter arripuit
uersus curiam ad perquirendam gratiam domini regis super
electione facta,[1] comitantibus secum H(erberto) priore, R(oberto)
sacrista, R(oberto) camerario, I(ohanne) postea abbate de Hulmo,[2]
I(ohanne) de Laueham, magistro Nicholao et magistro Thoma de
Walsingham. Et presentatus est ab istis domino regi per inter-
positas personas, cum et ipsi accessum ad eum non haberent. Sed
dominus rex, audita forma sub una persona, iratus noluit assentire.[3]
Quo uiso, et ibidem non sine magnis expensis moram fecisse, se^a
grauari sentiebant. Consilium inierunt[4] ut dominum S(tephanum)
archiepiscopum super hoc conuenirent per magistrum Nicholaum,
qui profectus est cum litteris domini prioris patentibus ac^b
sigillo suo signatis in hec uerba:^{c}

Reuerendo domino et patri sanctissimo S(tephano) Dei
gratia Cantuariensi archiepiscopo, sancte Romane ecclesie
cardinali et tocius Anglie primati, H(erbertus) prior sancti
Aedmundi et conuentus eiusdem loci debitam et deuotam
obedientiam cum salute.

Nouerit uestra paternitas^d quod nos una cum fratribus nostris
uniuersis, de pastore domui nostre preficiendo^e tractantes, in
loco^f quo fieri debet electio,[5] secundum Deum et canones
elegimus uirum honestum et approbatum et suffitientem,
dominum Hugonem de Norwalde, unanimi omnium uoto et
assensu. Quo electo nos omnes in eodem loco pro eo et pro
electione nostra appellauimus, ne quid fieret in preiudicium
eiusdem electionis. Ea propter dilectum fratrem nostrum magistrum Nicholaum monacum, capellanum nostrum, cum litteris
nostris patentibus eandem appellationem protestantibus,^{g} ut
sub tuicione nostra iam dictam innouet appellationem, desti-
namus.

Valeat paternitas uestra in Christo.^{h}

Quibus coram domino Cantuariensi perlectis, extendens manus
suas ad Deum dixit: 'Gloria sit Altissimo;[6] iam nunc in hac parte

After his election the worthy brother Hugh set out for the court, early in the morning of the day after Transfiguration, that is, the seventh of August, to obtain the king's favour for his election.[1] With him went Prior Herbert, Robert the sacrist, Robert the chamberlain, John later abbot of Hulme,[2] John of Lavenham, Master Nicholas and Master Thomas of Walsingham. And they presented Hugh to the king through intermediaries, since they were not allowed in to him. But the king, when he heard that they had adopted the procedure of choosing one person only, angrily refused his assent.[3] Because of this and the heavy expenses incurred by their stay at court, the monks were much aggrieved. They decided to consult Archbishop Stephen about it;[4] and so Master Nicholas was sent to him with letters patent from the prior and under his seal, reading thus:

> To his reverend lord and most holy father Stephen by the grace of God archbishop of Canterbury, cardinal of the Holy Roman Church, primate of all England, Herbert prior of St. Edmunds and the convent there send befitting and devoted obedience with their greetings.
>
> Know, father, that we and all our brothers, seeking a pastor to set over our house, chose, in the correct place,[5] according to God and the canons, and by unanimous consent, Hugh of Northwold, a man upright, approved, and competent. After his election we all appealed there for him and for our right of election, lest anything be done to prejudice it. For this reason we are sending Master Nicholas, our beloved brother and chaplain, with our letters patent defending the appeal, that under our protection he may renew it.
>
> Farewell, father in Christ.

When this had been read to the archbishop he raised his hands heavenward, saying: 'Glory to God the highest,[6] for in this way

---

[1] John was probably at Corfe (*Itinerary*).

[2] Made abbot October–November 1214, dying in December before receiving the episcopal blessing. *Heads of Religious Houses*, ed. D. Knowles, C. N. L. Brooke and V. London (Cambridge, 1972), pp. 68–9.

[3] The king expected at least to be offered a choice, as was Henry II at the election of Samson, Hugh's predecessor (*JB*, pp. 21–3).

[4] *Consilium inire* is a common O.T. expression used frequently by this writer, and a favourite of Jocelin's (*JB*, pp. 3, 21, 28, 49, etc.).

[5] i.e. where they could not be influenced by the secular power as at court, or in the king's chapel.   [6] Cf. Luc. 2: 14.

uincens ecclesia triumphauit!' Magister uero Nicholaus priori et
domino electo sociisque eorundem uerba domini archiepiscopi et
modum gratulacionis super cartam extremam[1] festinanter exposuit.
Qui mox regressi sunt omnes domum preterquam electus et
magister T(homas) de Walsingham et I(ohannes) de Laueham.[2]
Venientes uero domum statim dominus prior et sacrista, simulque
totus conuentus, introierunt capitulum; factoque summo silentio,[3]
precepit dominus prior ut sacrista que facta fuerant ad curiam[a] et
audita conuentui detegeret. Ille uero, non breui utens eloquio,
narrauit quomodo a magnatibus curie iam fame dispendium
propter electum incurissent, et non solum illi, sed et totus conuentus, dicens: 'Vbi membrum scandalizatur, ibi et totum corpus.'[4]
Audientes autem hec, commota est pars magna. Erigens tandem se
dominus I(ocelinus) elemosinarius petiit audientiam. Prorumpens
quidem in uerba, uoce flebilica recitare cepit, quomodo minus
circumspecte quam debuit facta est electio, et maxime de carta
conuentus de rato contra regium assensum et eius usitatam consuetudinem, et periculum quod inde iminere credebat proponens,
ad hoc utens ut cartam aliquo modo reuocaret; appellauitque pro
statu regio et eius usitata consuetudine, salua electione licet sero.
Quamobrem factus est illo die tumultus magnus in populo,[5] et sic
assurgens conuentus incipiendo 'Verba mea'[6] a capitulo discesserunt.

In crastino uero ante capitulum intrauit sacrista ad priorem,
f. 172ᵛ   ducens secum A(lbinum) subpriorem | atque[b] R(icardum) pre-
centorem et I(ocelinum) elemosinarium[c] et A(dam) infirmarium[d]
et P(etrum) de Wrthstede et multos alios; peciitque[e] ut littere
quedam ab eis composite pro saluacione domus — ut illi asserebant — et ordinate, sub sigillo conuentus munite, nostro dirigentur
electo. Quibus cum gratanter dominus prior adquieuisset, absen-
tans se tamen illo die a capitulo, reliquit domino A(lbino) suppriori omnem potestatem secundum regulam sancti Benedicti in
subiectos excercendam et ultra; scilicet ut quoscumque reperiret
huic consilio repugnantes sub anathematis sententia uinctos in-
nodaret; factumque est ita. Peractis omnibus ad ordinis rigorem

---

[a] H adds domini, *canc. by scribe and Hand C*   [b] quod H   [c] elemosinario H, *corr. by Hand B*   [d] infirmario H, *corr. by Hand B*
[e] multis aliis peciit quod H, *corr. and* et *added to* peciit *by Hand B*

the Church has at last triumphed in victory!' Master Nicholas lost
no time in conveying to the prior, the abbot elect and his friends
the archbishop's words and his joy at their latest charter.[1] They
then returned home, except for the abbot elect, Master Thomas of
Walsingham, and John of Lavenham.[2] As soon as they had arrived,
the prior and sacrist entered the chapter-house with the rest of the
convent. And amid deep silence[3] the prior instructed the sacrist
to tell the convent what they had done and heard at court. The
sacrist, in a lengthy speech, related how on the abbot-elect's
account they had been made fools of by the magnates there—and
not only they themselves but the whole convent, saying: 'Where
one member is held in ill repute, so is the whole body.'[4] Hearing
this, most of them were greatly disturbed. Jocelin the almoner rose
to his feet and begged a hearing. Breaking into speech, he exclaimed
in unhappy tones how the election had been less prudently conducted than was proper. He dwelt particularly on how the convent's charter of ratification went against the royal assent and the
king's traditional custom, so that they were threatened with
imminent disaster, as he thought. Of course his object was to have
the charter revoked by some means, and he appealed, although
belatedly, for the king's dignity and for his traditional custom,
without violation of their election. That day there was a great
tumult among the people[5] over these things, and so the convent
rose and left the chapter-house with the *Verba mea.*[6]

The next day before chapter, the sacrist went to the prior,
accompanied by Albinus the subprior, Richard the precentor,
Jocelin the almoner, Adam the infirmarer, Peter of Worstead,
and many others. He asked that a letter, which they had written
for the good of the house—so they said—be sent to the abbot elect,
protected and authorized by the convent seal. The prior gladly
agreed, but nevertheless absented himself from chapter that day,
leaving Subprior Albinus all the power afforded by the *Rule* of
St. Benedict—and more—to exercise discipline. For whomsoever
he found opposing this idea was to be bound under sentence of
anathema; and so it was done. When everything pertaining to the

---

[1] i.e. the chapter's charter of ratification.
[2] 19 August, as may be deduced from what follows.
[3] *Reg. Ben.*, c. 38.
[4] Marc. 9: 41–6; 1 Cor. 12: 26.   [5] Os. 10: 14.
[6] Ps. 5: 1, customarily sung at the conclusion of chapter (Lanfranc, *Constitutions*, p. xvii).

spectantibus, pretendit R(icardus) precentor litteras memoratas a magnatibus et sapientibus compositas—ut ipse asserebat— petiitque ut perlecte et sub sigillo conuentus impresse nostro dirigerentur electo. Fuit autem hic tenor litterarum:

> Mandamus tibi quatinus uisis litteris domum uenire omni occasione postposita festines. Habemus enim quoddam nego- cium terminandum, quod sine tua presentia non potest duci ad effectum.

Quibus perlectis, facta est inter eos dissensio magna, eo quod ex parte conuentus talia sine consensu eorum electo proposuissent[1] transmittere. Et assurgens magister T(homas) tertius prior, cum tribus sociis secum astantibus, appellauit ne quid in preiudicium electi fieret. Intuens eum unus de parte sacriste, repulit et manus iniecit[a] in eum,[2] scilicet Taillehaste. R(icardus) uero precentor, existimans quod non essent plures in congregatione quam isti tres, qui fidem Deo et sacramento in pleno capitulo facto, presente Dominico corpore et attestante, seruassent, circuiuit conuentum, singulos singillatim conueniens et interrogans cuius uel qualis esset oppinionis aut sententie. Et inuenti sunt illo die in capitulo numero quadraginta uiri, cum septem examinatoribus, pleni fide et ueritate,[3] qui pro morte nec pro uita a uia ueritatis et ab electo a Deo sibi dato nulla ratione nec uelle nec posse recedere pro- miserunt.[4] Vnde uenerabilis A(lbinus) supprior premeditatam super eos intulit excommunicationis sententiam quam, ut postea in pleno capitulo, ad presentiam coram eiusdem ductus, penituit se dedisse.[5]

Illo autem die post prandium[6] conuenerunt sacrista et R(icardus) precentor[b] et alii quinque in domum prioris, super hoc quod litteras predictas sigillo prioris munitas sub pristina[c] forma ex parte conuentus R(obertus) sacrista et R(icardus) precentor electo defferrent; factumque est ita. Concilium autem quinto die sequenti apud Lundoniam prefixum erat.[7] Venientes uero apud Lesnes electum ibi inuenerunt,[8] sed illo die ei communicare noluerunt.

---

[a] inietit H   [b] H adds coram, canc. by scribe and Hand C   [c] Twice H, first canc. by Hand C

[1] i.e. the sacrist and his followers.
[2] Marc. 14: 46.   [3] Cf. Ioh. 1: 14.
[4] Almost a year later (see below, p. 87) this number had fallen to 34. Six months later again, however, it had apparently increased again, probably to about the original 40 (see below, p. 121).
[5] Cf. Abbo of Fleury, *Passio Sancti Edmundi* (*Mem.* i. 22): 'qui inpremeditatus sententiam dedit, quam se dedisse postea . . . poenituit.'

rigour of their order stood in readiness, Richard the precentor presented the letter, written, so he said, by officials and wise men, and asked that after it had been read out it should be sent to our abbot elect impressed with the convent seal. Now this was the gist of the letter:

> We order you to hasten home when you have read this letter, abandoning all other matters, for we have some business to finish which cannot be properly dealt with without your presence.

When it had been read out there was great dissension because they[1] had intended to send such a letter to the abbot elect on the convent's behalf but without its assent. Master Thomas the third prior, rising to his feet with three friends in support, appealed against anything being done to the abbot elect's prejudice. One of the sacrist's party, a man named Taillehaste, seeing this, laid hands on him[2] and pushed him down. Now Richard the precentor thought that there were in the congregation only those three who, keeping their faith in God, were standing by the oath made on the host in full chapter. So he went round the convent, tackling each man individually and asking his opinion. And that day there were found forty men in the chapter as well as the seven electors who, full of faith and truth,[3] did not wish nor were able for life or death or any reason to abandon the path of truth or their God-given abbot elect.[4] So the worthy Subprior Albinus pronounced the prearranged sentence of excommunication against them, although he later apologized for this, in full chapter and in their presence.[5]

The same day after dinner,[6] the sacrist, Richard the precentor and five others met in the prior's house, intending that Robert the sacrist and Richard the precentor should take the letter from the convent to the abbot elect, unaltered and sealed with the prior's seal. And it was done. A council had been fixed to meet at London five days thence,[7] and so, coming to Lesnes, they found the abbot elect there,[8] but would not talk with him that day.

[6] 20 August, about 2 p.m.

[7] *Councils*, pp. 19–20. The council met on 25 August and discussed, *inter alia*, the repayment of sums extorted by the king from the clergy as a necessary preliminary to the lifting of the interdict.

[8] Lesnes in Kent being situated almost on a direct line from Canterbury to London, the archbishop was doubtless there on his way to the council; it was one of his manors.

Mane autem facto[1] R(obertus) sacrista et R(icardus) precentor coram domino archiepiscopo se ingerentes, electum instanter accusare ceperunt, nitentes eius canonicam improbare electionem que, secundum quod proposuerant, minus canonica quam debuit facta fuit, et quod plures de domo in generali examinacione fuerunt nominati ad officium pastorale et ad abbatiam quam electus, et quod septem examinatores periuros[a] probarent. Illis autem in eodem loco super hoc persistentibus, uenit electus tanquam a Deo missus.[2] Qui cum ad dominum archiepiscopum humili premissa salutacione esset ingressus,[3] dixit ad eum archiepiscopus:[b] 'Frater, quid est hoc quod audio de te? Aurum tuum uersum est in scoriam.[4] Ecce, in quantis isti te accusant!'[5] Et incipiens narrauit ei omnia que a duobus iam presentibus de eo erant prosecuta. Ille uero hiis auditis, pocius admiratione quam stupore repletus,[6] humiliter peciit ut ibi coram eo, ne diucius protelaretur, rei ueritati perquisite finem imponeret. Dominus autem archiepiscopus, pre tantis diuersisque negociis tota die emergentibus, coram eo circumspitiens non posse istud determinari, statuit eis iudices, uidelicet duos clericos, qui in crastino natiuitatis beate Marie apud sanctum Aedmundum uenientes,[7] rei ueritatem subtilius indagarent, et cognita ueritate auctoritate archiepiscopali finem imponerent. Quibus conuentui recitatis, conuentus nimis moleste pertulit quod scrutinium super uiros religiosos per manus clericorum, semper ad insidias eis assidentium,[8] aliqua condicione exerceretur.

Quid plura? In crastino uoluit dominus R(obertus) sacrista et R(icardus) precentor quedam proponere, absente electo. Sed sanior pars conuentus, licet non etate maturior, nequaquam consensit, ut eo absente ille uel alius aliqua que ad eius spectabant[c] electionem proponeret. Facta est illa hora dissensio magna[9] et diuisio, ita quod, a capitulo sine 'Verba mea' et animarum absolutione[10] discedentes, una pars, que cum sacramento firmiter

---

[a] per uiros H   [b] H *adds* pre tantis diuersisque negociis, *canc. by scribe and Hand C*   [c] expectabant H

[1] Num. 22: 41.   [2] Ioh. 1: 6.
[3] Cf. *lectio iii* for the office of the vigil of St. Edmund, cited above, p. 4 n. 2.
[4] Is. 1: 22.   [5] Marc. 15: 4.

The next morning[1] Robert the sacrist and Richard the precentor, thrusting themselves into the archbishop's presence, began unceremoniously to accuse the abbot elect, endeavouring to prove that the conduct of his election had been less canonical than was proper, that other members of the house besides the abbot elect had been nominated for the pastoral office and abbacy in general examination, and that the seven examiners had proved themselves perjurers. While they were still there persisting in this fashion, the abbot elect arrived, as though sent from God.[2] When he had entered and presented his humble greetings,[3] the archbishop said to him: 'Brother, what is this I hear about you? Your gold is become dross.[4] See how much they bring against you!'[5] And he began to tell the abbot elect everything of which the two still present had accused him. Hugh, when he had heard these things, was full of wonder, though not put to confusion,[6] and he asked humbly that, to avoid longer delay, the archbishop should then and there get to the bottom of the matter and pronounce judgement. But the archbishop, because of the mass of varied business which came before him all day long, found it impossible to give them his personal decision. Instead he arranged judges for them, two clerks who would come to St. Edmunds on the day after the Nativity of the blessed Mary,[7] investigate the facts of the matter more minutely, and after reaching a decision, pronounce judgement by archiepiscopal authority. When this was told the convent they were very annoyed that a scrutiny of religious should be conducted under any condition by clerks, who always lay in wait for them.[8]

Why say more? The next day Robert the sacrist and Richard the precentor wished to raise certain matters in the abbot elect's absence. But the wiser members of the convent, although not the maturer in years, disallowed any discussion relating to the election, by him or anyone else in the abbot elect's absence. At this point there was so much dissension[9] and division that, quitting the chapter-house without the *Verba mea* and absolution[10] the party

---

[6] Based on Act. 3: 10. In the Itala this reads 'repleti sunt pauore et admiratione', while the Vulgate has 'stupore et extasi'. An intermediate version, then, seems to be the source of the author's expression, which may have been proverbial at the time.

[7] 9 September.

[8] Ps. 10 (*sec. Hebr.*): 8.

[9] Act. 23: 10.   [10] See above, p. 15 n. 6.

f. 173 et inflexibiliter | stetit, ad electum in domo prioris confugit, altera
uero que sacriste erat, reclusit se in capella infirmorum, hostiis
reseratis, et custodibus ad hostia positis.¹ Ibi uero super hiis
sollicite tractantes, mandauerunt electum per dominum A(lbinum)
suppriorem et I(ohannem) de Laueham, ut ad illos solus uenisset,
nullo alio de suis secum comitante; ad quod fideles eius noluerunt
assentire, nisi omnes secum possent interesse. Talibus R(oberto)
domino sacriste et aliis ibi expectantibus renunciatis, discesserunt*a*
a capella psallendo 'Verba mea'.²

Euolutis paucis diebus et tumultu aliquantulum sedato, et
contramandatis clericis supramemoratis, electus iterato presentatus est apud Nothingham³ per dominum priorem et R(obertum)
sacristam et R(obertum) camerarium et magistrum T(homam)
tercium priorem et magistrum Nicholaum. Sed ibi per aliquot dies
morantes, cum se nichil aspicerent ad tempus proficere, domum
reuersi sunt, infecto negocio. Factumque est crastinum, et intro-
euntes in capitulum, facta est mentio per magistrum Nicholaum et
magistrum Thomam et alios plures super absentia electi, plurima
proponentes quod eius presentia magis expediret quam eius
absentia. Hucusque enim, postquam dominus H(ugo) electus fuit,
a capituli ingressu priuabatur. Quod tandem concessum est, et
uocatus collocatus est in dextera parte capituli iuxta priorem in
sede superiori.

Processu uero temporis uenit dominus S(tephanus) archiepiscopus apud sanctum Aedmundum, ob deuocionem et ueneracio-
nem ipsius, uigilia passionis eiusdem.⁴ In crastino quidem post
diem passionis uenit in capitulum,⁵ et ibi, refocillans uerbo Dei
gregem beati martiris, exhortabatur ut unanimes in domo Dei
permansissent,⁶ dicens: 'Si separabiles et superabiles, et si in-
separabiles insuperabiles usque*b* reperiemini.' Finito tandem
sermone super hoc, 'qualis est rector ciuitatis, tales et inhabitantes
in ea',⁷ flexis genibus coruit dominus H(erbertus) prior*c* coram eo,
rogans humiliter et supplicans pro electo. Post quem erexit se
R(obertus) camerarius et recitauit quomodo electio secundum
Deum processa est; rogauitque ut ob amorem Dei et eius genetricis et gloriosi patroni nostri Aedmundi,*d* partes suas fideles

---

dissesserunt H   *b* ut que H   *c* Added in marg. by scribe or
Hand A   *d* H adds ut, canc. by Hand C

¹ Iud. 16: 2.   ² See above, p. 15 n. 6.

who stood firmly and inflexibly by the election oath fled in a body to the abbot elect in the prior's house, while the sacrist's party shut themselves up in the infirmary chapel, placing guards at the open doors.[1] After earnest discussion there as to what was best to be done, they ordered the abbot elect, by Albinus the subprior and John of Lavenham, to come to them alone without any of his friends. To this his friends would not agree unless they could all be present. When this had been told Robert the sacrist and the others with him, they left the chapel singing the *Verba mea*.[2]

A few days later after the storm had calmed somewhat, and the clerks' visit had been countermanded, the abbot elect was again presented to the king at Nottingham[3] by the prior, Robert the sacrist, Robert the chamberlain, Master Thomas the third prior, and Master Nicholas. But after waiting there for several days, they saw that no progress could be made at that time, and so returned home, having achieved nothing. In chapter the next day Master Nicholas, Master Thomas and many others raised the matter of the abbot elect's absence, giving many reasons why it would be better if he were present. For from the time of his election up to that very moment, Hugh had been denied entrance to the chapter-house. This point was eventually conceded, and he was called and placed in the higher seat next to the prior's, on the right hand side of the chapter-house.

Some time later, on the vigil of the saint's passion,[4] Archbishop Stephen came to St. Edmunds, led there by devotion and venera-tion. On the day after the saint's passion[5] he entered the chapter-house, and there, refreshing the flock of the blessed martyr with the word of God, he exhorted them to be of one mind in the house of the Lord,[6] saying: 'If you are divided, you will be made subject, but if united, then you will never be placed in subjection.' His sermon ended on this note: 'Whatever the character of a city's ruler, so will be the character of its inhabitants'.[7] Then Prior Herbert sank down before him on bended knees, humbly pleading and supplicating for the abbot elect. After him Robert the chamberlain stood up and told how the election had been con-ducted, according to the will of God, and he asked that for the love of God, His Mother, and our glorious patron Edmund, he would

---

[3] John was at Nottingham 3 September (*Itinerary*).
[4] 19 November.   [5] 21 November.   [6] 1 Pet. 3: 8, etc.
[7] Cf. Walther, no. 30991d: 'Talis est ciuitas quales et principes.'

interponeret ad gratiam domini I(ohannis) regis captandam, quia non erat repugnantia, nisi in assensu solummodo domini regis. Steterunt omnes etiam cum eo, rei ueritatis sicut proposuit testimonio. Dominus uero archiepiscopus ob unitatis gaudium et integritatis, perhibens*a* quod uiderat et audierat,[1] uultu iocundo respondit et promisit sacramento, quod non minus pro causa nostra pro loco et tempore staret quam pro sua, que tamen spetialiter eum tangere uidebatur. Hiis uero rite peractis, in capitulo comite Rogero[2] et multis aliis tam monachis extraneis quam clericis et laicis existentibus, relinquens conuentui benedictionem discessit, iter tendens uersus Radinges. Ibi enim die sancti Nicholai proxima sequente prefixum erat concilium generale.[3]

In crastino uero post decessum archiepiscopi uenerunt tres littere, ut dictum est, singulis personis ex parte domini regis, uidelicet priori, sacriste et R(icardo) precentori. Quarum littere domini prioris in pleno capitulo lecte erant; alie uero nec audite nec uise ab aliquo fuere. Tenor autem litterarum prioris hic erat:

Miramur quod tantum distulistis firmam nostram de abbatia; unde mandamus ut uisis litteris ad nos inde responsuri uenire festinetis.

Alias litteras suscepit R(obertus) sacrista, ut scilicet prior et R(obertus) sacrista et R(icardus) precentor, uisis litteris, domino regi apparerent, responsuri quare firma eius de abbatia tam esset protelata. Preparantibus se, scilicet priore et R(oberto) sacrista et R(icardo) precentore domino regi in concilio apparere, perquirebant utrum electus ibi ueniret necne. Quibus cum respondisset se ire, commoti sunt; et cum pluribus sentenciis pariterque obiectionibus propositis, uiderent iter eius non posse impedire. Verumptamen et cum antea*b* semper palliarent quod interius non habebant (ut scilicet quod ore in antea pretendebant, in corde non habebant), diutius eum blandis pertrahere uolentes sermonibus, respondit sacrista se esse lese maiestatis reum si a domino rege perciperetur electo in itinere associari. Illic timore trepidans et formidine ubi non fuit timor,[4] concepto iam firmiter in animo suo et fidelium

---

a perhibentis H   *b* So H; *perhaps to be omitted?*

[1] Ier. 23: 18, etc. Also used by Jocelin (*JB*, pp. 16, 73).
[2] Roger Bigod (d. 1221), earl of Norfolk and Suffolk.
[3] 6 December. *Councils*, p. 21. This was the third of a series of fruitless

do his level best to obtain King John's favour, for there had been no obstacle to the election except the king's consent. Everyone supported him, testifying that what he said was true. The archbishop, pleased with their unity and singleness of purpose noted well what he had seen and heard.[1] He replied with a joyful countenance, swearing that he would give as much place and time to our affairs as to his own, since our cause was anyway so much his. After these matters, which were broached in the chapter-house before Earl Roger[2] and many clerks, laymen, and monks from other houses, the archbishop gave the convent his blessing and departed. He now made his way to Reading, where a general council had been arranged for St. Nicholas' day.[3]

On the day after the archbishop's departure, three letters arrived, so it has been said, addressed from the king to the prior, the sacrist, and Richard the precentor. The prior's was read in full chapter, but the others remained unseen and their contents were not disclosed to anyone. This was the gist of the prior's letter:

We are amazed that you have for so long delayed payment of our dues from the abbey; therefore we order you, when you have read our letter, to hasten to us to offer an explanation.

Robert the sacrist received another letter to the effect that the prior, Robert the sacrist, and Richard the precentor, after reading it, were to appear before the king to explain why the farm from the abbey was so long delayed. While these three were preparing to appear before the king at the council, they asked whether the abbot elect should accompany them or not. On his replying that he wished to, they were much disturbed, but when many opinions and objections had been aired, they saw that they could not stop his coming. However, as they had always been used to saying one thing openly while intending something else in their hearts, so now they tried for a long time to fool him with deceptive words. For the sacrist replied that he would be guilty of contempt of the king's majesty if he were seen in the abbot elect's company on the journey. But the abbot elect, trembling and fearful in the place where there used to be no fear,[4] resolved firmly, with his faithful

councils held between the king and lay magnates on the one hand, and the legate, archbishop, and clergy on the other, to discuss the repayment of the *ablata* and *damna* extorted by the king from the Church during the interdict.
[4] Ps. 13: 5.

amicorum usus consilio, ut se domino Nicholao legato et sancte
Romane ecclesie cardinali[1] in concilio se presentaret, rogauit humi-
f. 173ᵛ liter, qui ratione | imperare debuit, ut in itinere saltem domino
priori propter scandalum lese unitatis uitandum posset associari,
plurimas propenens rationes et non*a* ratione carentes,[2] quod pocius
simul apparere quam diuisim ire*b* possent et decentius. Sed in
uanum; non enim ratio potuit uoluntatem comprehendere.[3] Vnde
dominus H(erbertus) prior, consilio aquilonis a quo panditur
omne malum[4] suffultus et iam bene obnubilatus, minus circumspecte quam debuit et decuit dedit responsum, in hoc ei nec posse
nec audere condescendere. Quibus auditis, et iam omnibus ad iter
suum spectantibus paratis, assumpto secum R(oberto) camerario
et I(ohanne) de Laueham*c* firmario, plenam in Domino habentes
fiduciam, secure et audacter dominum E(ustachium) Elyensem[5]
apud quoddam manerium suum, scilicet Dittune,[6] adierunt. Quos
ut domnus Eliensis uidit, pre gaudio assurgens eis suscepit in
oscula. Prosequentes tandem inter cetera causam rei geste ordina-
tim et exponentes, consuluit uenerabilis Elyensis, ut electus cum
duobus sociis secum existentibus uenerabilibus N(icholao) legato
et S(tephano) archiepiscopo, Elyense episcopo duce, in concilio*d* se
presentaret; spem habens in Domino certam, et non de eius
misericordia diffidens, quod isti duo gratia Dei interueniente, iram
domini regis, quam per filios degeneres contra electionem suam
satis Deo dignam et causam ecclesie in animo conceperat, miti-
garent. Ille uero uir erat mire simplicitatis et mansuetudinis; in
his omnibus non est commotus, neque mutatus*e* est uultus eius.[7]
Consilio tandem domini Elyensis utpote sano inclinans, profectus
est apud Radinges.

Veniente uero apud Radinges, perrexit obuiam domino
N(icholao) legato, decem fere leucas extra Radinges, et se osculan-

---

a H *adds* sine   *b* diuisire H, *corr. Hand B*   *c* H *adds* ca, *canc.*
by scribe   *d* consilio H   *e* immutatus H

[1] Nicholas, cardinal bishop of Tusculum (1204–19), arrived in England as
legate some time in September. He was 'to confirm John's surrender of the
kingdoms of England and Ireland, to procure proper conditions for raising the
Interdict, to superintend the filling of vacant episcopal sees and abbacies, and to
take disciplinary action against those who had offended against the Church in
the last five years' (*Councils*, pp. 20–1).
[2] Cf. John of Salisbury, *Entheticus*, *PL*, cxcix, col. 978, ll. 613–14; Aldhelm,
Ep. 9, *MGH*, *Auct. Ant.*, xv. 502, l. 4.
[3] The relationship of *ratio* and *uoluntas* had exercised the minds of western
philosophers from Plato on, and was one of the great topics in the schools of

friends' advice, to present himself at the council before Nicholas, cardinal and legate of the holy Roman Church.[1] And he, who by right ought to have been giving the orders, asked humbly that he might be accompanied on the journey by the prior at least, to avoid scandalous rumours of their broken unity. And he advanced many arguments not devoid of reason[2] in support of this proposition—that it was better and more becoming for them to appear united than to journey separately. But in vain; for no argument could change their will.[3] Prior Herbert, supported and over-shadowed by the advice of that 'north wind' from which all evil is spread abroad,[4] replied, less prudently than became him, that he could not and dared not go with him. After this the abbot elect, having made all necessary preparations for his journey, took with him Robert the chamberlain and John of Lavenham the victualler. Trusting firmly in the Lord, fearless and confident, they came to Eustace, bishop of Ely,[5] at his manor named Ditton.[6] When the bishop saw them he rose joyfully and greeted them with a kiss. When at length they came to discuss, among other things, the sequence of events arising from the election, the good bishop of Ely advised the abbot elect and his two friends to present themselves at the council before the worthy legate Nicholas and Archbishop Stephen, with himself as their spokesman. For he had sure hope in the Lord's mercy, that by His grace and the mediation of those two men, the king's anger, aroused by base men against his church and divinely inspired election, might be appeased. Now the abbot elect was of wonderful simplicity and gentleness; he remained unmoved through all this, and the expression of his face did not change.[7] In the end, taking the bishop of Ely's advice, as it seemed sensible, he went to Reading.

On the way there, about ten leagues from the town, he met the legate Nicholas, and after greeting each other with a kiss, they

twelfth-century Europe. Anselm and Bernard, for instance, both wrote treatises on it. The writer's contrasting of the two here and later (p. 61) suggests that he was aware of the traditional debate.

[4] i.e. the sacrist. Ier. 4: 6, 6: 1. Cf. Abbo (*Mem.* i. 9): 'Denique constat iuxta prophetae uaticinium, quod ab aquilone uenit omne malum', and the anonymous Life of St. Edmund in New York, Pierpont Morgan Library MS. 736, p. 60, both referring to the Danes.

[5] 1198–1215. One of the very few English bishops whom the pope could entirely trust. He was bound to favour the cause of Hugh and his allies.

[6] Fen Ditton, Cambs.

[7] Dan. 5: 6. Cf. *JB*, p. 23.

tes inuicem perrexerunt tribus pene miliaribus simul loquentes, nullo alio mediante. Inter hoc dominus H(erbertus) prior et R(obertus) sacrista et R(icardus) precentor obuiam legato uenientes apparuere, et simul omnes pergentes uenerunt cum domino legato ad Radinges; ibique domino priore et H(ugone) electo sociisque eorum in una domo ospitantibus, licet uersus Radinges non simul comparerent, in crastino uero dominus H(ugo) electus, accepta licentia aᵃ domino N(icholao) legato, domum cum R(oberto) camerario et I(ohanne) de Laueham reuersus est. Dominus autem prior pariterque sacrista, propter magnas expensas, ut creditur, euitandas, et ut se exonerarent de censu abbatie, de quo paulo ante summonicionem super terminorum protelacione per breue domini regis acceperant, apud Londiniam iter suum deflexerunt. R(icardus) autem precentor solus apud Radinges ex parte eorum remansit, audiens, ut dicebatur, et expectans, quo fine illa summonicio clauderetur. Ingerente se postmodum coram rege per comitem Salesbere, precepit ei dominus rex ut, legato apud sanctum Aedmundum properanti, ibique Natale suum super custum domini regis sollempniter celebranti, associaretur; factumque est feria iii. instanti post festum sancti Nicholai apud Radinges.¹ Dominus uero prior et sacrista, apud Lundoniam nuntium suum expectantes, postquam tale susceperant mandatum, cum tota pecunia quam secum attulerant domum sunt reuersi, preparantes se ad suscipiendum legatum.²

Veniente quidem domino legato die sancti Thome apostoli ante Natale,³ honorifice ad processionemᵇ susceptus est ad portam ecclesie, precentore incipiente 'Summe Trinitati'.⁴ Quo sollempniter ab omnibus prosecuto, peruenit ante magnum altare, et facta oratione prosecutus est in cameram,⁵ preparans se ad ordines faciendos; fecit enim illo die ordines apud sanctum Aedmundum. In crastino uero uenit in capitulum, et predicabat uerbum Dei super hoc, 'Vigilate animo', etc.⁶

Peracto quidem sermone, precepit ut populus ibi assistens ammoueretur; habuit enim quoddam conuentus secretum preferendum, quod nullo alio licuit communicare. Ammotisque omnibus, facta est mencio super electione. Et exurgentes sex⁷

ᵃ *Added over line by Hand A*   ᵇ *recte* in processione?

¹ 10 December. John was at Reading 7–14 December (*Itinerary*).
² i.e. the dues which they had gone to London to pay would now be used to defray the cost of the abbey's hospitality to the legate.
³ 21 December. See also *Bury Chronicle*, p. 2.
⁴ 9th respond at matins on Trinity Sunday. In the Sarum rite it was sung in

continued on for almost three miles talking alone together. Meanwhile Prior Herbert, Robert the sacrist and Richard the precentor appeared, come to meet the legate, and so they all went on together, arriving at Reading with the legate. There the prior and Abbot elect Hugh with their retinues lodged in one house, although they had not travelled to Reading together. The next day Hugh, Robert the chamberlain and John of Lavenham returned home, with the permission of the legate Nicholas. But the prior and sacrist, to avoid great expenses, it is believed, and to pay the delayed dues from the abbey as instructed in the king's recent letters, made their way to London. Richard the precentor, however, remained at Reading on their behalf, to listen and watch, it is said, for the sequel to that summons. Not long after he came before the king through the earl of Salisbury, and was instructed to accompany the legate, who would soon come to St. Edmunds and celebrate Christmas with them at the king's expense. This was done on the Tuesday after the feast of St. Nicholas at Reading.[1] On hearing this order the prior and sacrist, who had been awaiting Richard's news in London, returned home, taking all the money which they had brought with them, and prepared to receive the legate.[2]

The legate, then, arrived before Christmas, on the day of St. Thomas the apostle,[3] and was received with due honour by a procession at the church door, the precentor leading in the singing of the *Summae Trinitati*.[4] When these formalities were over he came before the high altar, and after offering prayers proceeded to the chamber[5] where he prepared to carry out ordinations, which he did that same day at St. Edmunds. The next day he entered the chapter-house and preached the word of God on the text 'Be ye watchful in mind', etc.[6]

When his sermon was finished he asked the crowd present to withdraw, for he had a private matter to discuss with the convent which could not be made known to anyone else. After they had all gone out the matter of the election was broached. The six[7]

procession for the reception of a king and queen. F. Harrison, *Music in Medieval Britain* (London, 1958), p. 259 n. 1.

[5] In the west range of the cloister, over the cellar. Whittingham, pp. 176–7 and pl. xxi.

[6] 'Vigilate animo; in proximo est Dominus Deus noster', antiphon at lauds, Friday, the third week of Advent, according to the Sarum use. W. H. Frere, *Antiphonale Sarisburiense* (Nashdom, 1901–24), i, pl. 35.

[7] Hugh himself having been the seventh (see above, p. 9 n. 5).

examinatores, prostrati in medio, uoce clara modum electionis et susceptionis et appellationis pro electo et eius electione ceperunt exponere, nihil tamen omittentes de contingentibus. Quibus expositis, surrexit precentor in medio, et dixit quod primo appellauit contra, primamque uocem in omnibus precentoria dignitate sibi uendicabat, adhibendo*a* etiam de electione, quod sex

f. 174 examinatores pocius | simplicitate quam fraude uel dolo fuisse credebat circumuentos, supplicans ut ob honorem eiusdem curieque Romane subtilius per examinatores septem et totius rei ueritatem perquisisset et ueritate cognita determinasset; si tamen ad honorem regis et regni cedere properasset. Sacrista autem et eius parti inclinantes, licet sacramenti sui ueritati obuiantes, illud idem quod precentor proposuerat protestando petierunt. Maior pars conuentus et sanior[1] ueritati cum sex examinatoribus inflexibiliter perstiterunt et immobiles. Illo uero die abstulit legatus conuentui solitas misericordias.[2]

In crastino[3] quidem exurgens magister Nicholaus recapitulauit coram legato excelle⟨n⟩tissimo ydiomate modum electionis et appellacionis, et inprobauit precentorem non debere ulla ratione magis primam uocem sibi usurpare in aliquo loco, preterquam in ecclesia, quam aliquem alium.[4] Narratione sua tali modo super electione completa et improbacione, erexit se precentor in medio et dixit: 'Domine legate, Boloniam non uidi, nec leges scio.'*b* Plures autem, putantes se Babiloniam protulisse,*c* in tantam prosilierunt derisionem ut pre confusione dominus precentor a causa incepta penitus desisteret.[5] Sacrista autem aliqua ratione cupiens suffulcire, cepit proponere quod in carta conuentus de rato subintelligebatur assensus*d* regius. Et ut hoc uerum esse iudicaretur ab omnibus steterunt testimonium perhibentes: Albinus supprior, qui hoc idem affirmabat; Henricus, qui diffamare nitebatur electum; Aedmundus, qui dixit, in eo quod

a abhibendo H   *b* nescio H, *corr. by Hand C*   *c* procullisse H
d assentus H

---

[1] The traditional canonistic formula stipulating the amount and kind of support necessary for the legitimate election of an abbot. Lanfranc, *Constitutions*, p. 71 and n. 1.

[2] No letters survive charging Nicholas with the task of monastic reform, with which, however, as an ex-Cistercian, he must have been sympathetic, and with which Innocent had earlier been concerned (Cheney, *Letters*, nos. 462, 463, etc.). Besides Bury, he is known to have investigated life at Evesham and Westminster (see below, pp. 51–3, 62–5 and Whileblood, pp. 76–7).

[3] 23 December.

examiners, rising to their feet and prostrating themselves in the midst, explained clearly how the election, reception, and appeal for the abbot elect and his election had proceeded, without omitting anything relevant. After this the precentor stood up among them, stating that he had appealed from the first against the election, boasting that he had the right of first voice on all matters because of his position as precentor. He believed that the six examiners, by naïvety rather than by deceit or cunning, had been manipulated, and he besought the legate that, for the sake of his own honour and that of the Roman curia, he should examine more closely the seven examiners and the real facts of the whole matter, and that when he had found out the truth he should pronounce a judgement which would be to the honour of the king and his realm. The sacrist and his party, not keeping their oath, urgently seconded the precentor's request. But the wiser majority of the convent,[1] together with the six examiners, persisted immovably and inflexibly in their defence of the truth. Now that day the legate deprived the convent of their customary extra food allowances.[2]

The next day[3] Master Nicholas stood up and described again to the legate in most eloquent language how they had carried out the election and appeal, and he proved that the precentor had no more right than anyone else to first voice on any matter or in any place except within the church.[4] After he had concluded his account of the election process and arguments in disproof, the precentor rose in their midst and said: 'Lord legate, I have not seen Bologna, and I am no expert in civil law.' Many of them, however, thought he said 'Babylon' instead of 'Bologna', and there was such laughter that the precentor, in confusion, utterly lost his train of thought.[5] But the sacrist, wanting to bring some rational argument to his defence, declared that the king's assent was implicit in the convent's charter of ratification. And so that everyone would agree that this was true, the following men took their stand as witnesses: Albinus the subprior, who seconded him; Henry, trying to defame the abbot elect; Edmund, who said that the abbot elect did not

---

[4] Yet the precentor may have been within his rights according to local Bury custom. See *JB*, p. 128.

[5] The precentor's putative error was probably due to a stutter (see below, p. 125); the fact that Babylon was taken as the type of the worldly city, and that it was the contemporary western term for Saracen Cairo made his error doubly funny. At the same time the precentor's statement is almost unaccountable unless Master Nicholas *had* been trained at Bologna.

electus promocionem suam procurauit, demeruit; I(ocelinus) elemosinarius, qui nunquam pro regio assensu destitit appellare;
Ricardus Taillehaste, qui manum iniecit in tercium priorem;[1]
Adam infirmarius, qui omnia asserebat in irritum reuocare;
Philippus, qui se iactauit in capitulo dedisse consilium appellationis pro regio assensu; Ricardus Caluus, qui in porticu abbatis
coram omni populo abbati de Belloloco[2] non septem examinatores
sed seductores nominauit, addendo ibi quod licet uenerabilis
H(ugo) electus in baculo pastorali ad potestatem esset erectus
plenariam, in eo tamen quod cartam conuentus de rato in manus
domini archiepiscopi tradidit, demeruit; Walterus, Willelmus,
Adam, Thomas Capra, Gregorius et Galfridus, parti ueritatis in
insidiis assidentes,[3] clamauerunt nichil uerius his que a precentore
et sacrista proferuntur. Qui tamen uentilacione cupiditatis — ne
dicam infidelitatis — contra sacramenti sui ueritatem circumuenti,
tanquam arundo que a uento de facili huc illucque defertur, sunt
permutati.[4]

Dominus autem legatus, subtilius rei ueritatem cupiens indagare,
precepit textum[a] defferri, super quem prior totusque conuentus
cum septem examinatoribus iurauerunt, quod cum requisiti essent
de statu ecclesie et electione uerum confiterentur, nec omitterent
pro amore uel odio, prece uel precio, neque pro aliquo temporali
emolumento, quin ueritatem dicerent;[5] factumque est ita. Conuentus quidem exiens de capitulo uocatus est prior causa examinandi.
Tanta uero fuit mora in examinacione super inquisitis, ut illo die
ab hora matutinali usque ad horam reficiendi, qua conuentus
intrauit in refectorium,[6] non erant examinati nisi prior et electus.
In crastino quidem, scilicet uigilia Natalis Domini,[7] residui de
numero septenario examinati, eorum[b] examen pariterque predictorum in scriptum est redactum.

---

[a] precepitextum H   [b] eorumque H; *alternatively this may be correct, in
which case* sunt *should precede it*

---

[1] See above, p. 17.
[2] Hugh, a favourite of the king's, his nominee to his own foundation and
frequently employed on his business, for instance as ambassador at Rome
during the Canterbury election dispute of 1205–6. Of ill repute, therefore, in
the Church (*MO*, pp. 658–9). John had probably sent him to Bury to watch
Nicholas. The king was at Waltham, no doubt anxious to discuss with the legate
the implications of the papal decree *Cum non possit* (Cheney, *Letters*, no. 938),
the result of a recent legation to Rome in which Hugh of Beaulieu had taken
part (Whileblood, pp. 129–31).

deserve his promotion because he had worked for it himself; Jocelin the almoner, who never ceased to appeal for the king's assent; Richard Taillehaste, who had laid hands on the third prior;[1] Adam the infirmarer, who wished the whole thing revoked as invalid; Philip, boasting that he had advised appealing for the royal assent in chapter; Richard the Bald who, publicly in the abbot's porch, had told the abbot of Beaulieu[2] that the seven examiners were seven seducers—adding that although the worthy abbot elect Hugh had been elevated to the full power of the pastoral staff, yet he deserved to forfeit it because he had handed the convent's charter of ratification to the archbishop. Walter, William, Adam, Thomas the Goat, Gregory and Geoffrey, sitting in ambush for the party of truth,[3] asserted that nothing was truer than the statements of the sacrist and precentor. But it was greed—not to say infidelity—which moved these men to break their oath; for they had changed like a reed which is easily swayed this way and that by the wind.[4]

But the legate, wishing to delve into the facts of the matter in more detail, ordered the text of an oath to be brought, which the prior and all the convent, together with the seven examiners, swore; namely, that when required they would confess the truth about the state of their church and about their election without omitting anything for love or hate, gift or entreaty, or for any temporal emolument, but that they would speak the truth.[5] And so it was done. Then the monks left the chapter-house and the prior was called for examination. And that day so much time was taken up by the inquest, that from matins to dinner-time, when the convent entered the refectory,[6] only the prior and the abbot elect had been examined. However, the next day, Christmas eve,[7] the rest of the seven were examined and their evidence, together with that of the first two, was taken down in writing.

---

[3] Ps. 10: 8; cf. above, p. 19 n. 8. The writer's list is doubtless based on a written document.

[4] Evidently a proverb (perhaps ultimately based on Matt. 11: 7; Luc. 7: 24), although without exact parallel in the Bible or classical literature. Cf., however, Peter the Venerable, *Liber contra Sectam Saracenorum*, ed. J. Kritzeck, *Peter the Venerable and Islam* (Princeton, 1964), p. 237: '. . . more harundinis flatu quolibet agitatae hac illacque inflecti. . . .'

[5] The writer is evidently closely following the text itself.

[6] i.e. from about 6 a.m. to 2 p.m.

[7] 24 December.

Inter hec quidem dominus S(tephanus) archiepiscopus, quem ueritas electionis non latebat, transmisit litteras suas domino legato, supplicandi ne contra electum et eius electionem aliquid in sinistrum fieri permisisset, et ut electionem approbaret canonicam et a tanto conuentu fideliter processam;[1] eidem tenorem litterarum conuentus de rato et rescriptum litterarum domini prioris de renouacione appellationis pro eius electione destinauit. Abbas uero de Belloloco, ueniens ex aduerso, domino legato ex parte domini regis litteras huius pretendit, ut uisis litteris ad eum redire festinasset.[2]

In die autem crastino, scilicet Natali Domini, scilicet[a] tempore interdicti,[3] talem conuentui prestitit indulgentiam, ut eius auctoritate quilibet sacerdos de conuentu missam celebraret, alii autem f. 174ᵛ inferioris ordinis uiaticum susciperent. | Celebrauit et ipse illo die ad magnum altare, et cum fratribus in refectorio uescebatur. In crastino Natalis Domini,[4] ueniens in capitulo dominus legatus plurima commendabat qui uiderat et audierat,[5] preter quod inestimatam super electione reperiit dissensionem; et licet, ex diuersis emergentibus causis prepeditus, eam ad presens non posset diffinire, pro certo tamen in breui ad honorem Dei et ecclesie scirent terminandam. Hiis dictis erexit se abbas de Belloloco in medio, et pluribus ex parte domini regis super electione premissis, tanquam consulendo ammonuit rogauitque, ne libertatibus domini regis semper[b] usitatis in aliquo derogassent. Hoc enim, ut ait, erat uia iustitie, ius suum unicuique reddere,[6] 'Cesari que Cesaris', etc.[7] Vnde si quid minus prouide[c] actum fuit in electione et discrete quam debuit et decuit, dum licuit, reuocarent.[d] Exurgens quidem magister Thomas de Walsingham, singulis allegationibus pro conuentu sufficienter respondens, uoce clara ostendit coram domino legato qualiter domus ista ex dono et confirmacione illustris domini I(ohannis) regis predecessorum et regum antiquorum, ut et regis Cnut et sancti Aedwardi, diuersis esset munita

---

[a] So H; *perhaps to be omitted?*   [b] semperque H   [c] proinde H
[d] reuocassent H

---

[1] Mentioned in Major, *Acta*, Appendix I, p. 154, no. 2. The use of technical language suggests that the writer had access to the text.

[2] It is possible that the abbot of Beaulieu, who seems to have accompanied the legate to Bury (see above, p. 31), had this letter in his possession from the first, with orders from the king to present it if pressure was put upon the legate to confirm the election. This pressure had now been applied in the form of the archbishop's letter.

Meanwhile Archbishop Stephen, to whom the validity of the election was evident, wrote to the legate, asking him not to permit any unjust act which would harm the abbot elect or his election, and to approve the election as canonical and as having proceeded in good faith from so great a convent.[1] He also sent him the gist of the convent's letter of ratification and a copy of the prior's letter renewing the appeal for Hugh's election. Then the abbot of Beaulieu, in order to oppose the archbishop, handed the legate a letter from the king, demanding that he return to him without delay.[2]

The next day, that is, Christmas day, being in the time of the interdict,[3] he gave the convent an indulgence such that, by his authority any priest of the convent might celebrate mass, and others in lesser orders might receive the viaticum. He himself celebrated mass that day at the high altar and ate with the brothers in the refectory. The next day[4] he entered the chapter-house and commended much that he had seen and heard,[5] except the dissension over the election, which he had not expected to find. And although a number of factors prevented him from pronouncing judgement then and there, before long, he said, they would definitely know how the matter would be settled, to the honour of God and the Church. At these words the abbot of Beaulieu rose in their midst and had much to say about the election on the king's behalf; and pretending to offer advice he asked and warned them not to detract in any way from the king's customary liberties. For this, he said, was the way of justice, to render each man his due,[6] 'to Caesar what is Caesar's', etc.[7] And if the election had indeed been carried out less prudently and discreetly than was proper, then they could annul it while there was still time. But Master Thomas of Walsingham stood up and answered each of the allegations competently on the convent's behalf, describing clearly to the legate how the house had been provided and supported by the gift and confirmation of the illustrious King John's predecessors and of the ancient kings, especially Cnut and St. Edward, with various liberties, particularly that of electing a pastor. For

---

[3] The interdict was formally lifted 2 July 1214.
[4] 26 December.
[5] Ier. 23: 18, etc.; cf. above, p. 22 n. 1.
[6] Augustine, *De Civitate Dei*, PL, xli, col. 649; cf. Justinian, *Institutes*, i. i (and Rom. 13: 7).
[7] Matt. 22: 21; etc.

libertatibus et suffulta, et maxime de pastore eligendo, ut in carta
sancti Aedwardi Anglicano continetur sermone; scilicet quod,
uacante pastore, liceat eis unum de seipsis quem melius uoluerint
ad dignitatem predecessoris pristinam eligere.[1] Quam et uenera-
biles predecessores H(enricus) pater eius et R(icardus) frater eius,
reges Anglorum illustres, insuper et ipse carta sua singillatim
confirmauerunt, et sigillorum munimine corroborauerunt. Et ne
quis processu temporis super electione unica aliquid in sinistrum
posset obicere, auctoritate confirmationis domini I(ohannis) regis
eiusque predecessorum protecti in factum processerunt.

Hiis itaque coram domino legato legatis et responsis, dominique
prioris et septem electorum testimonio maiorisque partis conuentus et sanioris[2] super electione canonica confirmato, prout eidem
legato a summo pontifice potestas erat indulta super ueritate
electionis cognita rigorem iustitie exercere omnimodam dissimu-
lans, illo die, scilicet in crastino Natalis Domini, infecto reliquit
eos negocio, hospitans apud Meleford, quoddam manerium scilicet
abbatis sancti Aedmundi.[3] Quem[a] quidem prior et uenerabilis
H(ugo) electus sacristaque secum illuc comitabantur. Dominus
autem legatus, ad memoriam reducens fidelitatem quam super
electione in examinacione comperierat, atque proponens in animo
eandem electionem in H(ugonem) factam ad effectum perducere,
precepit domino H(ugoni) electo ut sibi uersus curiam associaretur,
confidens in Deum quod dominus rex eius meritis eundem electum
in gratiam susciperet et amorem. Quod cum sacriste auribus per-
flatum esset, qui tanquam uulpes in spelunca[4] semper dolum in
facie predulci texere contra electum nitebatur, eidemque H(ugoni),
postquam fuerat electus, sedens ad insidias et laqueos tendens[b]
ut eum illaquearet,[5] talibus dominum legatum allocutus est,
dicens: 'Domine pater, cum sit uerissimum et omnibus notorium,
nos omnes de domo nostra in electione H(ugonis) contra regias
dignitates semper usitatas facta odium principis incurrisse, non est
laudandum quod eidem H(ugoni) coram rege conductum prebeatis,
cum et uos honorem regis atque ius suum probati estis per omnia

---

^a Qui H   ^b tetendens H

[1] J. M. Kemble, *Codex Diplomaticus Aevi Saxonici* (London, 1839–48), iv,
no. 895. P. H. Sawyer, *Anglo-Saxon Charters* (London, 1968), pp. 311–12, no.
1045, lists no less than twenty-three surviving copies of this charter. The
earliest, P.R.O. Cart. Antiqu. R.15 no. 1, dating from *c.* 1200, is printed by

an English charter of St. Edward stipulated that in a vacancy they were permitted to elect whomsoever of their number they thought fit to the dignity previously held by his predecessors.[1] King John himself and his worthy predecessors, his father Henry and his brother Richard, illustrious kings of England, had each confirmed this charter, ratifying it by the affixing of their seals. Thus they had proceeded in their action authorized and protected by these confirmations of King John and his predecessors so that no one in the future would be able to assail their right to elect a single person.

After these charges and replies had been heard by the legate, and the testimony of the prior, the seven electors and the larger and wiser part of the convent[2] concerning the election's canonicity had been confirmed, although the pope had delegated to the legate the power to dispense the most rigorous justice once the truth was known, nonetheless he only pretended to exercise it. For that day, which followed Christmas day, he left them, although the matter had not been cleared up, and lodged at Melford, a manor of the abbot of St. Edmunds.[3] The prior, sacrist, and the worthy abbot elect Hugh accompanied him there. Now the legate, keeping in mind the good faith about the election which he had found in examination, and wishing to bring Hugh's election into effect, ordered the abbot elect to accompany him to court. For he trusted in God that the king would take the abbot elect into his favour and love because of his merits. When this came to the sacrist's ears, like a fox in his den,[4] concealing his evil purpose as always behind a smiling face, while sitting in ambush and setting snares[5] for the abbot elect, he said to the legate: 'Lord father, it is a fact very true and plain to all that we at St. Edmunds have all incurred our ruler's ill-will by electing Hugh contrary to his traditional custom. Therefore you would not be wise to present Hugh to the king, especially since you have been charged with maintaining the king's

J. C. Davies, *The Cartae Antiquae Rolls 11-20* (*PRS*, new ser. cxxi, 1960), p. 87. It is discussed by F. E. Harmer, *Anglo-Saxon Writs* (Manchester, 1952), p. 141 n. 2, who remarks that its authenticity in its extant form is more than doubtful. As Henry II is the earliest king mentioned above as having confirmed it, it may have been forged during his reign. Alternatively, given the date of the earliest extant copy, and King John's remarks about it (see below, p. 125), it may have been fabricated expressly for use in Hugh's own election.

2 See above, p. 28 n. 1.
3 Long Melford, Suffolk, about 13 miles south of Bury.
4 Ps. 10 (*sec. Hebr.*): 9.
5 Ps. 10: 8, 10; cf. above, p. 19 n. 8.

manutenere.'¹ Hiis igitur et aliis pluribus consimilibus dominus legatus a sacrista circumuentus, precepit ut dominus H(ugo) domum rediret, confitens ei per ordinem omnia que in animo disposuerat, si tamen sacrista permisisset ad effectum duxisse. Factumque est ut dominus H(ugo) electus domum in crastino rediret. Prior uero et sacrista domino legato usque Herlaue² associati, inde domum accepta licentia sunt reuersi.

In die uero sancte Prisce uirginis,³ ueniens sacrista in capitulo, uolens premeditatam explere maliciam, finxit se ire ad legatum pro negociis domus, et maxime pro coyn et pro moneta adquirenda.⁴ Dominus autem rex tunc temporis pro certo transfretare proposuit.⁵

Inter hec*ᵃ* quidem amici Dei et domini electi fideles, circum-spicientes quod sacrista, qui in omnibus aduersus eum dolose et fraudulenter contra sacramentum suum operabatur, donisque interpositis plurimis curiam corrupit et curiales contra eum excitauit, electum consuluerunt ut curiam Romanam per aliquem uel aliquos suorum fidelium festinanter super rem actam adiret, seque tantundem a domo sua, pro periculis instantibus euitandis, f. 175 donec nuntii sui a curia redirent, absentaret. | Itaque dominus H(ugo) electus domini S(tephani) Cantuariensis archiepiscopi, Elyensis et Lundonensis,⁶ aliorumque fidelium usus consiliis, transmisit magistrum Thomam de Walsingham et dominum Symonem cognatum eius⁷ et Stephanum clericum filium Rogeri de Walsingham summo pontifici, secumque deferentes litteras domini S(tephani) Cantuariensis et Lundoniensis et Elyensis episcoporum in testimonium tocius rei geste super facto electionis.⁸ Se quoque quinta die ante Purificacionem,⁹ percepta in choro benedictione, cum domino R(icardo) de Heingham a domo*ᵇ* absentauit; factumque est ita.

ᵃ hoc H   *ᵇ* domino H, *canc. and corr. in marg. by Hand C*

---

¹ Undoubtedly referring to *Cum non possit* (see above, p. 30 n. 2), whose contents would by now have been known to both him and the legate, through Hugh of Beaulieu. Vacant benefices were to be filled with clergy distinguished for their life and learning, but also loyal to the king, whose assent was to be sought.   ² Essex, about fifty miles south-east of Bury.

³ 18 January 1214. On 3 January John notified the prior and convent that he had committed the custody of their estates into the legate's hands, excepting the escheats and revenues of vacant churches (*Rot. Litt. Pat.*, p. 107b). On 25 January he issued a general mandate to the same effect (ibid., p. 109).

⁴ Technically, *coyn* refers to the die, *moneta* to the weight of the coinage (Latham, *Word-List*, s.v.). The abbots of Bury had been granted the right to a local mint by Edward the Confessor (Harmer, op. cit., p. 165, no. 25).

⁵ John sailed for France on 9 February (Wendover, ii. 98).

⁶ William de Sainte Mère Eglise (1198/9–1221), like Eustace of Ely, very much a 'papalist' bishop.

honour and rights in everything.'[1] By these and many other similar arguments the sacrist manipulated the legate, until he ordered Hugh to return home, telling him all that he had intended, if only the sacrist had allowed him to proceed. So Hugh the abbot elect returned home the next day. The prior and sacrist, after accompanying the legate as far as Harlow,[2] were also given permission to return to the house.

On the feast of the virgin St. Prisca[3] the sacrist, wishing to bring to fulfilment the malice which he had been plotting, entered the chapter-house and pretended that he was going to the legate on convent business, particularly to acquire equipment for the mint.[4] But at that time the king definitely decided to go overseas.[5]

Meanwhile those who were friends of God and loyal to the abbot elect learnt that the sacrist, who lost no opportunity to work against him maliciously, cunningly, and in violation of his oath, was corrupting the court with very many gifts and inciting the courtiers against him. So they advised the abbot elect to send quickly about his election to the Roman curia, acting through some person or persons loyal to him. And they said that to avoid imminent danger he should retire from his house until his messengers returned from the curia. The abbot elect Hugh, therefore, with the advice of Stephen, archbishop of Canterbury, the bishops of London[6] and Ely and other friends, sent Master Thomas of Walsingham, his kinsman Simon,[7] and the clerk Stephen son of Roger of Walsingham to the pope with letters from Archbishop Stephen and the bishops of London and Ely, testifying to all the facts of the election.[8] He himself, after receiving the blessing in choir, left the house with Richard of Hingham five days before Candlemas;[9] and thus it was done.

[7] Also a Bury monk (see below, p. 188). At the request of his kinsman he composed an extant Anglo-Norman metrical Life of St. Faith. D. Legge, *Anglo-Norman in the Cloister* (Edinburgh, 1950), ch. 2.

[8] The letters of Langton and Eustace of Ely are quoted in full in *Cronica Buriensis* (*Mem.* iii. 15–16); see Appendix I. Langton's is also edited in Major, *Acta*, pp. 13–14, no. 7. These letters suggest concerted action against the legate, possibly devised at the council of Dunstable, held in late January (*Councils*, pp. 21–3). Knowledge of them may have formed the basis of Wendover's, the only account of this council. Wendover, iii. 278; Whileblood, pp. 76–7.

[9] 29 January. On 26 January the king sent mandates to eight vacant cathedral and monastic churches, including Bury, ordering them to proceed to make elections in the presence of William Brewer and others (*Rot. Litt. Pat.*, p. 109). The result of this so far as Bury is concerned is not known. If anything did happen, it passes unmentioned by the author of the *Electio*.

Sed cum hoc dominum regem diu latere non possent, accedentes quidam ex suis exposuerunt ipsi regi secundum ordinem rem gestam et quomodo magister Thomas esset pro electione nostra transfretatus. Hiis uero sermonibus pro certo compertis, iratus est dominus rex ualde et turbatus. Interim quidem ueniens sacrista ad curiam domino regi extra premissa, ex parte domini prioris et cum^a humili salutacione se presentauit.[1] Dominus uero rex, pre magna ira quam de magistro Thoma conceperat nondum animo sedatus, specialiter benedixit priorem, omnesque alios de domo sine ulla excepcione maledixit, inproperans eidem sacriste, per commune consilium contra libertates eius esset magister Thomas transfretatus. Sacrista uero, uolens domino regi satisfacere, cepit iurare et detestari[2] quod ille nec alius pro causa electi promouenda per eum, unquam extra domum pedem extulerat. Sed cum sic nec sacramento neque alia re ad presens cognouisset gratiam domini regis captare, neque animum eius ab ira concepta posse^b leuigare, quin eundem sacristam inter alios super assensu electionis contra regiam dignitatem, ut asserebat, sibi aduersantes connumeraret, pre magna confusione subtraxit se, et ad dominum Wyntoniensem,[3] non, ut creditur, manu accedens uacua, utpote a quo salus sperabatur,[4] rogauit ut apud dominum regem super exprobratis haberet excusatum, eundemque regem super coyn, si expedire uideret, conueniret. Dominus autem Wyntoniensis, ob amorem et reuerentiam gloriosi patroni nostri, sinistra tamen benedictione interposita coram domino rege pro negociis domus, et maxime pro coyn impetrando, audacter se optulit, exponens ei negocia domus pro quibus sacrista uenerat, excusacione ⟨scilicet⟩ de magistri Thome itinere atque^c consensu electionis unice premissa. Sed cum hec^d omnia rite a domino Wyntoniensi, licet in uanum, essent prosecuta, dominus rex talia eidem sacriste per dominum Wyntoniensem destinauit responsa: 'Si sacrista conuentusque suus cupiunt ut eos in negociis uariis exaudiam, et ad gratiam meam reformentur pristinam, satisfaciant mihi de electione secundum antiquam consuetudinem et semper usitatam; sin autem, incassum ulterius pro aliquo negocio, licet minimo, ad me redibunt.'

---

^{a} quam H ^{b} H *adds* benignare, *canc. by scribe* ^{c} itinere atque
nos; itinerisque H ^{d} hoc H

---

[1] Cf. *lectio iii* for the office of the vigil of St. Edmund, cited above, p. 4 n. 2.

But since they could not keep this from the king for long, some of his courtiers told him what had happened and how Master Thomas had gone overseas to forward our election. When he had checked the truth of this report the king became intensely angry and exasperated. Meanwhile the sacrist, who had come to court on his own initiative, presented himself on the prior's behalf with humble greetings.[1] But the king, not yet calmed of the great rage which he had conceived against Master Thomas, blessed the prior alone, but cursed the rest of the house without exception, reproaching the sacrist because Master Thomas had gone overseas by the advice of the whole convent, contrary to his liberties. The sacrist, wishing to pacify the king began to curse and swear,[2] saying that neither he nor anyone ordered by him had ever set foot outside the house to promote the abbot elect's cause. But when he saw that neither his oath nor anything else was sufficient to gain the king's favour or calm his anger at that time, but on the contrary that the king numbered him, as he said, among the others who opposed his rights regarding the election, he withdrew in great confusion. Going to the bishop of Winchester,[3] not, it is believed, with empty hands, hoping for salvation from him,[4] he asked to be excepted from the king's reproach; and, if it seemed necessary, he was willing to come to an arrangement with the king about the die for the mint. And the bishop of Winchester, out of love and reverence for our glorious patron—but accepting the bribe all the same—spoke courageously to the king about the business of the house and the die for the mint. He explained how the sacrist had come to excuse Master Thomas's journey and to ask his consent for their election of a single person. But all this, so eloquently explained by the bishop of Winchester, was in vain, for the king sent this reply to the sacrist by the bishop: 'If the sacrist and his convent want me to attend to their various pleas and restore them to my former grace, then they will satisfy me by celebrating their election according to ancient and well-tried custom; but if not, it will be useless for them to come to me again about any matter, be it never so trivial.'

[2] Matt. 26: 74.
[3] Peter des Roches (1205–28), the king's loyal official and a churchman in little more than name. He succeeded Geoffrey FitzPeter as justiciar in February 1214. He and William Brewer were in charge of the government of England while the king was in Poitou.
[4] 2 Macc. 13: 3.

Cum hoc sacrista percepisset, et se in uoluntate nihil proficere circumspexisset, inanibus iam sumptibus deductis omnino, penitus infecto negocio domum reuersus est. Veniens quidem domum die Purificacionis[1] accessit ad complices suos, premeditatum eius errorem contra sacramenta sua fouentes, et ut eosdem ad maiorem protraheret malitie accensionem, apposuit lignum et stipulas,[2] uerba inferendo uidelicet comminatoria ex parte domini regis uniuersis electionem secundum Deum in uenerabilem fratrem H(ugonem) factam fouentibus, aliis uero gratiam suam in omnibus suis agendis consequi et beniuolentiam; hec enim proposita maioris constantie in mala[a] causa fuerunt. Introgressus capitulum in crastino[3] cepit retractare que ei a domino rege super negociis domus per dominum Wyntoniensem fuerunt responsa, et quomodo domus nostra, ob furorem et iram quam dominus rex aduersus nos propter electionem unicam, quam et per magistrum Thomam de Walsingham curie Romane secundum Deum et canones iterantem iam conceperat, protestans,[b] nisi diuina impediretur misericordia, in dispendium in breui esset casura.[c] Ad hanc uocem dominus I(ocelinus) elemosinarius, A(dam) infirmarius et Aedmundus, licet non mundus, aliique de numero eorum,[4] sicut prouisum fuit, in uocem clamosam erexerunt se, dicentes: 'Dignus est puniri qui talia sine consilio nostro et inconsulto conuentu consequi probatur. Vnde in argumento fidei[5] f. 175[v] habere possumus, illum pocius contra nos et | libertates ecclesie nostre et regis libertates fore directum quam pro ecclesie libertatibus fouendis uel adquirendis.' Sed cum insipientes et qui Dei sunt non sapientes,[6] turbarentur in quo pocius gaudere debuerant et letari,[7] cum a diuersis matribus procreati, diuersa sentientes diuersas dedere sententias. Quidam enim a domo sua eum abiudicauerunt; quidam uero habitu priuari monachico; quidam autem ut in reditu omnis ei negaretur introitus. Sic itaque lupi rapaces[8] in ouem, impii in pium, indisciplinati et incompositi in uirum honestum et omni bonitate repletum[9] seuientes, absque misericordia in absentem contra legum instituta et[10] canones sententiam iniuste et indiscrete prolatam confirmare nitebantur, et mala pro bonis

---

[a] malo H   [b] perceperat protestatam H   [c] cassura H

[1] 2 February.   [2] 1 Cor. 3: 12, etc.   [3] 3 February.
[4] *De numero eorum* is a common O.T. expression found elsewhere in the *Electio*.
[5] Gen. 39: 16.   [6] Rom. 1: 14, etc.   [7] Thren. 4: 21, etc.
[8] Cf. Matt. 7: 15.   [9] Ps. 103: 28.

When the sacrist heard this and saw that nothing would advance his desires, having been put to utterly useless expense by his unsuccessful mission, he returned to the house. Arriving there on Candlemas day,[1] he went to his accomplices, who encouraged him in the deliberate breach of their oath, and in order to arouse them to a greater degree of wickedness, he placed before them wood and stubble;[2] that is, he passed on the king's warning to all those who supported the election of the worthy brother Hugh (chosen by God's will), and his grace and favour to the rest in all their actions. This, then, was made known so that there would be greater constancy among those who supported the evil cause. The next day[3] he entered the chapter-house and repeated what the king had replied to him about our business through the bishop of Winchester. And he declared that our house would soon be in dire straits unless saved by the divine mercy, on account of the rage and fury which the king had conceived against us because of our election of a single person and Master Thomas of Walsingham's journey to the Roman curia—both done according to God and the canons. At this Jocelin the almoner, Adam the infirmarer, and Edmund the impure, with others of their number,[4] rose up as prearranged, shouting: 'The man deserves to be punished for doing such a thing without our consent and without consulting the convent! For we can prove by sound argument[5] that he is bringing destruction upon us and upon the liberties of our church and king rather than supporting or augmenting our privileges.' But because they were foolish rather than wise in the things of God[6] they grew agitated when they should have rejoiced and been glad;[7] and because they were born from different mothers, having diverse thoughts, they brought forth diverse opinions. For some condemned him while absent from his house, others wanted him unfrocked, and yet others would have denied him entrance on his return. Thus, as ravening wolves[8] vent their fury on a sheep, or as impious men attack a devout one, or as undisciplined and restless people take part against an upright man, one full of goodness,[9] so these men laboured pitilessly to confirm the sentence which they had unjustly and imprudently pronounced against the absent man, in defiance of the institutes of the law[10] and the ecclesiastical

[10] It is just possible, given the distinction from *canones*, that the writer is referring specifically to Justinian's *Institutes*. Under this title it appears in the twelfth-century Bury library-catalogue (James, *On the Abbey*, p. 30).

retribuere,[1] dicentes: 'Ponamus lignum in panem eius, et ab-
radamus eum de numero nostro,[2] contrarius enim est operibus
nostris',[3] qui tamen pro causa domus sue et fratrum suorum Deum
timentium[4] innocens profectus erat. Pars quidem ueritatis, cum ad
tantam conspiceret eos aspirare maliciam ut nec timore diuino nec
mundialis terrore pudoris ab incepta desisterent malicia, quam ab
aquilone haurierant,[5] causam magistri Thome, que eorum fuit,
uiriliter defendentes, iterque suum protegentes, sic a capitulo
discesserunt.

Sed aquilo (id est sacrista, qui pocius dicitur a Christo segrega-
tus quam sacratus) eiusque fautores, pre tanta concepta malitia in
electum et eius partem seuientes, cum super hiis necdum quieuis-
sent, consilium illo die inierunt,[6] quod litteras ex parte conuentus
sub eorundem sigilli impressione domino pape per magistrum
Willelmum de Bancs[a] sub hac forma transmitterent: uidelicet
quod magister Thomas inconsulto priore et conuentu iter uersus
curiam Romanam arripuisset, nec aliquid quod per dictum Thomam in itinere presenti factum esset, aut ab aliquo mutuatum, pro
rato haberent. Sed cum, fama uentilante, ista auribus fidelium et
Deum timentium[7] patefierent, exurgentes magister Thomas
tercius prior et magister Nicholaus, sine mora priorem in locutorium minutorum[b] conuocabant, et ut 'minus lederent iacula
que preuidentur',[8] coram eo pro sigillo conuentus appellauerunt,
ne quid per idem sigillum fraudis uel doli contra electum et
electionem eo consentiente fieri permisisset. Magister quidem
Thomas in crastino appellationem coram priore et suppriore pro
sigillo die precedente factam renouauit; magister uero Nicholaus[c]
post capitulum, assumpto secum Nigello in testimonium, coram
suppriore pro eius claue appellauit. Tercio quidem sequenti die, in
translacione sancti Botulfi,[9] erexit se magister Nicholaus in pleno
capitulo, presente priore, et appellauit pro sigillo conuentus
propter quod tercio die precedente a quodam, nullo tamen
nominato, audierat: si in una claue ad conceptam corroborandam
nequiciam esset repugnantia (subaudis in claue tertii prioris),

---

[a] Bans H, *with contraction sign;* ancs *added opposite in outer marg. by Hand A;*
beginning cut away by binder   [b] minute H   [c] Nichalus H

---

[1] Ps. 30: 24, 34: 12.   [2] Ier. 11: 19.   [3] Sap. 2: 12.
[4] *Reg. Ben.,* c. 65; cf. above, p. 7 n. 7.

canons. Thus they returned evil for good,[1] saying: 'Let us place wood in his bread, and cast him out from among us,[2] for he is against our works',[3] although he, innocent man, had been sent to defend the cause of his house and of those of his brothers who feared God.[4] But the party of truth saw that the others were aspiring to such evil that neither from the fear of God nor of earthly shame would they turn from the wickedness which they had drawn from that 'north wind'.[5] And so, bravely defending Master Thomas's journey and cause (which was their own), they left the chapter-house.

But that 'north wind' the sacrist, segregated from Christ rather than consecrated to Him, together with his followers, ravening with hatred against the abbot elect and his party, and not yet calmed down over these matters, decided[6] that day to send letters to the pope on the convent's behalf and impressed with its seal, by Master William de Bancs, to this effect: that Master Thomas had gone off to the Roman curia without consulting the prior and convent, and that nothing which Thomas did on this journey, and no money which he had borrowed from anyone had their authority. But when the wafting of rumour brought this to the ears of the faithful and godfearing,[7] Master Thomas the third prior and Master Nicholas, rising up without delay, met the prior in the parlour, and that 'the missiles which they had anticipated might cause fewer wounds',[8] they appealed in his presence for the convent seal, so that it could not be used with his consent for any malice or trickery directed against the abbot elect or the election. The next day Master Thomas renewed his appeal, made before the prior and subprior on the previous day, and after chapter Master Nicholas, taking Nigel with him as a witness, asked the subprior for his key. Three days later, being the translation of St. Botolph,[9] Master Nicholas stood up in full chapter before the prior and appealed for the convent seal; for three days earlier he had heard from someone, not named, that if the custody of a key was opposed because it aided an evil purpose (meaning the third prior's), it

[5] Ier. 6: 1; cf. above, p. 25 n. 4.

[6] A common O.T. expression; cf. above, p. 13 n. 4.

[7] *Reg. Ben.*, c. 65; cf. above, p. 7 n. 7.

[8] Gregory, *Hom. in Evang.*, *PL*, lxxvi, col. 1259. A proverb cited also by John of Salisbury and Gilbert Foliot. *The Letters and Charters of Gilbert Foliot*, ed. A. Morey and C. N. L. Brooke (Cambridge, 1967), p. 250 n. 5.

[9] 8 February.

clauem regis facerent. Hoc autem dixit Walterus subsacrista
coram magistro Nicholao. Sacrista autem, cum uideret priorem et
custodes clauium appellationi defferre illos, et pocius timore quam
amore premeditatam arcius mutare maliciam, moleste tulit. Et
tamen ⟨cum⟩ per duos dies tocidemque noctes non reperisset
qualiter electo siue parti eius posset nocere, nouam a cista*ᵃ* fellis
extraxit plagam et inauditam, ut per eam, si tamen ad effectum
perduxisset, tota domus processu temporis grauius inde a domino
papa lederetur: ut*ᵇ* tempore interdicti infra gremium ecclesie beati
Edmundi uno die et una ebdomada due celebrarentur misse; una
scilicet a Godefrido clerico suo ante crucem, alia uero illo die a
monacho ad magnum altare, cum tantum una missa per ebdomadam domibus conuentualibus ex permissione summi pontificis et
executorum interdicti esset specialiter indulta.¹ Huic consilio
aquilonis adquieuerunt prior*ᶜ* et supprior, precentor et A(dam)
infirmarius, W(alterus) subsacrista et Aedmundus, I(ocelinus)
elemosinarius et Ricardus Taillehaste, cum*ᵈ* obliquis de numero
eorum² existentibus, licet indiscrete. Illo quidem die proposuit
dominus Henricus de Londonia missam primam cantare, sed
propter clericum passus est a sacrista repulsam.

Pars quidem ueritatis, sacramentum electionis obseruantes,
f. 176 intencionem | sacriste intuentes, quod rem istam non ob aliam
causam ad effectum ducere conaretur nisi ob detrimentum domus
et electi, ut hoc audito ab executoribus et a curia Romana perinde
protelaretur promocio, nitebatur contra simulque appellauit. Sed
supprior Albinus, alas habens binas ut hinc inde uolaret,³ cui
etiam potestas illo die erat in capitulo commissa, albini⁴ obceca-
cione uoluntati sacriste omnino deditus, licet pre multitudine
fidelium in ea non posset ex toto proficere, quosdam, ut alios
perinde compesceret,*ᵉ* sententiauit, scilicet Ricardus de Saxham
et Hugonem de Theforde. Prior uero in crastino ueniens in
capitulum, nimis credulus uerbis⁵ sacriste ob eiusdem ammoni-
cionem, utpote qui semper electo atque*ᶠ* parti eius sedit ad insidias⁶,

---

ᵃ cisti H   *ᵇ* nec H   *ᶜ* H *adds* et subprior   *ᵈ* H *adds* eorum
ᵉ compescerit H   *ᶠ* electoque H

---

¹ See C. R. Cheney, 'King John and the papal interdict', *Bulletin of the John
Rylands Library*, xxxi (1948), 295–317. There was actually some confusion about
the provisions of the interdict, and the sacrist was perhaps trading on the privi-

might be made over to the king. (In fact this had been told Master Nicholas by Walter the subsacrist.) The sacrist, however, was annoyed when he saw the prior and the keepers of the keys grant the appeal of these men, restraining the wickedness which they had planned from fear rather than love. For two days and nights he sought unsuccessfully for some way to harm the abbot elect and his party, and at last brought forth from his box of nasty tricks a new and unheard-of scourge, such that if he had been able to carry it into effect the whole house would eventually have been severely punished by the pope. His proposal was that two masses on one day of the same week should be celebrated at St. Edmunds during the interdict, one by Godfrey his clerk before the Cross, the other on the same day by a monk before the high altar. But one mass only per week had been specifically granted to the conventual houses by the pope and the executors of the interdict.[1] The prior, subprior, precentor, Adam the infirmarer, Walter the subsacrist and Edmund, Jocelin the almoner and Richard Taillehaste with the rest of their wrong-headed tribe[2] there present imprudently agreed with this suggestion of the 'north wind'. Indeed Henry of London proposed to sing the first mass that day, but he allowed himself to be repulsed by the sacrist on the clerk's account.

But the party of truth (those who kept the election oath) realized that the sacrist's intention in pursuing this matter was to harm the house and the abbot elect, for any progress over the election would be delayed once the executors and the Roman curia heard of it. So they opposed it and appealed against it. But Albinus the subprior, having as it were two wings with which he flew hither and thither,[3] to whom authority over the chapter had been committed that day, blindly obeyed the will of that alien[4] sacrist. Although restrained to some extent by the number of the faithful, he nevertheless disciplined a couple of them, Richard of Saxham and Hugh of Thetford, as examples to the rest. The next day the prior entered the chapter-house and, placing too much trust in the sacrist's admonition[5]—for he always lay in wait[6] for

leges bestowed on the house by earlier popes, by which the monks had the right to celebrate mass in time of interdict (*PUE*, iii, no. 187, etc.).
   [2] A common O.T. expression; cf. above, p. 40 n. 4.
   [3] Is. 6: 2.
   [4] *Albinus* is given as an alternative to *alienus* in Latham, *Word-List*.
   [5] Gen. 39: 19; cf. above, p. 4 n. 4.
   [6] Ps. 10: 8; cf. above, p. 19 n. 8.

manum suam super innodatos iniuste et iusta causa domum suam
protegentes aggrauabat,[1] cum de iure ex quo appellauerant et in
persecucione appellacionis perstiterunt. Teste Iustiniano, non licuit
pro causa appellata sententiam inferre.[2] Sed^a H(ugo) de Theford,
illius non immemor prophetici dicentis, 'Obedientiam malo
plusquam sacrificium',[3] necnon et beati patris nostri Benedicti in
regula, 'In omnibus obediendum est abbati nisi in manifestis
contra Deum',[4] ait in capitulo: 'Et ego pro causa electionis nostre,
ut per hoc tamen malicia sacriste et supprioris eorumque extin-
guatur sequentium, libenti animo uultuque iocundo in nomine
Domini suscipio'; sic itaque, licet per duos dies in ultimo gradu ad
aquam[5] et in leui culpa[6] pro causa sententiatus congnita, non
tamen ad tantam malitiam temperabatur^b contentam expiandam,
nec unquam postea septena dierum duorum, iudicio meo, suffecit
dieta. Factumque est hoc die tertia ante primam ebdomadam
quadragesime.[7]

In sequenti quidem ebdomada misit sequestratus ille Taupe et
Hugonem Canem garciferos^c suos uersus curiam Romanam, ea,
ut a laicis dicebatur, de causa, quatinus Thome sociisque eius
obuiando, uel ubi in itinere reperiendo, aliquod conferrent
inpedimentum. Tuleruntque idem secum litteras priori⟨s⟩,
clausasque^d magistri R(oberti)[8] officialis ex questu domini prioris
litterasque prioris de Theford[9] aliorumque plurium in testimonium
domino Norwicensi,[10] ⟨ut⟩ firmius aduersando electioni staret
et immobilius. In crastino uero Passionis Domini[11] magister
Thomas de Becles, magister Nicholaus, P(etrus) celerarius, H(ugo)
de Theford, R(icardus) de Saxham, H(ugo) de Hastinges,
Nicholaus Romanus aliique prouectionem^e electi cupientes, com-
munique utentes consilio, petierunt per^f magistrum Thomam et
R(icardum) de Saxham ut prior istis litteris sub hac forma magistro
R(oberto)[12] legato electionem nostram secundum Deum et canones

---

^{a} H *adds* licet ^{b} tempore abbatis H; *my emendation is conjectural, but*
probably more is needed to make sense of this corrupt passage ^{c} carciferos H
^{d} clausisque H ^{e} prouectiones H ^{f} *Twice* H

---

[1] 1 Reg. 5: 6.
[2] *Digest*, 49, 1 ff. deals with appeals. The writer might just as relevantly have
quoted canon law on this point (e.g. *Corpus Iuris Canonici*, i. 2, 2, 6, 2; ii. 28,
16, etc.), and it is interesting that he does not do so.
[3] Cf. 1 Reg. 15: 22; Os. 6: 6; Matt. 9: 13, 12: 7.
[4] *Reg. Ben.*, c. 4, paraphrased with the meaning rather more precisely
specified, probably reflecting the influence of local custom.
[5] Probably referring to the ritual washing at the lavatorium.
[6] A technical term referring to a class of offences for which light penalties
were prescribed, distinguished in *Reg. Ben.*, c. 44, from *grauis culpa*.

the abbot elect and his party—he came down heavily and unjustly upon those who had been disciplined,[1] although they were defending the just cause of his house, because they stood firmly by the law under which they had put forward and maintained their appeal. As Justinian has it, 'Sentence is not to be imposed in a case under appeal.'[2] But Hugh of Thetford, not forgetting the saying of the prophet, 'I prefer obedience to sacrifice',[3] and of our blessed father Benedict in the *Rule*, 'In all things obedience is owed to the abbot, except in what is obviously contrary to the will of God',[4] said in chapter: 'In God's name and for the sake of our election I accept my punishment with good will and a cheerful countenance, to silence the malice of the sacrist and subprior and their following.' And so, although sentenced to the last place at the washing[5] for two days (for a minor fault,[6] as all knew), moderation was not shown him in his expiation for such malice. Not for a fortnight after, in my opinion, was his diet sufficient. Now this was done three days before the first week of Lent.[7]

During the following week the sacrist secretly sent Mole and Hugh the Dog, his lackeys, to the Roman curia so that, meeting Thomas and his friends on the road, they might devise some impediment to his mission—according to local gossip. They took with them letters from the prior, letters close of Master Robert[8] the advocate on the prior's business, and supporting letters from the prior of Thetford[9] and many others addressed to the bishop of Norwich,[10] to make him stand firmly and immovably against the election. On Easter Saturday[11] Master Thomas of Beccles, Master Nicholas, Peter the cellarer, Hugh of Thetford, Richard of Saxham, Hugh of Hastings, Nicholas Roman and others who desired the abbot elect's advancement asked the prior, by common agreement, through Master Thomas and Richard of Saxham, to impress with his seal a letter addressed to Master Robert the legate,[12] protesting our election valid according to God and the

---

[7] 9 February.

[8] Robert de Areines? See below, p. 152.

[9] There were three male priories in Thetford, so that this man cannot be identified.

[10] John de Gray (1200–14), a royal appointee and friend of the king, whose candidate he had been in the Canterbury election dispute.

[11] 17 March.

[12] Cardinal Robert de Courçon, legate of France; an eminent canonist and friend of Stephen Langton.

protestantibus, sigillum suum inponeret, ut exinde maiore concepta
constantia, ⟨cognita⟩ ueritate*ᵃ* super electione, amore Dei et cause
nostre iusticia libentius ad effectum ducere niteretur. Quo tandem
fauente perrexerunt in domum que fuit quondam uetus infir-
marium¹ ibique sigillo suo muniuit, adiungendo ne cui illud
reuelarent, ne forsitan partis aduerse odium incurreret. Hoc
autem dixit quia sibi timebat eo quod sigillum suum sepius hinc
inde dederat superius in contrarium, ne perinde, si tamen aliis
patefieret, in fame dispendium incurreret. Quibus cum litteris
egressis et iam in uoluntate sua in parte maxima promotis, con-
suluerunt super hoc, si expediret litteras sub sigillo conuentus sub
forma pristina petere. Cui consilio fideles adquiescentes ut per hoc
tamen inter fideles et infideles maiorem haberent discrecionem,
facta est eo die mencio coram priore in capitulo per magistrum
Nicholaum sub forma prescripta; petiitque humiliter ut littere
coram omnibus legerentur, et si quid reprehensibile in eisdem
reperiretur, per commune deleretur consilium; sin autem, cum et
omnes singillatim faterentur promocionem electionis se uelle
procurare, quid contra? Opere enim erat Dei monstranda dileccio
ne esset infructuosa nominis appellatio. Ad hoc sacrista, seu
aquilo, a quo omne malum² et a cuius puteo uniuersa hauritur
malicia, appellauit ne impetrata aliqua uel impetranda alicuius
suggestione falsa ad effectum ducerentur. Post quem neque
⟨cessum, erexit se(?)⟩ alter eiusdem peruersitatis instructus,³ scilicet
R(icardus) de Sterteford qui, ut superius habetur, non septem
electores set seductores uocauit,⁴ appellauitque ne electus ulterius
f. 176ᵛ promoueretur; | quorum uidelicet appellationibus iustis nos omnes
deferentes, ita supplendo appellauimus cum eis ne quid suggestione
falsa perquisitum seu, ne electus ad altiorem dignitatem, ut in
episcopatum, alicubi a nobis sublatus ulterius promoueretur.

Existente interim concilio apud Norhamtun⁵ R(icardus) precentor ibidem se presentauit, ut in insidiis assidens⁶ perpetraret in
occulto quod exequi non licuit in aperto; salua tamen gratia prioris,

ᵃ ueritatis H

---

¹ Built 1107–c. 1114, between the river and the monks' cemetery, i.e. east of
the church; burnt c. 1150 and repaired. The 'new infirmary' was built just north
of it under Abbot Samson (1182–1211). Whittingham, p. 181 and pl. xxi.
² Ier. 6: 1; cf. above, p. 25 n. 4.
³ Cf. Abbo (*Mem.* i. 8): '. . . eiusdem peruersitatis homine . . .'.
⁴ See above, p. 31.
⁵ *Councils*, p. 21 n. 6. The *Winchcombe Annals* are the only other source to

canons. They hoped that this letter would encourage him to work
enthusiastically to see justice done in our cause, for the love of God
and because of our election's validity. When at length the prior
agreed to this, they proceeded to the house which used to be the
old infirmary[1] and there he affixed his seal, asking that they would
not reveal his action in case he incurred the anger of the opposing
party. This he said fearing loss of face if it were disclosed to the
others, because he had frequently used his seal for both sides and
for contrary purposes. When they had gone out with the letter,
having now got their way to a great extent, they discussed whether
it would be advantageous to ask for the letter to be sent, with its
contents unaltered, under the convent seal. To this the faithful
party agreed, hoping by this means to bring about better relations
between the faithful and unfaithful parties. So Master Nicholas
brought it up that day in chapter before the prior, as agreed. He
asked humbly for the letter to be read out before them all, so that
anything objectionable found in it might be deleted by the community's advice; if, on the other hand, each and all declared that
they wished to procure the election's fulfilment, what objection
could there be to it? For God's preference ought to be openly
demonstrated, lest the appeal defending his nomination should be
in vain. At this the sacrist, like the north wind, from whence comes
all evil,[2] and from whose depths all malice is poured forth, appealed
against anything being permitted which had been procured or was
to be procured by anyone's evil suggestion. Hardly had he finished
when another, possessed by the same perversity,[3] Richard of
Stortford who, as mentioned earlier, had called the seven electors
seven seducers,[4] appealed against the abbot elect's being given
any further assistance. We for our part granted their just appeals,
appealing with them against anything being attempted by false
suggestion, and against the abbot elect's being advanced to any
higher dignity, such as the episcopate, with our support.

Meanwhile Richard the precentor presented himself at the
council being held at Northampton[5] so that, lying in ambush,[6]
he could perpetrate in secret what he was unable to perform
openly. He had, however, leave of the prior, who was too prone to
grant such indulgences to him and to the others who opposed the

mention this council whose purpose and membership, apart from the archbishop of Canterbury and the two persons mentioned above, are unknown.
[6] Ps. 10: 8; cf. above, p. 19 n. 8.

qui eidem et aliis electioni contra Deum et sacramentum obuianti-
bus (ut ei aliquando per H(ugonem) de Theforde improperabatur),
in talibus nimis pronus repertus erat licentiis, cum et pocius eorum
habenas restringere debuisset quam relaxare. Factumque est,
precentore ⟨in⟩ concilio existente, nuntius quidam domini
R(oberti)^a citra montes legati litteras ex parte domini sui legato
Anglie pretendisset, in cauda quarum continebatur ⟨quodam⟩ pro
domo sancti Aedmundi. Auertens se quidem legatus quod electionem tangerent, conuocauit episcopum Wyntoniensem et fracto
coram illo sigillo tradidit eidem ad^b legendum. Quibus perlectis
et super hiis quid esset consulendum interrogans, respondit episcopus: 'Domine legate, peticio tanti uiri satis nobis expressum
debet esse preceptum; quod nullo beneplacito nostro occurrit
eidem super significatis respondere uestrum est prouidere.' Sed
legatus Anglie, tanti uiri non immemor peticionis, humili tamen
premissa salutacione[1] remandauit quod, quantum cum Deo posset,
preces eius in electione promouenda exaudiat sicut in casu con-
simili uice uersa uellet exaudiri.[2] R(icardus) uero precentor, cui
necdum ista patebant, accedens^c propius aduocauit dominum
Wyntoniensem sub piro quadam, sciscitans ab eo qualiter pro
regia dignitate contra electionem esset operandum. Dominus
autem episcopus, intuens quod si ad tempus differretur electionis
promocio, non tamen processu^d auferetur, primoque denudans ei
litterarum contentum pro electione et electo tunc perlectarum,^e
dixit ei: 'Frater, cum omnibus res gesta sit facti uestri notoria
tanquam a Deo processa, insuper ⟨et⟩ ad eiusdem H(ugonis)
electionem confirmandam cartam conuentus habeat de rato, non
inuenio qualiter sit subtrahendum quod tanto testimonio iam sit
confirmatum, qualiter resistendum quod cunctis eminet a Deo et
canone fore processum.' Ad que R(icardus) precentor, licet in
responsis nimis festinus et minus quam eius deceret persone
prouidus, cum iam sibi uniuersorum consilium contra unguem
cedere conspiceret, dixit: 'Per os Domini, antequam ei H(ugoni)
liber pateat ingressus, ictus dabuntur grossi!' et eo dicto domum
redire festinauit.

Ingressus quidem capitulum salutaciones ex parte legati
premisit,^f subsequendo quod cum super solitarum relaxacione
misericordiarum fecisset mencionem, qualiterue eius prohibicio, ne
solite repeterentur commessaciones, esset supplenda — tanquam

---

^a regis H, *canc. and corr. over line by scribe*   ^b *Added over line by Hand A*
^c accederes H   ^d *So* H; *Hand C adds* s   ^e H *adds* et   ^f primisit H

[1] See above, p. 4. n. 2.

election contrary to God and their oath. From time to time he was reproached over this by Hugh of Thetford, for he had relaxed their reins when he ought to have shortened them. While the precentor was at the council a messenger from Robert, legate on this side of the Alps, presented a letter from his lord to the English legate, at the end of which were some remarks favouring the house of St. Edmunds. The legate, reckoning that the letter might refer to the election, called the bishop of Winchester, and breaking the seal in his presence, handed it to him to read. When he had read it and was asked his advice about its contents, the bishop said: 'Lord legate, a petition addressed to us from so great a man is to be understood as an order; but the duty of replying to him about it is not mine, but yours.' So the English legate, not esteeming lightly the petition of such an important man, wrote back to him, conveying his humble greetings[1] and saying that, as far as he could, by God's help, he would take note of his request for the election's promotion just as, if their positions were reversed, he would wish his own prayer to be considered.[2] Now Richard the precentor, to whom they had not yet shown the letter, came up and met the bishop of Winchester under a pear-tree, inquiring earnestly of him how best to work against the election in support of the king's dignity. The bishop, knowing that even if the election's promotion was being delayed at that time, nonetheless eventually it would be carried through, revealed to him the contents of the letter which he had just read, supporting the abbot elect and the election. 'Brother,' said he, 'as it is evident to all that your deed proceeded from God, and since the convent has a charter ratifying Hugh's election, I do not see how it can be annulled, especially now that it is confirmed by such testimony, or how resisted, when it has obviously proceeded according to God and the canons.' At this Richard the precentor, more hasty and less prudent in reply than he ought to have been, seeing everyone's opinion going against him, said: 'By the Lord's face, before that fellow Hugh is permitted free entry, heavy blows will be dealt!' After saying this, he hastened to return home.

Entering the chapter-house he presented the legate's greetings and made known his reply to the question about the relaxation of their usual food-allowances, that is, how his prohibition of the accustomed food-allowances was to be enforced—as if this had

[2] The writer may have had access to the text.

non alia profectus esset ad curiam de causa — respondit legatus: 'Et ego omnibus carnium commessaciones prohibui et adhuc prohibeo eis et successoribus eorum in eternum preter quod prior, cum fuerit in camera, quos uoluerit de fratribus ad se conuocet per tres uel per quatuor; similiter in domo infirmorum dum non ad consequenciam trahatur[1] ad naturam refocillandam.' Videntes quidem Pharaonis sequaces partim uel nichil in uoluntate sua se posse proficere, excusacionem de peccato querentes, ut perinde facilius nequiciam infunderent proprie malicie in alios, dixerunt: 'Domine prior, ne miremini si quid fecimus non agendum cum et ab aliis sepius minati, ut si quando electus preualeret, a domo culpis nostris exigentibus expelleremur'; nitentes ad hoc ut propriam in aliquem effunderent maliciam, more primi parentis nostri Ade qui postquam transgressus et in ictu oculi nudus effectus, ait illi Dominus: 'Quid fecisti?' Ille quidem uolens in Dominum culpam retorquere propriam ait: 'Domine, mulier quam fecisti michi' etc.,[2] tanquam diceret: 'Si eam mihi non dedisses, in te penitus non peccassem.' Similiter: 'Si delictum sacramenti non exprobrassent nobis, utique cum electione stetissemus.' Cum hoc manifeste ficticium et inuentorium esset, ut uidelicet,[a] sedatis omnibus, ab incensa facilius ueniam consequerentur malicia. Ab inicio enim, postquam dominus H(ugo) electus fuit, semper dolose contra | eius electionem operantes inuenti sunt et maliciose. Vnde probatur eorum testimonium in hac parte non esse conueniens quia nec habiti fideles sunt in testimoniis suis.[3]

f. 177

Dominus quidem H(ugo) electus tunc temporis in partibus transmarinis exspectans, inopiam suam litteris diuersis priori et sacriste significauit, eorum suffragium petens. Sed cum R(obertus) sacrista ad locutorium in claustro quid super litteris electi esset consulendum interrogasset — licet irronice — respondit Ricardus de Sterteford, qui se aliis preminere in sensu iactabat et consilio: 'Non est tutum neque sani capitis consilium, inimicos domini regis in aliquibus contra eius libertates extollere, cum et ille H(ugo) de Norwolde, quem nonnulli false nominant electum, inconsulto priore et conuentu a domo sua recessisset', orando sine excepcione

---

[a] *Some words may be missing here* H

been the only reason for his journey to court. The legate had said: 'I have forbidden meat dishes to everyone, and therefore I still forbid them to you and your successors for ever, except that the prior, when he is in his chamber, may choose three or four brothers to have with him; and the same exception applies to the infirmary, if it seems that any of the inmates are not recovering quickly enough.'[1] Now the followers of Pharaoh, seeing that they were unable to get their own way even in part, looking for an excuse for their sin and to throw the blame for their own evil onto others, said: 'Lord prior, it is no wonder that we did what was forbidden, seeing that we had been threatened so often by the others; for they said that if the abbot elect were eventually to prevail, we should be driven from the house for our sins.' Their object was to blame someone else for their evil, like our first parent Adam who, after he had sinned and become naked in the twinkling of an eye, was asked by the Lord: 'What have you done?' And he, wishing to blame his own sin on the Lord, replied: 'Lord, the woman whom you made for me' etc.,[2] as if to say: 'If you had not given her to me, I would not have sinned against you.' Just so these men were saying: 'If the others had not reproached us with breaking the oath, we would have supported the election.' As this was so obviously a lie and invention . . . everyone calmed down and they were readily pardoned for their wickedness. For right from the start, ever since Hugh's nomination, they had worked cunningly and maliciously against his election. So their testimony in this regard is proved unreliable, for they had not remained faithful in their witness.[3]

Now the abbot elect Hugh, waiting overseas at the time, wrote to the prior and sacrist of his needy state and asked for their aid. But when Robert the sacrist in the cloister parlour asked—although ironically—what was to be done about the letter, Richard of Stortford, a man who thought himself superior in intellect and counsel to the others, replied: 'It is not prudent nor the counsel of a sane mind to support the king's enemies in anything against his liberties, especially as Hugh of Northwold, whom some falsely call abbot elect, left his house without the consent of prior and convent.' And he prayed that whoever should continue to name him as abbot elect might without exception incur the five hundred

---

[1] Cf. *JB*, p. 98: 'ne talia trahantur ad consequentiam'.
[2] Gen. 3: 12.　　　　　　　　　　　　　　[3] Ps. 77: 37.

illum quingenta Dei incurrere odia[1] qui eum pro electo ulterius nominaret. Rogerus quidem de Stanham inter alia quedam de electo non retrahenda, in comparatione quadam coram pluribus in parlorio proposuit. Hoc scilicet non ad retrahentiam uindicte, sed ut per hoc alias retractata ipsi in consimilibus rubore saltem perfusi reperiantur prudentiores, scribere duxi. Sed 'quo semel est imbuta recens' etc.,[2] cum et aquilo omni imbutus malicia et a quo omne pandetur malum,[3] succensos in satis cognita amplius accendere malicia nondum quiesceret;[a] ut ⟨quidam⟩ qui[b] ignem sub lebete accensum, apponendo lignum et stipulas ad maiorem combustionem accendere desiderat,[4] eo eorum maliciam, donis et promissionibus interpositis, ad maiorem iniquitatis combustionem ignire non distulit.

Effuso enim hac de causa metallo replicato et sepius repetito, insuper et se cum eisdem in omni loco ubicumque electioni nocere credebat, presentante, cum per hoc eius cordi non suffecit peruerso, protraxit intra se quod unum ex suis, Ricardum scilicet Caluum, die Iouis ante Pascha[5] populo faceret predicare, ut predicando per circumlocuciones et exempla[6] super electione corda audientium a ueritate cognita et per uniuersum orbem iam diuulgata distorqueret. Sed sicut ait apostolus, 'Nihil absconditum quod non reuelabitur'.[7] Cum et hoc aures fidelium[c] iam fama perflaret uentilans et eo iam bis in capitulo sermocinante ut eo coram populo audacior reperiretur, prouidendo fideli[d] consilio et salubri erexit se H(ugo) de Theford appellauitque contra eum in capitulo ad legatum Anglie, ne ulterius, propter maliciam cognitam sepiusque expertam et diffamacionem et famosum libellum quem idem Caluus abbati de Belloloco tradiderat, sermocinaret. Stetitque secum Ricardus de Flammeuille ad eius confirmandam appellationem; factusque est super hac appellatione tumultus magnus in populo peruerso.[8] Conferentes tandem inter se si deferendum esset appellationi, timore pocius quam reuerentia ipsius legati appellationi detulerunt. Sacrista uero, licet non sine graui cordis amaritudine, cum in locutorio paruo ante capitulum[9] iterato pre cordis

---

[a] quiesseret H, *corr. in marg. by Hand B*   [b] quo quos H   [c] fideles H, *corr. over line by Hand B*   [d] fidelium H

[1] I cannot find the origin of this curious expression.
[2] Hor., *Ep.* i. 2, 69; Walther, no. 25711.
[3] Ier. 6: 1; cf. above, p. 25 n. 4.
[4] Conflated from various biblical passages, e.g. 1 Cor. 3: 12, etc.

hates of God.[1] But Roger of Stanham, before many of the brothers in the parlour, suggested a certain amount of provision along with a few other items of which he thought the abbot elect ought not to be deprived. Now I have thought it worth while to record this not to lessen the blame which these men deserve, but that through this others who might refuse in similar circumstances should eventually be filled with shame and restored to prudence. But 'the jar will long preserve the odour', etc.,[2] for the 'north wind', absolutely saturated with evil, spreading his wickedness everywhere,[3] lost no opportunity to inflame those whom he had already set on fire to yet greater evil. As a man lights a fire under a cauldron and feeds it with wood and stubble to make it still hotter,[4] so by gifts and promises he hastened to inflame them to a greater pitch of infamy.

Again and again he and his party used tactics cast in the same mould, wherever he thought it would harm the election. But thinking in his perverse heart that this was insufficient the sacrist decided that a man of his, Richard the Bald, should preach to the people on Maundy Thursday,[5] in order to turn the minds of the congregation from the truth of the election, which was now spread abroad throughout the land, by preaching through examples[6] and circumlocutions. But as the apostle says: 'Nothing is covered which will not be revealed.'[7] For when this rumour reached the ears of the faithful, and when Richard had preached twice in the chapter-house so as to be bolder in speech before the people, Hugh of Thetford rose in chapter to offer faithful and beneficial counsel, and appealed to the English legate against Bald's continuing to preach, because of his well-known and often-endured malice, because he had spread slander, and because of the notorious libel which he had uttered before the abbot of Beaulieu. Richard de Flamvill stood with him, seconding the motion; and there was a great tumult among the perverse[8] because of that appeal. At length, after discussing among themselves whether they ought to give in to it, they decided to do so, more from fear of the legate than from reverence for him. For the sacrist, in great bitterness of heart, sought his party's advice again and again in his perplexity, in the small parlour before the chapter-house,[9] and he reasoned

---

[5] 27 March.

[6] A technical term from the *Artes Praedicandi*. P. B. Roberts, *Stephanus de Lingua Tonante* (Toronto, 1968), pp. 79–89.

[7] Cf. Matt. 10: 26 and Marc. 4: 22 (cf. Luc. 12: 2). Also quoted in *JB*, p. 109.

[8] Os. 10: 14; cf. above, p. 15 n. 5. [9] See above, p. 3 n. 7.

angustia super hiis a suis peteret consilium, omniaque eis super
casu presenti acciditura pariterque pro et contra coram eis satis
allegans sufficienter, appellationi deferre timore pocius quam
amore decreuerunt legati. Ita tamen ut idem sacrista, ad suorum
corda infidelium corroboranda, baculum scilicet predicatorium
illo die assumeret; factumque est ita.

Et extrahente quidem sacrista sermone ad hoc: 'Christus
descendit mundum redimere ut liberaret a morte homines',[1]
conatus est non modicum, quantum in se, tam clericos quam
laicos de medulla horum uerborum[2] interioris intellectus reficere;
cum et furfur pro farina, paleam pro grano, abscinthium pro uino,
auribus audientium plurima proponendo inconuenientia propi-
nasset, et a similaginario camulum pro simila discumbentibus
distribuisset.[3]

Sed ne infidelium in sua infidelitate corda persistentium[a]
corroboracione, fideliumue in[b] simplicitate manencium per ⟨uerba⟩
reiterata a sacrista contra fidem et ad memoriam reducta debilem,
f. 177ᵛ   quedam, licet | plurima omittens, ut in consimilibus fideles in fide
reperiantur[c] feruenciores, proponam. Solent enim contraria ad
maiorem efficatiam sepius contrariis opponi.[4] Cum itaque de
incarnacione Domini ad trium mortuorum resuscitacionem fecisset
descensum,[d] seruum centurionis predicauit a Domino inter alios
primo fore resuscitatum; cum et contra hoc satis expresse inueni-
antur Scripture, non enim a morte sed ab infirmitate corporis
perhibetur a Domino liberari, ut hic: ' "Domine, puer meus iacet
paraliticus in domo et male torquetur." "Amen, dico tibi, ego
ueniam et curabo eum" ',[5] non 'resuscitabo'. Dixit etiam et
Christum a crismate dictum,[6] cum secundum fidem nostram et
Scripturarum testimonium Christus semper manet in eternum;[6]
antequam crisma conficeretur fuit Christus qui omnia creauit ex
nichilo; ergo incongrue Creator a creatura potest dici, sed sicut

---

[a] ipersistentium H, *corr. by scribe*   [b] *Twice* H   [c] periantur H,
corr.   [d] decensum H

[1] This is not a biblical text (though cf. Ioh. 3: 16–17). Cf. the text of a
melisma sung at the end of an Easter Alleluia, *Pascha nostrum*, at St. Martial
of Limoges: 'Christus uenit in mundum ut redimeret genus humanum' (J.
Chailley, *L'École Musicale de Saint Martial de Limoges*, Paris, 1960, p. 297).
The sacrist may thus be quoting the text of an Easter trope sung at Bury.

with them, weighing the pros and cons of the situation. In the end they decided to grant the appeal, more from fear than from love of the legate—on condition, however, that the sacrist himself, to raise the spirits of his wicked band, would assume the preacher's rod on that day; and so it came to pass.

The sacrist preached on the theme: 'Christ came to redeem the world and to save men from death',[1] and he tried hard, as far as he was capable, to edify both clergy and laity by extracting hidden meaning from the depths of these words.[2] But, by propounding many fallacies, he fed the ears of his audience, as it were, with bran instead of flour, chaff in place of grain, wormwood for wine; and he distributed 'small beer' made of the fine flour rather than the flour itself to the feasters.[3]

I shall set down some of the sacrist's sermon, although omitting much, not to aid the unfaithful who persisted in their disloyalty, nor to support those of the faithful who were led astray in their naïvety by the sacrist's repeated onslaughts on their faith, but in order to encourage faithful men to more fervent loyalty in similar circumstances. For contraries are often opposed for greater efficacy.[4] For instance, he preached that when our Lord while here on earth revived three dead men, the centurion's servant was one of the first to be raised, when the Scriptures clearly state the contrary, for he was not freed from death but from bodily infirmity—' "Lord, my servant lies at home sick of the palsy, grievously tormented." And Jesus said to him: "Truly I tell you I will come and heal him" ',[5] not 'I will raise him.' He also said that Christ was so named after His anointing,[6] when according to our faith and the testimony of Scripture Christ is so named from eternity;[7] Christ who created all from nothing existed before the first chrism was made; so it is incongruous for the Creator to be

---

[2] Cf. Aulus Gellius, 18, 4, 2.

[3] Cf. Ioh. 6: 11, and the less elaborate figure employed by Gregory (*MGH, Epistolae Selectae*, ii. 252–3, ll. 30–2): 'Sed si delicioso cupitis pabulo saginari . . . patriotae uestri opuscula legite et ad comparationem siliginis illius nostrum furfurem non quaeritis.'

[4] The reference is to a common dialectical topos, the most likely source being Boethius, *De Differentiis Topicis, PL*, lxiv, cols. 1191C–D, 1198A, etc. It is also found in sermon-literature; see H. Caplan, 'The four senses of scriptural interpretation and the medieval theory of preaching', *Speculum*, iv (1929), 282.

[5] Matt. 8: 6–7.

[6] Act. 4: 27, etc.   [7] Ioh. 12: 34.

christianus a Christo, ita crisma a Christo deberet predicari.[1]
Vnde uidetur in hoc eum erasse. Dixit etiam Lazarum in mortali
peccato fore decessum; propter quod Dominus eundem suscitatu-
rus inuenit in monumento fetidum quatriduanum ⟨se⟩ habentem,[2]
existentibus ibi Roberto filio Rocelini, magistro Gilberto, magistro
Waltero scolarum rectore, Waltero de Disce aliisque pluribus.[3]
Aliud quidem, licet inconuenienter, de Willelmo Barbato de
Londonia monachis Cantuariensibus exemplum conformauit in
hec uerba:[4] 'Sunt quidam canes talis modi, quibus cum propria
non sufficiat*a* malicia, de patria sua ad aliam confugientes similibus
se copulant et alliciunt, et eos ad caulas ouium secum attrahentes,
eos suffocant pariter et interimunt.[5] Sic', aiebat, 'contigit de
W(illelmo) Barbato, qui contra dominum regem ciuitatem Lun-
donie subuertendo, subuertebatur laqueoque suspendebatur per
dominum Cantuariensem. Sic et de monachis Cantuariensibus, qui
sublato pastore contra dominum regem de preficiendo alio sine
assensu regio tractantes certamen inierunt; unde domus eorum
clarescentibus culpis, nisi diuina impediretur misericordia,[6] fere
ad nichilum fuit redacta.'[7] Hec autem*b* omnia ex deliberacione
maxime premeditacionis auribus proposuit audientium, ut pro
electione nostra idem domui nostre, nisi cicius uoluntati regis
conformaremur, intra se quilibet fore emersurum iudicaret, et
electionem sine assensu regio*c* factam omnino uacuam esse et
nullam. Qui, habitus sui ratione, talem comparationem de uiris
religiosis utpote canibus pocius subterfugisse deberet, quam
coram clericis et laicis retraxisse.

---

a sufficit H, *corr. over line by Hand B(?)*   *b* H *adds* coram, *canc. by*
scribe and Hand C   *c* H *adds* tractantes, *canc.*

---

[1] The sacrist's statement is perfectly in harmony with the teachings of both
the Fathers and medieval theologians. Among many, see Augustine, *In Ioh.
Evang.*, xxxiii. 3, and Isidore, *Etymologiae*, vi. 19, 50. On the other hand, no
authority for the writer's view appears in the *PL* indexes, although it may have
been discussed in the schools at the time.

[2] Ioh. 11: 17–44. A gross confusion, if fairly reported, between the literal
and moral sense of the story as interpreted by the Fathers and medieval theologians. Lazarus' death typified *morally* the state of the soul in mortal sin.
B. Smalley, *The Study of the Bible in the Middle Ages* (Oxford, rev. edn., 1952),
p. 23.

[3] FitzRocelin is otherwise unknown. Master Gilbert of Walsham, who
witnesses many charters of Abbot Samson between 1182–1211 (*Kalendar*, nos.
1, 18, 26, 57–8, 93, 119, 121–2, 150) and appears in one of Hugh of Northwold's,
c. 1217–20 (Cambridge University Library MS. Ff. ii. 29, f. 129), may have been

named after the creature. Rather, just as 'Christian' should be said
to derive from 'Christ', so also should 'chrism'.[1] Thus you may see
that in this his preaching went astray. Again, he said that Lazarus
had died in mortal sin, for the Lord when about to raise him from
the tomb four days later, found that he stank.[2] Present at the
sermon were Robert FitzRocelin, Master Gilbert, Master Walter,
head of the school, Walter of Diss, and many others.[3] Again he
drew an incongruous example from a comparison of William the
Bearded of London[4] with the monks of Canterbury, in the following words: 'There are certain dogs of such a kind that when their
own evil does not suffice they leave their country and establish
themselves in another, joining and allying to themselves dogs of the
same kind, and enticing them to the sheep-folds in their company,
they strangle and kill them along with the sheep.[5] Thus', he said,
'was the case of William the Bearded who tried to turn the London
citizenry against the king, but was overturned himself and hanged
on the gallows by the archbishop of Canterbury. So also with the
Canterbury monks, who after their pastor's death, thought that
they could appoint another without the king's consent and began
a contest against him; whence through their obvious guilt their
house would have been reduced almost to nothing,[6] had not the
divine mercy defended them.'[7] Now he addressed all this to his
audience by design, meaning that he could predict what would
happen unless we quickly conformed to the king's will regarding
our election, and that our election, made without the royal assent,
was wholly null and void. But, as a sensible man, he ought to have
altogether avoided such a comparison of religious to dogs, let
alone to have made it before clerks and laymen.

---

a local vicar. Master Walter would have been head of the Bury grammar-school.
Walter of Diss was vicar of Chevington on Abbot Samson's presentation (*JB*,
p. 44).

    [4] William was a demagogue who roused the London citizens against the heavy
taxation of the ruling oligarchy in 1196. He was captured and hanged by
Archbishop Hubert Walter. C. R. Cheney, *Hubert Walter* (London, 1967),
pp. 93–4.

    [5] If the implication is that William the Bearded was a foreigner, there is no
mention of this in contemporary chronicles.

    [6] Cf. Abbo (*Mem.* i. 9): '. . . nisi diuina impediretur miseratione'.

    [7] Referring to the election dispute of 1205–6, which resulted in the papal
appointment of Stephen Langton. F. M. Powicke, *Stephen Langton*, pp. 75–101,
and D. Knowles, 'The Canterbury election of 1205–6', *EHR*, liii (1938),
211–20.

In crastino quidem Pasche[1] sacrista, assumpto secum Ricardo
Caluo, habenas suas domino legato Anglie deflexit.[2] Cuius causa
itineris, ut a Willelmo Disce percipiebatur, fuit hoc: proposuit
autem transmittere Ricardum Caluum ad dominum regem cum[a]
litteris[b] legati, ut per eas saltem aliquid in contrarium electioni
machinaretur. Sed, ut postea declaratum est, ipsi obuiantes
lepori, sicut uulgari habetur prouerbio, infecto negocio, cum super
hoc dominus legatus non consentiret, domum reuersi sunt, ut
infra determinatur.

Post quorum uero recessum, cum et Albinus supprior, ratione
donorum a sacrista, ut dicebatur, interpositorum, parti electionis
sederet in insidiis,[3] nominauit quodam die in capitulo fratrem
Hugonem de Theforde solo nomine sine uerbo adiuncto, sic:
'Domine Hugo'; cumque ille responderet: 'Quid?' clamauit eum,
qui exurgens stetit in medio ut decuit. Suscepit ab eo disciplinam
regularem,[4] propter quod dixit 'quid'. Sed cum Albinus in hoc non
sibi adiudicasset satis fecisse, precepit ut illo die pane tantummodo
et aqua contentus sicut penam purgaret responsionis 'quid', cum
et totum capitulum eius iudicium indiscrete latum, odio pocius
quam fraterni amoris correpcione, iudicaret, et iniuste. Quam
quidem sententiam, quia plane iniustam, omnino renu⟨it⟩ subire,
dicens: 'Deus neminem punit bis in idipsum.'[5] Persistente uero
suppriore in ira concepta, idem in crastino premissam[c] a duobus
disciplinam,[d] licet sine ratione, repeciit. Qui causam malicie et
radicem huius clarius intuens persecucionis plane subire recusauit,
nisi manifestam premonstrasset rationem. At ille sine more[e] dispendio sententiam excommunicationis, cum et hoc spectet solummodo ad abbatem in arduis et maioribus culpis,[6] inferre in eum
non distulit. Hoc iam ter[f] post electionem factam | in diuersis
personis, uoluntate magis operante quam ratione,[7] meminimus
intulisse. Subsecuto die tercio conuenerunt supprior, I(ocelinus)

f. 178

[a] per H	[b] litteras H	[c] premissa H	[d] disciplina H
[e] moris H	[f] tercio H		

[1] 31 March.
[2] Variants of this phrase are common in classical authors, e.g. Virgil, *Aen.*
xii. 471; for a medieval example, cf. *Waltharius* (*MGH, Poetae Aevi Carolini*,
vi. i. 26, l. 42 and n.).
[3] Ps. 10: 8; cf. above, p. 19 n. 8.
[4] A technical term for certain kinds of punishment from *Reg. Ben.*, c. 54,
c. 62, etc.

On Easter Monday[1] the sacrist, taking with him Richard the Bald, directed his horses' heads[2] towards the English legate. The cause of his journey, as William of Diss perceived, was this: he proposed to send Richard the Bald to the king with a letter from the legate, by means of which something might at last be devised against the election. But as was afterwards said in the words of the common proverb, they went on a wild goose chase, for the legate would not agree to this plan. So they returned home, their business unaccomplished, as is related below.

After their departure Albinus the subprior, who had accepted gifts, as was said, from the sacrist in return for hindering the election party,[3] called to brother Hugh of Thetford one day in the chapter-house, by his name alone, without any other words, thus: 'Dom Hugh.' And when Hugh answered: 'What?' he called him; and he rose and stood in the midst as he ought. Because he had said 'what' he received regular discipline[4] from the subprior. But Albinus thought that this was not enough, and sentenced him unjustly to be content that day with bread and water alone, until he should be cleansed of replying 'what'. The whole chapter judged this sentence to be imprudent and unjust, motivated more by hate than by brotherly love. Because it was so patently unfair, Hugh utterly refused to undergo it, saying: 'God does not punish anyone twice for the same offence.'[5] But the subprior, persisting in his anger, ordered discipline to be administered again the next day by two monks, giving no reason. Hugh saw clearly the cause and root of his malicious persecution and stoutly refused to submit to discipline unless manifest reason were shown him. The subprior promptly excommunicated him, although this punishment is only supposed to be administered by the abbot for very serious sins.[6] I recall that after the election this sentence was passed three times on various people, by force of will rather than the operation of reason.[7] Three days later the subprior, Jocelin the almoner, and others of

[5] A corruption of Nahum 1: 9 in the Septuagint version as given by Jerome. With *iudicat* instead of *punit* it appears in the *Decretum* (*Corpus Iuris Canonici*, i. 2, 13, 30), and in the various Lives of St. Thomas Becket (*Materials for the History of Thomas Becket, RS,* i. 28; iii. 281). The *punit* form was employed by Paris Masters in the late twelfth century, e.g. Peter the Chanter in his *Verbum Abbreviatum* (*PL,* ccv, col. 547). The words are no doubt the writer's, and may suggest his connection with the Continental schools. Powicke, *Stephen Langton,* pp. 60-1.

[6] *Reg. Ben.,* c. 24.

[7] Cf. above, p. 24 n. 3.

elemosinarius aliique de numero eorum[1] super hoc in locutorium paruum.[2] Sed non inuenientes causam qualiter in hac parte maliciam apertam exercuissent, insuper cum et ad omnia flagella eundem H(ugonem) humiliter tolleranda pronum reperissent, discordie fomitem dissimulando, de pace simulabant tractare. Tandem propter humilitatem Hugonis preostensam, ut super hoc suppriori satisfacerent, iudicauerunt laudaueruntque ut[a] in capitulo satisfaciens ueniam peteret, et perinde omnia perpetue obliuioni tradita, osculantes se[b] inuicem ex utraque parte remitterentur. Victus tandem prece magistri Nicholai eis adquieuit, factumque est hoc coram priore capitulum regente.

In die tercio sequenti redierunt sacrista et Caluus, unus socius eius a curia domini legati, deferentes secum breue eiusdem legati domino priori quod ad eorum peticionem fuerat dictatum. Sed quia prior, inspecto breue, illud pocius ad commocionem quam ad pacem uiderat operari, nemini reserans preterquam suppriori penes se inclusit. Sacrista autem hoc uidens, premissa in capitulo ex parte legati salutacione, monuit conuentum quatinus sic se haberent adinuicem, ne eorum fama in aliquo posset deperiri uel minui. Vnde per hec uerba plures colligebant quod super restrictione fouentium sacramentum electionis breue loqueretur legati. Adiunxit etiam sacrista super ⟨negotio⟩ solitarum misericordiarum dominum legatum taliter dispensasse, tanquam ad curiam, scilicet apud Cirencestre, hac specialiter de causa iter suum superius direxisset: uidelicet quod prior sollicitam curam circa ualidos haberet, ut in Dei seruicio fortiores inuenirentur, et circa debiles, ut conualescerent et uires pristinas recuperarent prout uiderit expedire. Dum ne prohibite repeterentur commessaciones, in domo infirmarii ad naturam refocillandam conuocaret quociens expediret. Hoc autem preceptum, ex quo presente legato notum a conuentu fuit in capitulo quomodo fuit obseruatum usque[c] ad primum Pascha.[d] Ab illo uero die, locum tantummodo mutantes solitum in domo infirmarii per viii. et x. et duodecim, priore duce, pristinas ita reuocabant[e] commessaciones, ut cum clerici uel laici in refectorio ad mensam aliquando ob honorem essent conuocati, in dedecus et in fame dispendium uertebatur, cum non ex una parte

---

[a] H *adds* idem H. humiliter tolleranda pronum reperissent, *canc. by scribe*
[b] H *adds* in   [c] *om.* H; *added in marg. by Hand A*   [d] *Something like* non ultra parebatur *may be missing here* H   [e] reuocabat H

their number[1] met together in the small parlour to discuss this matter.[2] But not perceiving how to exercise open wickedness in it, especially as Hugh humbly submitted to all scourges, they pretended not to be fomenting discord but to be pressing for peace. At length, because of this humility of Hugh's, and to satisfy the subprior, they decided and recommended that he should ask pardon in chapter by way of reparation. Then, consigning the whole matter to perpetual oblivion and exchanging the kiss of peace, each party would forgive the other. Eventually, persuaded by the prayer of Master Nicholas, the subprior agreed to this and it was carried out in front of the prior presiding over the chapter.

Three days later the sacrist and his single ally Bald returned from the legate's court, bringing with them a writ which he had drawn up at their request, addressed to the prior. But because the prior, after reading the writ, saw that it would lead to strife rather than peace, he kept it in his possession, showing it to no one except the subprior. But the sacrist, seeing this, delivered the legate's greetings to the chapter, and warned the convent that they ought to behave in such a way that by no means would their reputation be impaired or destroyed. From these words many inferred that the legate's writ was directed at those who continued to adhere to the election oath. The sacrist also announced the legate's reply to their query about their accustomed extra meal-allowances—as though this had been the sole object of his journey to the court at Cirencester: namely, that the prior was to exercise careful supervision of the healthy, to ensure that they remained vigorous in the service of God, and of the sick, to ensure the recovery of their former strength, just as seemed necessary. While the prohibited private meals were not to be resumed, in the infirmary he could administer as many as seemed necessary for the restoration of the inmates to health and strength. This order the legate himself had given the convent in their chapter-house, to be observed up to the following Easter . . . But from that very day, changing their customary eating-place to the infirmary one by one, led by the prior, first eight of them, then ten, then twelve, they resumed their customary private meals. So when from time to time clerks or laymen were received at the refectory table as a mark of respect, it was turned to shame and loss of reputation, for from one side of

[1] A common O.T. expression; cf. above, p. 40 n. 4.
[2] See above, p. 3 n. 7.

chori ibidem ad mensas nisi vi. monachi pre uacuacione comes-
sacionum solitarum iam tunc inceptarum essent relicti, nullo
tamen claustrali reclamante preterquam Radulfus de Londonia et
Petrus de Len, sacramentum electionis fouentes, absque breue
super hoc a domino legato specialiter de uoti huius relaxacione ad
eas commessaciones^a nolentes accedere.¹

In die uero sancti Alphegi² uenerunt littere domini legati
Francie priori et conuentui sancti Aedmundi pro electo. Erat
quidem primus dies minucionis prioris.³ In crastino autem cum
per manum Ricardi de Saxham eidem priori littere essent porecte,
destinauit eas suppriori^b in capitulo legendas. In quibus uidelicet
omnes sacramento electionis obuiantes et contra factum proprium
temere uenire presumentes,^{c 4} cum decenter corripuisset, ait
Walterus subsacrista: 'Hec auribus nostris infusa contra dominum
regem et sine assensu capituli a nobismetipsis processerunt.'
Sacrista uero, quia eius personam specialiter tangebant ait:
'Infructuoso adquieuit consilio et fatuo' (subaudis electus),
'quando, relicto magnatum^d regni et sapientum consilio, stultorum
quorundam adherendo, a terra se alienauit Anglicana.' Cui
Ricardus de Saxham, qui in responsis non tepidus sed festinus
probatur, talia festinanter reddidit responsa: 'Ex diuina constat
emanasse prouidentia, quod inter uos diutinam non fecit moram.
Si enim aliquantulum diucius esset moratus, a uobis proculdubio
foret oppressus et suffocatus.' Que cum sic in pleno capitulo |
sacriste eiusque complicibus improperasset, et a sacrista pre cordis
angustia istud probrosum uerbum esset sepius recitatum, quidam
sociorum Ricardi, precauentes ne ista processu temporis per
legatum, a quo peruersorum spes pendebat, eidem possent in
malum retorqueri, ita se dixisse supplebant, quod' si ille (subaudis
electus) diucius inter uos esset moratus, eius electio quantum ad
uos esset iam oppressa et suffocata'; licet Ricardus de suffocaci-
one corporis mencionem fecisset. I(ocelinus) elemosinarius, uir
dupplex animo⁵ et uarius, subsecutus dixit: 'Vnum est quod
omnibus affirmare cupio, quod neque pro legato neque pro archi-

f. 178ᵛ

^a commessiones H   ^b supprior H   ^c Some words may be missing
here H   ^d nunquam H

¹ The other two journeys of the precentor and sacrist (see pp. 51, 67) must
have been attempts to have the legate's ordinance mitigated. The writer attempts
to link the keeping of the election oath with obedience to the legate's reform
decrees; but the connection is hard to see when only eight monks obeyed the
legate by continuing to eat in the refectory.
² 19 April.

the choir there were only six monks who remained, owing to the prohibition of the private meals, now recommenced. Nor did any of the cloister-monks protest, except Ralph of London and Peter of Lynn, keepers of their election oath; they would not agree to private meals without a writ from the legate in answer to their entreaty, specifically pronouncing a relaxation.[1]

On St. Alphege's day[2] a letter favouring the abbot elect arrived from the French legate, addressed to the prior and convent of St. Edmunds. But it was the first day of the prior's blood-letting,[3] and the next day, when the letter was handed to him by Richard of Saxham, he ordered the subprior to read it in chapter. In it all those who opposed the election oath and heedlessly presumed to go against their own deed . . .[4] When he had quite properly reproved them Walter the subsacrist said: 'These things which have just been brought to our ears were elicited by some of our number, contrary to the king's wishes and without the permission of chapter.' The sacrist, because the letter was directed against him in particular said: 'He' (meaning the abbot elect) 'listened to unfruitful and foolish advice when, forsaking the counsel of the wise and great of the realm and adhering to that of a few ignorant fellows, he quitted the land of England.' To whom Richard of Saxham, ever unfaltering and ready in reply quickly returned answer: 'It was certainly providential that he did not stay longer among you, for if he had but stayed a little longer you would have set upon him and choked him, that's for sure.' Now when he had thus upbraided the sacrist and his accomplices in full chapter, and the sacrist in the anguish of his heart had more than once repeated his abusive words, some of Richard's friends, concerned lest the others should turn them to an evil purpose through the legate, in whom the hope of the perverse party lay, altered what he had said; namely, that 'if he (the abbot elect) had stayed any longer with you, you would by now have most certainly assailed and choked off his *election*'. But Richard had meant the choking of the body. Jocelin the almoner, a man false and unstable by nature[5] followed them, saying: 'There is one thing which I want everyone to know; that neither on the legate's account, nor on the archbishop's, nor

---

[3] i.e. the prior was too weak to attend to business. *Licencia minutionis* lasted three days, during which no work was done. *MO*, p. 455.

[4] From the technical wording of what remains, it appears that the writer had access to the text of this letter (cf. below, p. 155). [5] Iac. 1: 8.

episcopo neque pro papa eidem H(ugoni) electo absque assensu regio unquam*a* in hac domo patebit introitus.' Qui saltem dominum papam, utpote qui regibus dominatur et principibus ratione preminentis dignitatis, excepisse debuisset. Nec mirum; quia, 'sicut aquila prouocans ad uolandum pullos suos et super eos uolitans',[1] sic aquilo (id est sacrista), pullos praui nominis et peruerse ad uolitum innate malicie, ne elemosinarius et alii ab ea desisterent, prouocans, cura uigilanti super eosdem uolitabat, ut per eos que de electione secundum Deum facta fuerunt peruerteret et suppeditaret.[2]

Vnde cum magister Henricus Plumbe et W(illelmus) de Bec,[3] senescallus domini Cantuariensis, singulis litteris et nuntiis super electionis confirmacione ueritatem amicis et fidelibus electi significare*b* festinassent peruersique de numero sacriste, pre timore nouitatis audite trepidantes, contraria contrariis mendaciaque ueritati opponentes, illa per quosdam satellites et satis in malicia latentes, ficticia et in cellario monachorum fore repert dederunt intelligere, insipientes itaque et maligni, uehementi iocunditate, hec*c* ad alterutrum inter se tanquam uera conferentes, moram aduentus ipsius legati, quem sibi profuturum indubitanter asserebant, non sine cordis tedio acriter reprimendo expectabant. Prolocutum enim fuit ⟨quod⟩ apud Glastenesberi inter legatum et sacristam e⟨s⟩t prouisum ut ante Ascencionem Domini legatus ad ecclesiam beati Aedmundi accederet, nouumque substitueret prelatum et intruderet, quassata omnino prima electione, celerarium uero et camerarium, ratione familiaritatis electi deponeret. Dominum H(ugonem) electum et omnes electioni eiusdem inclinantes excommunicaret. Et subinde ad maiorem huius falsitatis constanciam, idem sacrista super aduentu legati litteras ipsi priori portauit.

In spe quidem huius exultationis cum per tres ebdomadas pars fatua*d* existeret atque sacrista utensilia ad abbatem spectantia, ut bigas et alia similia contra aduentum legati tanquam ad opus proprium preparasset, casu superuenerunt fortuito*e* duo burgenses de uilla, qui sacriste super electione a domino pape confirmata

---

a nunquam H   *b* singnificare H, *corr. by scribe*   *c* hoc H
d futua H   *e* fortuitu H

---

[1] Deut. 32: 11.
[2] An ironical imitation of the technique of glossing a scriptural text, suggesting the writer's familiarity with the discipline of biblical studies (cf. below, p. 71 n. 4).

on the pope's, will the abbot elect Hugh ever be allowed to take office here without the king's assent!' But he ought at least to have excepted the pope, since because of his pre-eminent dignity he holds dominion over kings and princes. No wonder, however; for 'as the eagle encourages her chicks to fly and flies over them herself',[1] so Robert the sacrist, that north wind, encouraged his brood, evil and perverted in name, to take off on a flight of innate malice, and sought to prevent the almoner and the others from faltering in it. He flew watchfully over them so that by their agency he might pervert and undermine those actions in the election which had been undertaken according to God's laws.[2]

So when Master Henry Plumbe and William of Bec, the archbishop of Canterbury's seneschal[3] hastened to the abbot elect's faithful friends with letters and messages stating that the election was confirmed, the perverse members of the sacrist's party, trembling with fear at this news opposed the truth by contradictions and lies. They made out (through certain low fellows, skilled in concealing their evil intentions) that they knew these tidings to be a fraud, concocted in the monks' cellar. These worthless and deceitful men, full of glee, passed this around among themselves as though it were really true and waited, severely restraining their impatience, for the legate's arrival, from which, they asserted, they would surely profit. For at Glastonbury the legate and the sacrist had openly discussed and arranged for the legate to come before Ascensiontide to the church of the blessed Edmund, where he would substitute and intrude a new prelate, annul the first election, depose the cellarer and chamberlain because of their intimacy with the abbot elect, and excommunicate Hugh and all those who supported his election. Soon after, to give greater substance to this nonsense, the sacrist handed the prior a letter about the legate's arrival.

But when for three weeks the party of the worthless had waited in hope of this triumph, and the sacrist had prepared materials belonging to the abbot, carts and the like, as if for his own work but really for the legate's arrival, two burghers of the vill turned up by chance, who told him the certain news that the pope had

---

[3] This must be William of Bec from Kent, prominent in the public records of the time (e.g. *Curia Regis Rolls*, v, 1931, pp. 173, 288; vi, 1932, p. 221; cf. K. Major in *EHR*, xlviii (1933), 540). Neither of these men appears in Major, *Acta*.

noua et certa referebant. Quod iam fama crebrescente, cum
crederet, et in eisdem rumoribus minime gauderet sacrista, pre
cordis*a* tumore ⟨haud⟩ omnino silere necdum eundem H(ugonem)
electum nominare potuisset, ait illis: 'Alterum ab eo quem uos
electum dicitis et confirmatum hucusque semper de biga ista
putabam sedare.'

In die uero sancti Iohannis ante portam Latinam[1] uenit
W(illelmus) de Bec, senescallus domini Cant(uariensis), uerba ex
parte domini sui deferens priori. Sed quando eundem minime
reperiit neque pre arduis domini sui Cant(uariensis) negociis
diucius apud sanctum Aedmundum potuit morari, fidelibus, scilicet P(etro) celerario magistroque Nicholao uices suas super significatis priori ex parte domini Cant(uariensis) fideliter commisit
exequendas. Fuit autem hic tenor mandati, licet in uanum:[2]

> Mandamus tibi, priori, quatinus monachorum tue subiectioni
> subditorum habenas, contra ecclesiasticas libertates repugnan-
> tium, compescas; ne, quod absit, si per eos aliquando inter
> regnum et sacerdocium iterato fu⟨er⟩it suborta discordia, in te
> culpa delinquencium tanquam consentientem retorqueatur.

Veniens autem P(etrus) celerarius premisit in pleno capitulo ex
parte domini Cant(uariensis) salutaciones multiplices et horta-
tiones, ut scilicet in Deum spem plenam habentes sustinerent
patienter[3] et expectarent eius*b* misericordiam,[4] qui non despicit
sperantes in se; quia ubi concordia fratrum, ibi caritas, et ubi
f. 179   caritas, ibi Deus[5] implebit | in bonis desiderium nostrum;[6]
adiungendo ut si quid alicui siue regi siue duci pro negociis domus
esset destinandum, in publica*c* causa pretenderetur primo, et sic
demum unam uiam consilio proficeretur. Hoc autem dixit propter
quod cantor iam se consilio inueterate malicie ad curiam ire
latenter parauerat, causa adquirendi litteras magnatum ad dominum regem, ne electus per confirmacionem domini pape in
baroniam suam extenderet potestatem; idem rex pro ea appellare

---

a H *adds* que, *canc. by Hand C*   *b* *Twice* H, *second canc. by Hand C*
c publico H

---

[1] 6 May.   [2] Major, *Acta*, p. 54, no. 3.
[3] A conflation of a number of common biblical phrases.
[4] Iud. 1: 21.

confirmed the election. Because these rumours were gaining substance the sacrist began to believe them, and they gave him little cause for rejoicing. His swelling heart would not permit him to remain silent, and yet he could not mention the abbot elect by name, so he said to them: 'Hitherto I had always thought fit to drive a cart such as this quite a different sort of man from him whom you say the pope has confirmed as abbot elect.'

On the feast of St. John before the Latin Gate[1] William of Bec, the archbishop of Canterbury's seneschal, arrived with a message from his lord to the prior. But the prior was not to be found, and since the seneschal was unable to stay long at St. Edmunds because of the heavy round of duties for his lord, he commissioned loyal men, Peter the cellarer and Master Nicholas as his deputies to notify the prior faithfully of the archbishop's message. This was the gist of the mandate, although it had no effect:[2]

> We order you, prior, to shorten the reins of those monks committed to your charge, who are acting contrary to the church's liberties, lest (God forbid) if at any time discord between the royal and ecclesiastical powers rise up through them, the blame attached to such delinquents should be laid on you personally, as much as if you had aided and abetted them.

Then Peter the cellarer presented many greetings and exhortations on the archbishop's behalf in full chapter, to this effect: that having full hope in God they were to hold firm with patience,[3] awaiting His mercy,[4] for He does not despise those who hope in Him. For where there is unity among brothers, there is love; and where love is, there God[5] will satisfy our mouths with good things.[6] And this in addition, that if anything concerning our house's affairs were to be directed to a king or noble, it should first be aired in public debate, so that eventually it might be put forward with unanimity. This was because the precentor, prompted by his inveterate wickedness, had secretly prepared to go to court in order to acquire letters from the magnates to the king, aimed at preventing the abbot elect from coming into his baronial power because of the papal confirmation; for the king had hastened to

[5] Cf. the refrain of the 'Hymn of Charity' sung by the Benedictines at the weekly Maundy: 'Vbi caritas est uera, Deus ibi est', composed in the time of Charlemagne (F. J. E. Raby, *A History of Christian-Latin Poetry to the close of the Middle Ages* (Oxford, 2nd edn., 1953), pp. 157–8). Cf. also 1 Ioh. 4: 8, 16.

[6] Ps. 102: 5.

festinasset. Hoc quidem consilium processit ab aquilone, a magistro mali, a ministro doli; ab inuentore huius malicie qui successorem (id est electum) more heredis timens et de infinitis malis ueniam promereri desperans, inimicicias multiplicare non distulit et augere iniquitatem.[1] Protestatus est etiam ibidem celerarius electionem a domino papa iam confirmatam, ut perinde timorem aduersariis incuteret. Ad que Philippus, hucusque electioni sedens in insidiis,[2] tanquam brucus tota die uolitans per amena ad uesperam se in fimum demergit,[3] sic ipse, ex quo malicia aduersus electionem pululauit, quodammodo uolitu palliationis uerborum se protegens, in fimum nunc plane reuelationis et concepte iniquitatis demersit.[4] Nitebatur enim palam sic contra, quod nondum eius electio fuit confirmata nec ulterius potestate alicuius confirmaretur. Sic alii aliis contradicentes, exeunte conuentu a capitulo cum 'Verba mea',[5] magister tamen Nicholaus et Philippus nondum quieuerunt quousque ante sedem prioris in claustro peruenerunt.

Euoluto tempore peruentum est ad anteuigiliam uigilie Pentecostes,[6] in qua facta est questio in pleno capitulo ⟨su⟩per I(ohannem) de Laueham et Ricardum firmarios,[8] consilio praue nacionis[7] (id est sacriste), et peruerse, eo tamen et eius complicibus ibidem presentibus, utrum summa que a dominis dictis firmariis in augmentum ad ceruisiam emendendam et murmur extinguendum de ceruisia[9] constituebatur, daretur ulterius, cum et conuentus nullus*a* se gaudebat fructus percepisse, eorumque obedientia exinde onerata*b* et inutili esset tributo subiugata;[10] adiungentes quod Ricardus de Saxham, tunc subcelerarius, illud augmentum omnino per aliam suscipere recusauit mensuram quam per regiam, cum et una sipha mensuram de Cokefeld[11] excederet regia mensura, semperque per eandem antea susciperet. Ad que sacrista opponens

---

a nullos H   *b* honorata H

[1] Gen. 17: 20, 48: 4.
[2] Ps. 10: 8; cf. above, p. 19 n. 8.
[3] This strange behaviour of the *brucus* is unmentioned in the Bestiary or its sources, but is noticed in the *Scivias* of Hildegard of Bingen (2, 6p., 5, 13c), commenting on Ioel 2: 25: '. . . ubi locusta negligentiae . . . utilitatem bonorum fructuum aufert, ibi et bruchus foeditatis in faece inmunditiae se inuoluit'. MSS. of her work were spread throughout western Europe, although Bury is not known to have had one.

appeal for the barony. This idea, of course, had come from the 'north wind', that master of malice, that servant of sin, that inventor of evil, who did not hesitate to multiply enmities and increase iniquity,[1] for he feared the successor, that is, the abbot elect, as though he were an heir, and despaired of obtaining pardon for his infinite crimes. At the same time the cellarer announced that the election had now been confirmed by the pope, so as to strike fear into the hearts of his adversaries. Now Philip had always sat in ambush for the election.[2] Just as the locust, after flying through the countryside all day plunges himself into the dung-heap in the evening,[3] so he, although bursting with evil against the election, had covered himself wherever he flew with smooth words; but now at last he plunged into the dung, fully revealing the evil which was in him.[4] For he spoke openly against the election, saying that it had not yet been confirmed, nor would it ever be confirmed by anyone's say-so. Thus, contradicting each other, the convent left the chapter-house singing the *Verba mea*,[5] but Master Nicholas and Philip had still not calmed down when they were come before the prior's seat in the cloister.

With the passing of time came the day before the vigil of Whitsun,[6] when an inquiry was made in full chapter, by the urging of that 'depraved nation',[7] namely the sacrist and as many of the perverse party as were present, about John of Lavenham and Richard, the victuallers.[8] The question was raised as to whether the amount which these two had fixed to correct the augmentation of the ale-allowance[9] and to silence murmuring ought to be dispensed any longer. None of the convent, they said, was happy with the present state of affairs because their obedience was burdened by it and useless tribute laid on them.[10] And they added that Richard of Saxham, then subcellarer, had refused to dispense the augmentation by any other measure than the king's, because one pipe by measure of Cockfield[11] exceeded the king's measure, and he had always used the latter. The sacrist opposed this, as if it were his

---

[4] Note the ironical use of the glossing method, this time not employed on a scriptural text (cf. above, p. 66 n. 2).

[5] See above, p. 15 n. 6.   [6] 16 May.   [7] Phil. 2: 15.

[8] See above, p. 8 n. 4.

[9] Ale (without hops), not beer, which was not introduced into England until the fourteenth century. L. F. Salzmann, *English Industries of the Middle Ages* (Oxford, 1923), p. 294.

[10] *Reg. Ben.*, c. 40.

[11] A manor belonging to the abbey, about 5 miles from Bury.

se, tanquam ad eum specialiter pertinuisset istam diffinire questionem, cum pocius odio quam amore caritatis, propter ipsum
Ricardum super celerarii officium loqueretur. Sed cum idem
Ricardus diucius improbitatem sacriste minime sufferret, eoque
eum magis clamosum quo celerarium et magistrum Nicholaum
absentes esse uideret, hiis uerbis allocutus est sacristam: 'Vt quid
magis super obedientiam nostram quam nos super ⟨tuam⟩ loqueris?'
Ob quam causam prior clamauit Ricardum et sine more*a* dispendio
ab officio subcelerarii absoluit, precipiens in ui obedientie ut
redderet claues. Ac ille uero cum omni celeritate,*b* sine uerborum
repugnantia aut more*c* dispendio in manus prioris claues tradere
festinabat. Celerarius uero domum rediens illo die, finito capitulo, pocius in facto gaudere uidebatur quam dolere. Cui tamen
camerarius et Rogerus refectorarius et tercius prior et H(ugo) de
Theford accedentes, rogauerunt ut eum ad pristinam reformaret
societatem, quem pro defensione ipsius obedientie nouerant iam
depositum. Quibus responsa, licet tepida, super propositis reddens,
respondit se tandem cum priore locuturum, facturumque quicquid
cum consilio suo sibi intelligeret cedere ad honorem. Sed cum nec
illo die per celerarium neque in crastino Pentecostes[1] per camerarium et tercium priorem, comitante sibi celerario, Ricardus gratiam
prioris inueniret, obiurgantes*d* priorem eo quod iram indiscrete et
sine aliqua ratione aduersus eum conceptam non mitigasset,
turbati*e* sunt ualde.[2] Quibus prior subnixo sacramento respondit,
quod nulla ratione nullaue condicione neque modo neque in
futuro adquiesceret ut idem Ricardus ad aliquam promoueretur
obedientiam, quousque in electum oculorum defixisset*f* intuitus.

   In die quidem Pentecostes[3] uenit Stephanus de Walsingham a
f. 179ᵛ curia Romana, | deferens secum litteras commissorias ex parte
domini pape H(enrico) scilicet abbati de Wardone et R(icardo)
priori de Dunestaple et R(icardo) decano de Salesberi[4] in hec
uerba:[5]

---

a moris H   *b* sceleritate H   *c* moris H   *d* obiurgentes H
e turbatique H   *f* deffigasset H

---

[1] 19 May.   [2] Ps. 6: 3.   [3] 18 May.
[4] Henry was abbot *c.* 1212–15 of Wardon or St. Mary de Sartis, a Cistercian
house in Beds. Richard de Morins (or Mores) was prior of the Benedictine
abbey at Dunstable 1202–42. He was often cited by Innocent as a judge
delegate (Cheney, *Letters*, nos. 751, 788, 808, 901, 999, and Sayers, *Judges
Delegate*, pp. 296–301). Before his priorate he was a well-known canon and civil

special prerogative to decide the issue and, more from hate than love of charity, he made remarks about the office of the cellary, really aimed at Richard himself. But when Richard could no longer bear the sacrist's allegations, whose clamouring was all the louder as he saw that the cellarer and Master Nicholas were absent, he said to him: 'Why do you prate to us so much more about our duties than we do about yours?' For this the prior summoned Richard and deposed him without delay from the office of sub-cellarer, ordering him by his obedience to return his keys. And truly, with all speed and without opposition of word or deed, he hastened to deliver the keys into the prior's hands. The cellarer, returning home that day after chapter had ended, seemed to rejoice rather than sorrow at the news. Nevertheless, he was approached by the chamberlain, Roger the refectorer, the third prior, and Hugh of Thetford, who asked for Richard to be re-instated to his former association with him, for they knew that he had only been deposed for the defence of his obedience. In reply to their request, although not enthusiastic, he said that he would speak with the prior and do whatever seemed honourable, with his advice. But neither that day when approached by the cellarer, nor on the day after Whitsun[1] when besought by the chamberlain, third prior, and cellarer, would the prior restore Richard to his favour, and rebuking him for continuing in his indiscreet and unreasonable anger, they were very grieved.[2] For the prior said to them, with an oath, that not for any reason, or on any condition, either then or in the future, would he agree to promote Richard to any obedientiary office, until he had fixed his eyes upon the abbot elect.

On Whitsunday[3] Stephen of Walsingham returned from the Roman curia with letters of commission from the pope to Henry abbot of Wardon, Richard prior of Dunstable, and Richard dean of Salisbury[4] in these words:[5]

lawyer, having been to Bologna and lectured at Oxford. A number of his writings are extant. S. Kuttner and E. Rathbone, 'Anglo-Norman canonists of the twelfth century', *Traditio*, vii (1951), 279–358, espec. 329–38. Richard Poore, afterwards bishop of Salisbury (1217–28), was known as an able, pious, and learned man. He had suffered already at the hands of John, having been disappointed of the bishopric of Winchester. He had attended Langton's lectures in Paris (Gibbs, *Bishops*, pp. 25–7).

[5] Cheney, *Letters*, no. 970. For elucidation of the legal proceedings which occupy so much of the writer's attention from this point on, see Sayers, *Judges Delegate*, pp. 65–99.

Innocentius etc.

Ex parte celerarii et prouisorum monasterii sancti Aedmundi fuit propositum coram nobis quod, bone memorie eorum abbate uiam uniuerse carnis ingresso, prior et conuentus eiusdem monasterii potestatem eligendi abbatem in septem monachos contulerunt, promittentes sub uinculo iuramenti quod personam que ab illis septem denominaretur eisdem reciperent in pastorem. Electores autem, Spiritus Sancti gratia inuocata, fratrem Hugonem de Norewolde eiusdem monasterii monachum ⟨et⟩, ut asserunt, uirum prouidum et honestum, in abbatem regulariter elegerunt, uoce appellationis ad nos emissa, ut nullus in contrarium aliquid attentaret. Cuius electioni ab uniuerso conuentu recepte^a karissimus in Christo filius noster I(ohannes) illustris rex Anglie differt plus debito, sicut accepimus, regalis assensus fauorem, machinantibus quibusdam hoc monachis, sicut dicitur, qui prius uerbo et facto consenserant in eandem.

Nolentes igitur eidem monasterio, quod ad sedem apostolicam immediate dinoscitur pertinere,[1] deesse diucius sollicitudine^b pastorali, discretioni uestre per apostolica scripta mandamus, quatinus uocatis qui fuerunt euocandi et auditis hinc inde propositis, electionem ipsam, si eam inueneritis de persona idonea canonice celebratam, auctoritate apostolica confirmetis, contradictores, si qui fuerint, per censuram apostolicam sublato appellationis obstaculo compescendo. Regem autem prefatum diligenter et efficaciter moneatis, ut ipsi electioni sine difficultatis dispendio suum impartiatur assensum. Ceterum si quid post appellacionem ad nos legitime interpositam inueneritis perperam^c attemptatum, in statum debitum appellatione remota reuocetis.

Nullis litteris etc. Quod si non omnes etc. Datumque etc.[2]

Igitur predictus Stephanus in eadem ebdomada cum litteris istis uersus iudices profectus est, comitante secum magistro Nicholao. Inter hec uenit dominus H(ugo) electus in Angliam cum ii. sociis suis, Ricardo scilicet de Heingham et Symone monachis, moram faciens apud Bellum et Westmonasterium, donec delegatis tradita esset commissio. Peracto itinere commissionis a supradictis, uenit dominus H(ugo) electus domum Sabbato octauarum sancte Trinitatis,[3] deferens secum litteras ex parte delegatorum priori et

---

^{a} recepto H ^{b} sollicitudinis H ^{c} properam H

[1] The traditional formula for describing an exempt and papally privileged house such as Bury was. *PUE*, iii. nos. 187, 217, 232, 403, etc.

[2] Customary formulae, of which the first two when expanded would read

Innocent etc.

It was declared in our presence on behalf of the cellarer and prudent men of the monastery of St. Edmunds that, their abbot of blessed memory having gone the way of all flesh, the prior and convent of that monastery transferred the power of electing an abbot to seven men, binding themselves with an oath that they would receive as pastor the person named by those seven. The electors, then, having invoked the grace of the Holy Spirit, chose brother Hugh of Northwold, according to the *Rule*, a monk of that monastery and, as they assert, a man upright and prudent, appealing to us that no one attempt anything against him. To his election, accepted by the whole convent, our most dear son in Christ John, illustrious king of England, delays the favour of royal assent, so we hear, more than he ought, certain monks conniving at this, it is said, although they had earlier agreed with the election in word and deed.

Not wishing, therefore, that that monastery, which is deemed worthy to pertain directly to the apostolic see,[1] should be any longer without pastoral guidance, we order you by papal letter to summon in your wisdom as many as you find necessary and hear the statements of both sides; and if you find the election to have been celebrated canonically in a fit person, you are to confirm it by the papal authority. If any oppose your decision, you are to subdue them with apostolic censure, appeal disallowed. Moreover, warn the king diligently and efficaciously that he ought to give his assent to the election without hesitation. And if after you have legitimately sought our aid by appeal you find wrong still committed, you are to recall them to a state of obedience, appeal disallowed.

No letters etc. And if not all etc. And given etc.[2]

Stephen took the letters to the judges that week, accompanied by Master Nicholas. Meanwhile the abbot elect Hugh returned to England with his two companions, the monks Richard of Hingham and Simon, staying at Battle and Westminster until the commission had been delivered to the delegates. When this had been done the abbot elect came to the house on the Saturday after Trinity,[3] with

more or less as follows: 'Nullis litteris ueritati et iustitiae preiudicantibus a sede apostolica impetratis; quod si non omnes hiis exequendis potueritis interesse, duo uestrum ea nihilominus exequentur.'

[3] 31 May.

conuentui commonitorias, quatinus idem sic se ad alterutrum haberent,*a* ut cum ad locum execucionis causa de mandato domini pape accessissent, de eorum caritate mutua et dileccionis integritate Deum et patronum suum sanctum Aedmundum laudare famamque debitam possent commendare.[1] Ne uero pretermittatur quod cum idem H(ugo) electus x. fere miliariis a uilla esset remotus, clerici de uilla pariterque burgenses eidem festinabant occurrere, nullo tamen monacho preterquam solo camerario, licet omnibus magnatibus, ut sacrista, Adam infirmario, Waltero subsacrista, Ricardo precentore, Willelmo pitantiario, Iocelino elemosinario, domi existentibus, uolente occurrere. Et ut eorum diutina malicia clarius innotesceret*b* 'lippis et tonsoribus',[2] dominus H(ugo) electus eosdem ut illo die secum communicarent inuitabat, qui sine omni excepcione aut ratione preostensa, tanquam uniformiter in eadem malicia instructi, secum commedere uel communicare refutauerunt. Acceptoque priore mandato trium executorum absentauit se in crastino a capitulo, transmisitque suppriori litteras illas ut presente capitulo perlegeret. Quibus perlectis, erigens se magister Nicholaus, pretendit*c* eidem suppriori ex parte delegatorum transcriptum tenoris mandati domini pape, in quo*d* etiam diem eorum aduentus conuentui prefixerunt. Factumque est hoc die ⟨Dominica⟩ octauarum sancte Trinitatis.[3]

Die quidem Mercurii proxima subsequenti,[4] accedentes ad capitulum sancti Aedmundi H(enricus) abbas de Wardone et R(icardus) prior de Dunestaple et R(icardus) decanus Salesberi causa execucionis, ad instantiam tocius capituli in primis dederunt sententiam excommunicacionis, accensis candelis, cum monachis f. 180 eiusdem | capituli, in omnes illos qui ab illo die in antea pacem Dei et ecclesie istius maliciose perturbarent uel impedirent, precipue quantum ad electionem H(ugonis) confirmandam uel infirmandam, uel qui contra conscientiam suam scripto uel dicto falso*e* allegando, uel falsam narracionem facti proponendo, uel uerum celando cum super hoc essent interrogati, uel quodcumque impedimentum impetrando, quo minus uel tardius mandatum domini pape eisdem tribus commissum execucioni mandetur, quicquam maliciose fuerint machinati.[5]

Post hoc autem preceperunt omnes, tam clericos quam laicos et uiros religiosos qui de gremio ipsius capituli non essent, ammoueri.

---

a habentes H   *b* innotessceret H, *corr.*   *c* pretenditque H
d quoibus H, *corr. by scribe*   *e* falsa H

---

[1] No doubt a paraphrase of the actual text.

letters from the delegates to the prior and convent, admonishing them to behave towards one another in such a fashion that when they arrived there to carry out the papal mandate, they would be able to praise God and their patron St. Edmund for their mutual love and pure devotion, and to commend their reputation as well deserved.[1] Now I must tell you that when the abbot elect was about ten miles distant from the vill, the clerks and burghers hastened to meet him, but no monks cared to come except the chamberlain alone, although all the officials, such as the sacrist, Adam the infirmarer, Walter the subsacrist, Richard the precentor, William the pittancer, and Jocelin the almoner were at the house. And that their habitual evil might be clearly visible even to 'blear-eyed men and barbers',[2] when Hugh invited them to talk with him that day, they refused to eat or talk with him, without exception or reason given, as if uniformly instructed in the same wickedness. The prior, after receiving the mandate of the three executors, absented himself from chapter the next day, and gave the subprior the letter to be read out. When it had been read Master Nicholas, rising to his feet, presented the subprior, on the delegates' behalf, with a copy of the papal mandate to which the day of their arrival at the convent was appended. This was done on the Sunday after Trinity.[3]

On the following Wednesday[4] Henry abbot of Wardon, Richard prior of Dunstable, and Richard dean of Salisbury entered the chapter-house of St. Edmunds to carry out the mandate. At the request of the whole chapter, they first pronounced sentence of excommunication, assisted by the monks of that body carrying lighted candles, against all who, from that day on, wickedly impeded or disturbed the peace of God and of that church, especially regarding Hugh's election, whether it was to be confirmed or invalidated; or who made any statement in speech or writing contrary to what he knew to be the truth; or who told a false and concocted story; or who concealed the truth when asked for it; or who set up any impediment or attempted any wicked connivings which delayed or made less effective the execution of the papal mandate committed to those three men.[5]

After this they ordered all clerks, laymen, and religious not of that house to withdraw. When this had been done they began by

---

[2] Hor., *Sat*. i. 7, 3; Walther, no. 13866a.   [3] 1 June.
[4] 4 June.   [5] Evidently closely following a text.

Quibus ammotis, ceperunt inquirere de sacrista, utrum carta conuentus de rato, quam dictus H(ugo) electus habuit, de consensu totius capituli eidem esset tradita uel non. Quibus interrogatis, cum subticuisset sacrista dare responsa uerumque confiteri cum super hoc esset interrogatus, ait decanus Salesberi: 'Frater, qui eroneam habet conscientiam in sententiam iam incidit latam, sicut qui falsa pro ueris proponit'; non enim aliter eum denunciauit in*a* excommunicationem incidisse. Itaque illo die in causa nichil amplius profecti sunt.

In crastino quidem pretendit magister Nicholaus alias litteras eisdem iudicibus ex parte domini pape super correctione prauarum consuetudinum domus, sub hoc tenore:[1]

Innocentius episcopus etc., dilectis filiis etc.

Ex parte celerarii et prouisorum monasterii sancti Aedmundi fuit propositum coram nobis quod in eodem monasterio quedam praue consuetudines, immo pocius corruptele, contra monastice religionis obseruantiam obrepserunt,*b* que nisi cicius euelantur, tanquam robur auctoritatis et quasi priuilegium delinquendi a transgressoribus assumentur. Quia*c* uero melius est ante tempus uel in tempore saltem occurrere huius⟨modi⟩ corruptelis quam remedium querere postquam more dispendio inuilescant, discretioni uestre per apostolica scripta mandamus,*d* quatinus ad locum personaliter accedentes, inquisita*e* super hoc ueritate,*f* sollicite quod regulare fuerit appellatione postposita statuatis.

Facientes etc. Nullis litteris etc. Quod si non omnes etc. Tu denique, fili abbas etc.[2]

Datum Rome apud sanctum Petrum ix. kal. Aprilis pontificatus nostri anno xvii.[3]

His itaque perlectis, preceperunt iudices ut conuentus a capitulo egrederetur, et ⟨ut⟩ unusquisque post alium in suo ordine rediret, super interrogatis eisdem responsurus. Facta est*g* illo die ista examinacio a singulis singillatim, prestito tamen sacramento quod nullus odio uel amore falsa diceret uel uera celaret, cum ab eisdem super ueritate esset requisitus. Sic super hoc continuatis duabus diebus peruentum est ad diem tercium. In quo cum nichil nouum

---

a *Added in marg. by scribe*   *b* obreperunt H   *c* Qua H   *d* madamus H   *e* quisita H; in- *added over erasure by Hand C*   *f* H *adds* hoc   *g* H *adds* que, *canc. by Hand C*

---

[1] Not in Cheney, *Letters*.
[2] Customary formulae: 'Facientes quod statueritis per censuram ecclesiasticam firmiter obseruari; tu denique fili abbas super te ipso et credito tibi grege taliter uigilari procures, extirpando uitia et plantando uirtutes, ut in nouissimo

inquiring of the sacrist whether the convent's charter of ratification, held by Hugh, had been handed to him by consent of the whole chapter or no. And when the sacrist hesitated to reply and confess the truth of this, the dean of Salisbury said: 'Brother, whoever knowingly withholds information has already incurred the full sentence just as much as he who states a falsehood instead of truth', thus denouncing him as excommunicate. Nothing further was done in the inquiry that day.

The next day Master Nicholas presented another letter from the pope to the judges, concerning the correction of bad customs in the house, in these words:[1]

Innocent bishop etc., to his dear sons etc.

We have been notified on behalf of the cellarer and prudent men of the monastery of St. Edmunds that certain evil customs, or rather corruptions, have crept into their house, contrary to the observance of monastic religion. And unless they are eradicated with all speed, the strength of authority, as it were, and the privilege to disobey will be assumed by the transgressors. For truly it is better to obviate this kind of corruption before or in time, than to seek a remedy after it has grown worse through time wasted in delays. Therefore we order you in your wisdom by papal letter, to go to the place in person and seek the truth, causing to be observed only that which is regular, appeal disallowed.

Causing etc. No letters etc. And if not all etc. You lastly, son abbot etc.[2]

Given at Rome at St. Peter's, 24 March, in the 17th year of our pontificate.[3]

When this had been read out the judges ordered the convent to leave the chapter-house and return one at a time to reply to questions put to them. That very day this examination of each individual one by one was carried out, after an oath was taken that neither for love nor hate would they tell lies or conceal the truth when correct information was sought from them. This continued for two days and was concluded on the third, when, not wanting

districti examinis die coram tremendo Iudice qui reddet unicuique secundum opera sua, dignam possis reddere rationem', and see above, p. 74 n. 2.
[3] 24 March 1214.

super obiectis et responsis sine omni deliberacione uellent constitu-
ere, renouauerunt sententiam prescriptam, adiungentes ut si quid
aliquis infra diem adquireret uel adquisitis uteretur, quo minus uel
tardius etc., ut supra.[1] Post hoc admonuerunt uniuersos ad pacis
composicionem, in qua cum tunc proficere non possent, dederunt
diem partibus, scilicet diem Veneris proximam post festum sancti
Barnabe apostoli[2] ad tractandum iterum de pace. Coram quibus
sacrista ita respondit quod salua conscientia et saluo canone[a] in
quantum posset ad pacem niteretur, licet eam semper magis
studeret perturbare quam ad mentis tranquillitatem reformare.
Cumque prior de Dunestaple omnes sibi circumsedentes uideret
pre falso Latino in publico prolato sacristam deridere, ita suppleuit
pro sacrista: 'Salua conscientia et saluo iure.'[3] Datus est itaque dies
ille ad pacis reformacionem, in qua si non possent proficere de
consensu partium, statuerunt eisdem diem peremptorium, scilicet
uigiliam[b] apostolorum Petri et Pauli apud Liutone,[4] H(ugoni)
scilicet electo et sex electoribus eius, et omnibus illis qui se duxerint
opponendos electioni prefati H(ugonis), ut comparerent coram
eisdem die et loco, per se uel sufficientes responsales monachos,
mandatum domini pape alias eis editum audituri, et iuri parituri. |

f. 180ᵛ   Statuerunt etiam illo die ut de communi ⟨consensu⟩ partium[c]
⟨electus⟩ prouideretur in sumptibus sufficientibus ad totam causam
illam, et si qua dilatoria excepcio[5] deberet opponi, omnes illo die
proponerentur.

    In crastino quidem, antequam a loco recederent iudices, uenit
Iohannes de Pakeham nuntius sacriste[6] a domino legato Anglie,
deferens secum litteras domini Wyntoniensis iusticiarii domini
regis, Phillipo de Brunham[7] et Iohanni de Cornherde[8] custodibus
abbacie in hec[d] uerba:

    Mandamus uobis quatinus sine dilatione capiatis in manum
    domini regis abbaciam de sancto Aedmundo cum baronia ad

---

    canones H   ᵇ uigilia H   ᶜ partibus H   ᵈ hoc H

[1] See above, p. 77 n. 5.
[2] 13 June.
[3] *Canon* in the singular refers to one particular statute, thus making nonsense
of the sacrist's statement, whereas *ius* may stand for a body of law, or for rights
in general.
[4] 28 June. Luton is in Beds., about 50 miles south-west of Bury.
[5] A 'dilatory exception' was a formal protest made by the defendant against
the conduct of the action. Sayers, *Judges Delegate*, pp. 80–3; *Corpus Iuris
Canonici*, ii. 2, 25.

to proceed further on the basis of the charges and replies without much deliberation, they renewed the earlier sentence, adding that if anyone from that day on procured or caused anything to be done which made slower or of less effect etc., as above.[1] After this they admonished everyone to keep the peace, and as they were unable to continue the proceedings at that time, they appointed a day for the parties, namely the Friday after the feast of St. Barnabas the apostle,[2] to try again to reach a peaceful settlement. The sacrist replied to them that, without violating his conscience and the canon, he would strive to keep the peace as far as possible— although all the time he was trying to stir up trouble, rather than bring the community back to a tranquil state of mind. When the prior of Dunstable saw all those sitting around deriding the sacrist for speaking such bad Latin in public, he corrected him thus: 'Without violating your conscience and the law.'[3] So that day was appointed on which to work for a peaceful settlement. But in case they were unable to bring the parties to an agreement on that day they appointed another, the vigil of the feast of the apostles Peter and Paul at Luton,[4] on which the abbot elect Hugh, his six electors and all the leaders of the opposition to his election were to come to them in person, or send competent representative monks to hear the papal mandate put into effect and to submit to the law. They also determined then and there, with the common consent of the parties, that the abbot elect should be provided with sufficient money to cover his expenses for the whole suit, and that if a dilatory exception[5] were to be submitted, they would make it known on that day.

The next day, before the judges had left, John of Pakenham,[6] the sacrist's messenger, arrived from the English legate, with a letter from the bishop of Winchester, the king's justiciar, to Philip de Burnham[7] and John de Cornard,[8] the guardians of the abbey, in these words:

> We order you to take the abbey of St. Edmunds with the barony pertaining to it into the king's hand without delay,

[6] 8 June. He appears as a witness in charters of Abbot Samson, 1196–c. 1206 (*Kalendar*, nos. 58, 60, 119).

[7] De Burnham seems to have been replaced by the following year, since *Pipe Roll 16 John* (*PRS*, new ser. xxxv, 1959, p. 177) records a return of £105. 10s. made by John de Cornard and Thomas of Barrow from the abbey lands (cf. below, p. 169 n. 5).

[8] Sheriff of Norfolk and Suffolk since 1204.

eam pertinente, et omnibus rebus et tenementis ad monacos eiusdem loci pertinentibus, et eam*a* ad opus domini regis*b* custodiatis donec inde mandatum aliud habueritis, saluo ratio-nabili monachorum predictorum estouerio; quoniam abbaciam illam cum pertinenciis suis uobis et Iohanni de Cornherde ex parte domini regis commisimus custodiendam.*c* In agendis domini regis ad predicte abbatie custodiam pertinentibus, consilio prioris et sacriste eiusdem domus precipue adquiescatis. Peruenisset. Supersedit eam.[1]

Vnde postea manifestum fuit eorum questu hec fore perquisita,*d* licet contra sententiam a iudicibus in pleno capitulo paulo ante prolatam. Quod cum iudicibus esset declaratum, admiratione pocius quam stupore nimirum repleti,[2] dicebant adinuicem: 'Quisnam, putas, est hic filius perdicionis,[3] ire et superbie, qui suppeditata*e* sententia et postposita talia procurare presumpsit? Non enim manus Domini est cum eo!'[4] Ingemiscentes itaque non minus super infortunio mandati quam si eisdem personaliter accidisset, precauentes tamen ne aliquod periculum per diem partibus constitutum apud Luitone posset imminere, in instanti locum premutantes, diem reuocauerunt in capitulum sancti Aedmundi. Hiis itaque a iudicibus prosecutis, reuersi sunt ad propria.

Die igitur predicto, uigilia scilicet apostolorum, constitutis*f* in presentia eorum apud capitulum sancti Aedmundi H(ugone), scilicet eiusdem loci electo et sex electoribus eius et aliis qui se duxerunt opponendos eidem, domini regis iusticiarii, scilicet episcopus Wyntoniensis et W(illelmus) Marescallus comes de Pembroc et R(ogerus) Bigot et ⟨Saherus⟩*g* comes Wyntonie et R(obertus) filius Walteri et I(ohannes) de Basseingburc[5] cum aliis multis et magnis constanter proposuerunt coram iudicibus quod dicta controuersia dominum regem tangebat; et hac ratione precipue, quod post mortem S(amsonis) abbatis nihil fuerat regi de electione abbatis facienda intimatum, secundum quod moderno iure summi pontificis declaratum est debere fieri.[6] Et quia sic spreto rege processum erat, dixerunt irritum esse fundamentum

a ea H   *b* H *adds* saluo   *c* custodiam H; -end- *suppl. in marg. by*
Hand C   *d* perquisita H; *corr. to* perquisitanda *by Hand C*   *e* sub-
pedita H   *f* constitutus H   *g* .R. H

together with all the goods and holdings belonging to the monks of that place, and to maintain it for the king's work, until you receive a further mandate, saving, however, the monks' reasonable maintenance. For we have committed that abbey with its appurtenances to you and John de Cornard to guard on the king's behalf. In the king's business concerning the custody of the abbey, listen chiefly to the advice of the prior and sacrist of that house. *Peruenisset. Supersedit eam.*[1]

This, as the mandate made clear, had been brought about at the request of the prior and sacrist, contrary though this was to the sentence pronounced by the judges in the chapter-house just a moment before. When it had been told the judges they, greatly astonished but not put to confusion,[2] said: 'Who on earth, do you think, is the son of perdition,[3] wrath, and pride, who has presumed to bring this to pass, disregarding and trampling on our judgement? Truly the hand of the Lord is not with him!'[4] And so, complaining of the unhappy mandate as much as if it had been directed at them personally, and anxious in case danger should threaten the parties on the day appointed at Luton, they changed the place immediately to the chapter-house of St. Edmunds. After this the judges returned each to his own place.

On the vigil of the apostles the abbot elect Hugh, his six electors and the leaders of his opponents appeared before them in the chapter-house of St. Edmunds, together with the king's justices, namely the bishop of Winchester, Robert FitzWalter and John de Bassingbourne[5] with many other great men who firmly maintained before the judges that the controversy directly involved the king. The most important reason was this, that after the death of Abbot Samson nothing had been told the king about the election of an abbot, although according to a recent law of the pope[6] this ought to have been done. And because it had proceeded

---

[1] Formal clauses, whose complete form cannot be determined. In *Rot. Litt. Pat.*, p. 135, is an order, dated 4 May, for the knights of St. Edmunds to go to the vill to hear John de Cornard's orders respecting the care of the abbey lands. The mandate given in the text doubtless bore the same date.

[2] For this proverb, see above, p. 19 n. 6.

[3] 2 Thess. 2: 3.   [4] Act. 11: 21.

[5] Of these men now supporting the king, Bassingbourne, William Marshal and Peter des Roches were on his side in the civil war. Bigod, FitzWalter and de Quency were three of the twenty-five barons of the Charter.

[6] Referring to *Cum non possit* (see above, p. 30 n. 2).

electionis, et regem esse uocandum ad causam. Quibus a regalibus sic coram iudicibus in capitulo prosecutis ex parte domini regis, dixerunt iudicibus et omnibus aliis qui de gremio capituli speci-aliter non erant, ut inde ammouerentur, dicendo: 'Habemus quedam secreta domino H(ugoni) electo et conuentui ex parte domini regis detegenda, nullo alio immediate existente.' Quibus egressis, W(illelmus) Marescallus comes de Pembroc taliter allocutus est conuentum: 'Nostis, domini, quot et qualia beneficia dominus rex et predecessores sui domui huic contulerint; unde uestrum est eius priuilegia et libertates illesas et illibatas conseruare, ne gratiarum ingrati uel beneficiorum immemores, penam repor-tetis ingratitudinis. Vt igitur manifestari possit qui libertatem regis fouere uelint et qui ei aduersari, auctoritate regia precipimus ut separentur ab inuicem fauttores regis et non fauentes eidem, scilicet qui sunt electioni facte consentientes.' Hiis dictis Albinus supprior, Henricus Ruffus, Iohannes de Dice, Aedmundus, Walterus, Iocelinus elemosinarius, Herbertus subrefectorarius, W. de Bosco, Ricardus Taillehaste, Rogerus Ruffus, Ada⟨m⟩ nutritus Hugonis, Ricardus precentor, Petrus de Wridewelle, Willelmus subcamerarius, W. laicus, Adam infirmarius, Thomas Capra, Salomon, Ricardus subsacrista, H(enricus) de Len, Alan Walensis, Petrus de Thifteshale, Gregorius subcentor, | Willelmus Mothes, Galfridus, R(icardus) de Stortesforde, Rogerus de Stanham, W. sacerdos de hospitali,[1] Phillipus et Osbertus, qui ante diuisionem et post semper se habuerunt[a] ex parte aduersa, licet in diuisione de capitulo extitissent[b] statim, sinistram partem eli-gentes. Subito et clammosa uoce, coram dictis baronibus et aliis laicis quampluribus ibidem existentibus, Iocelinum de Altari et Iohannem de Laueham ad se attraxerunt inuitos. Sicque facta per eos diuisione in domo Domini,[c] quod prius latuit manifestatum est scisma, et partium ad edictum nobilium facta ⟨est⟩ descriptio, singulis singillatim in scriptum redactis, procurante hoc Ricardo precentore, sub Pontio Pilato, id est subsacrista, ut maior eiulatus et confusio fieret[2] in domo Domini. Facta itaque separacione, ut dictum est, edictum regalium, surrexerunt Iocelinus de Altari et Iohannes de Laueham in medio coram eisdem et dixerunt quod

f. 181

---

[a] habuit H   [b] exisset H   [c] domino H

---

[1] The hospital of St. Saviour at Babwell, outside Bury; a dependency of the abbey, founded by Abbot Samson (*JB*, p. 45).

thus in contempt of the king, they said that the election was invalid from the start, and that the king had to be summoned to the case. After the royal officials had declared this on the king's behalf to the judges in the chapter-house, they asked them and all others not members of the chapter to retire, saying: 'We have something private from the king to reveal to the abbot elect Hugh and to the convent, no others being present.' When they had gone out, William Marshal earl of Pembroke addressed the convent thus: 'You know, lords, how many and what sort of benefits have been conferred on this house by the king and his predecessors; for this reason it behoves you to preserve his privileges and liberties unhurt and unimpaired; otherwise, being ungrateful for his favour and unmindful of his benefits, you may suffer the penalty for your ingratitude. So that we can see who wish to support the king's liberties, therefore, and who oppose them, by the royal authority we order the king's followers to separate from those who do not favour him—that is, from those who consent to the election as carried out.' At this Subprior Albinus, Henry Rufus, John of Diss, Edmund, Walter, Jocelin the almoner, Herbert the subrefectorer, W. du Bois, Richard Taillehaste, Roger Rufus, Adam foster-son of Hugh, Richard the precentor, Peter of Wordwell, William the subchamberlain, W. the lay-brother, Adam the infirmarer, Thomas the Goat, Solomon, Richard the subsacrist, Henry of Lynn, Alan of Wales, Peter of Tivetshall, Gregory the succentor, William Mothes, Geoffrey, Richard of Stortford, Roger of Stanham, W. priest of the hospital,[1] Philip and Osbert, who before and after the division always held to the adverse party, now made their stand publicly, choosing the left side of the chapter-house. And suddenly, with much shouting, in front of the barons and many other laymen there present, they pulled across to their side the unwilling Jocelin of the Altar and John of Lavenham. And thus, by the division made by them in the house of the Lord the schism, earlier concealed, was made evident. A record of the parties was made by the command of the nobles, each name being taken down in writing. Richard the precentor undertook this task at the command of that Pontius Pilate the subsacrist, that there might be greater confusion and lamentation[2] in the house of the Lord. After the separation had been made at the courtiers' command, Jocelin of the Altar and John of Lavenham rose in their midst and said that they had

[2] Cf. Abbo (*Mem.* i. 10): '. . . ut maior esset eiulatus'.

cum domino rege et eius libertatibus semper steterunt et starent; sed si de ueritate electionis canonice facta est inquisitio, proculdubio scirent ueritatem non posse aliquo metu interposito nec uelle celare.

Isti sunt ex parte dextera capituli collocati, qui a sacramento electionis prece uel pretio[1] nunquam potuerunt auelli, sed firmiter cum eo se habentes in hoc perseuerauerunt: Petrus celerarius, Ricardus de Heingham, Rogerus filius Drogonis, Robertus camerarius, magister Henricus de Hehy, Hugo de Theford, Hugo de Hastinge, Ricardus de Flameuille, Robertus de sancto Butulfo, Symon, Radulfus de Londonia, Ricardus de Saxham, Ioseph, R. de Oxonia, magister Nicholaus, Petrus de Len iuuenis, Willelmus de Thomeston, magister Thomas de Walsingham, magister Thomas tercius prior, Nicholaus Romanus, Karolus, Ranulfus, Rogerus de Norwolde, Iohannes de sancto Aedmundo, Radulfus, magister Alanus, Nigellus, Iacobus, Alanus de Broc, Wydo, Willelmus iuuenis de Stanhonne, Mauricius iuuenis.[2]

Post hec sacrista et sui (utinam boni) emulatores,[3] in dictos electi fauttores uerba contumeliosa et probrosa coram dictis regalibus et aliis laicis quampluribus ibidem existentibus intulerunt, dicentes: '⟨O⟩ Proditores, O ueritatis inimici, O seductores, amici nequicie, uiri dolosi, qui circumuenistis nos et inique egistis nobiscum,[4] de cetero nichil proderit uobis malicia uestra!' Sed quid? Licet multa talia opprobria ab eisdem sepius perpessi essent, non est mutatus uultus eorum,[5] quia pro ueritate et iusticia que eosdem liberauit[a6] firmiter steterunt. Post hoc quidem ut dictus comes de Pembroc maiorem adhuc parti ueritatis timorem incuteret dixit: 'Quoniam dominus papa testificatur litteras istas per quosdam prouisores fore perquisitas, uolumus ut illi nobis manifestentur.' Cui uero pars aduersa mox in uocem erupit clamosam,[b] dicens: 'Ne dominum regem et uos eiusdem fideles lateat, istius maliciosi questus contra eundem proditores fuisse et auctores; diucius celerarium huius rei specialiter extitisse auctorem.' Cumque celerarius in medio uocatus plenus fide[7] stetisset et imperterritus, taliter allocutus est eum Comes Bigot: 'Frater karissime, cum ad nos omnes libertates beati martiris spectet

---

[a] liberabit H   [b] clamosa H

[1] A play on words as old as Cicero, but by this date become a common proverb (cf. *JB*, pp. 13, 15, 105). It seems to have passed into the text of ecclesiastical oaths (see above, p. 8 n. 1), and this could be the source of the author's acquaintance with it.
[2] The writer evidently had access to the original record of the division.
[3] 1 Pet. 3: 13.

always stood and always would stand by the king and his liberties, but if they wanted to know whether the election had been truly canonical, then let them be assured that they neither wished nor were able by any intimidation to conceal the fact.

Gathered on the right side of the chapter-house were those who had never been able to tear themselves from the election oath for gift or entreaty,[1] but who firmly persevered in holding by it: Peter the cellarer, Richard of Hingham, Roger FitzDrew, Robert the chamberlain, Master Henry of Ely, Hugh of Thetford, Hugh of Hastings, Richard de Flamvill, Robert of St. Botolph, Simon, Ralph of London, Richard of Saxham, Joseph, R. of Oxford, Master Nicholas, young Peter of Lynn, William of Thompson, Master Thomas of Walsingham, Master Thomas the third prior, Nicholas Roman, Charles, Ranulf, Roger of Northwold, John of St. Edmunds, Ralph, Master Alan, Nigel, James, Alan of Brooke, Guy, young William of Stanhoe and young Maurice.[2]

Then the sacrist and his (would that they were good) imitators[3] cast accusatory and provocative words at the abbot elect's followers before the royal officials and the many other laymen present, saying: 'O you betrayers and enemies of truth, O you seducers, friends of evil, men of guile, you who tricked and dealt wickedly with us,[4] from now on your evil will avail you nothing!' But to no purpose; for although the others had long endured many such reproaches, their countenances remained unchanged,[5] and they stood firm in the truth and justice which made them free.[6] After this the earl of Pembroke, to strike the hearts of the truthful party with greater fear, said: 'Since the pope testifies that his letter was sought by certain "prudent men" we wish them to show themselves to us.' At once the adverse party burst out into shouting, saying: 'Let it not be hidden from the king or from you his followers, who they are who have been wicked traitors and instigators of this business against him; the cellarer especially has been for a long time conspicuous as its chief promoter.' When the cellarer was summoned, he stood in the midst unafraid and full of faith,[7] and Earl Bigod said to him: 'Dearest brother, although it is our common duty to keep the blessed martyr's liberties intact and

---

[4] *Agere inique* is a common O.T. expression.
[5] Dan. 5: 6; cf. above, p. 25 n. 7.
[6] Ioh. 8: 32.
[7] Act. 6: 5.

illesas conseruatas et illibatas ⟨custodire⟩, gregique*a* eius in arduis
consulere, michi tamen, cuius signifer iure hereditario existo[1]
dominoque Roberto filio Walteri*b* presenti, hominibus et fidelibus
eiusdem, incumbit specialius. Vnde est quod monemus fideliterque
exhortamur, ne mediante alicuius fatui et insipientis consilio,
domini regis maliuolentiam fouendo aliquid seu contradicendo
contra eiusdem libertates usitatas, incurras.' Quibus tandem
celerarius sic ora resoluit:[2] 'Domini mei et fideles ecclesie, cum sit
unus Dominus dominantium et Rex regum,[3] qui etiam unicuique
ius suum, "Deo scilicet que Dei et Cesari que Cesaris" attribuere
precipiat,[4] dominusque noster rex electionem nostram secundum
tenorem carte sancti Aedwardi[5] scripto iam confirmauerit,
sacramentique*c* uinculo, sicut et omnes alii, astringar, ut quem
septem nominarent pro electo haberem, non mihi uidetur, si placet,
posse sane resilire sacramento, nisi saltem precessisset*d* absolucio,
f. 181ᵛ neque libertatibus domini regis in aliquo | contraire, cum et
foueam quod idem mera dilectione scripto, ut dictum est, beato
iam contulisse dignatus est Aedmundo. Vnde insuper, si domino
priori nostro ueniat ad beneplacitum et eius intersit potestatis,
peto cum confratribus nostris ut a dicto sacramento, ab eodem
uidelicet iam primo prestito, nos absoluat; et sic demum uni
consilio uobiscum adherentes super instituendis*e* siue destituendis
diligenter conueniemus.' Quibus sic propositis non habentes quid
conuenienter responderent exierunt a capitulo, super obiectis et
responsis dominum Wintoniensem ratione maioris cautele consulere uolentes. Adhuc quidem omnibus in eodem loco persistentibus dictus comes de Pembroc, Willelmus scilicet Marescallus,
parti electionis ob eorundem constantiam et immutabilitatem ait:
'Triduanas damus inducias; si quis tuicionem libertatis regie uelit
accedere, tutus accedat.' Communicato quidem consilio cum
Wyntoniensi, tunc regis iusticiario,[6] reuersi sunt in capitulum

----

a H *adds* in, *canc. by scribe*   *b* Waltero filio Roberti H   *c* sacramen-
toque H, *corr. by scribe*   *d* precepisset H, *corr. in marg. by Hand C*
e instittuendis H, *corr. by scribe*

----

[1] Within the eight and a half hundreds over which the abbot of St. Edmunds
exercised the rights of royal jurisdiction, Roger Bigod held three knights and
FitzWalter one (*JB*, pp. 120–2); hence their connection with St. Edmunds.
The Bigods claimed the hereditary office of bearer of St. Edmund's standard

unimpaired and to advise his followers in hard cases, this especially applies to me as his standard-bearer by hereditary right,[1] and to Robert FitzWalter here present and to his men and followers. This is why we sincerely exhort and warn you not to incur the king's ill will by taking the advice of any vain or stupid person, or by persisting in anything contrary to his customary liberties.' To this the cellarer made reply:[2] 'My lords and faithful members of the Church, as there is one King of kings and Lord of lords[3] who orders that each be given his right, namely to God what is God's and to Caesar what is Caesar's,[4] and because our king has provided written confirmation of our right of election as bestowed in St. Edward's charter,[5] and because I am bound under oath, together with all the rest of us, to accept him whom the seven nominated as abbot elect, it does not seem possible or sensible, begging your pardon, to go back on our oath, at least unless absolution were to be provided first. This does not seem to run counter to the king's liberties, for I am supporting what he himself deigned to confer in writing recently on the blessed Edmund, out of pure devotion, it is said. Now therefore, if it seem good to our prior, and if it lie in his power, I together with our brothers ask that he absolve us from our first oath, so that eventually, adhering with you to one counsel, we may seriously discuss appointing or abandoning.' Not knowing what appropriate reply to make to this proposal they left the chapter-house, wishing for greater security to consult the bishop of Winchester about the charges and replies. But the earl of Pembroke, William Marshal, because of the election party's firmness and constancy, said to all those who remained there: 'We give you a three-day amnesty; if anyone decides to change his mind and defend the royal liberties, he may do so under our protection.' After taking counsel with the bishop of Winchester, at that time the king's justiciar,[6] they returned to the chapter-

after Roger Bigod, father of the above, had carried it at the battle of Fornham in 1173. Jordan Fantosme, *Chronique*, in *Chronicles of the Reigns of Stephen, Henry II and Richard I*, RS, iii. 283–97; Benedict of Peterborough, ibid. i. 61–2; *JB*, p. 57.

[2] A common Virgilian phrase, e.g. *Georg.* iv. 452, etc. Also used by Abbo (*Mem.* i. 12).

[3] 1 Tim. 6: 15.

[4] Augustine, *De Civ. Dei* xix. 21, 1; Matt. 22: 21; cf. above, p. 33 n. 6.

[5] See above, p. 34 n. 1.

[6] He was replaced by Hubert de Burgh in June 1215 (Painter, p. 328). The writer's use of *tunc* suggests that he was writing at a later date.

pariter cum delegatis. Et uidentes iudices quod illo die pre magnatibus non possent in causam procedere, et quidam ipsum regem opinabantur esse uocandum, alii uero in contrarium senserunt, nec poterant alicuius periti consilium habere quin alterutra pars illum repelleret ut suspectum, articulum illum distulerunt diffinire, donec super hoc consilium haberent maturius. Partibus autem diem constituerunt in crastino sancti Iacobi[1] coram regalibus apud sanctum Albanum in ecclesia beati Petri[2] peremptorium, omnimodo sub ea forma qua dies superior fuerat constituta.

Verumtamen quoniam difficilimum erat tot monachos tam longe proficisci,[a] ideo ibidem in crastino coram eisdem pars electi tres procuratores constituit pro tota parte sua, saluo sibi beneficio, ut si opus esset ex aliis testes producere possent, ita siquidem, quod si omnes tres interesse non possent, duo uel unus ex illis ad idem plene sufficeret. Similiter et pars opposita alios tres sub simili forma constituit. Nomina procuratorum partis electi sunt Petrus celerarius, Ricardus de Heingham, magister Nicholaus de Dunestaple. Nomina procuratorum partis opposite sunt Ricardus precentor, Robertus sacrista, Adam infirmarius.

Hiis itaque ad uotum singulorum rite constitutis et concessis, erexit se Ricardus de Neuport, tunc subsacrista,[b][3] prostrauitque se coram iudicibus, ueniam humiliter petens de transgressione sepius facta contra sacramentum electionis ab eodem superius prestitum; cuius penitentiam suscipientes gaudendo, presente ibidem toto conuentu, data absolutione iniunctaque satisfactione, plene in fide iam instructum dimiserunt. Quo facto, mox petitum[c] est ex parte electi quod contradictores electioni sue iurent quod non maliciose moueant ei questionem. Cui obiectum est, quod ei[4] sub forma iudicii non esset respondendum, sed quasi extra iudicium. Respondit[5] quod dictum iuramentum simile est iuramento calumpnie, quod non debet prestari nisi post litem contestatam et hoc, si prestari debet et potest, prestari ab actore uniuersitatis;[6] altera

---

[a] proficissci H, *corr. by scribe*   [b] sacrista H, *corr. over line by Hand B*
[c] H *adds* iudicium. Respondit quod dictum iuramentum, *canc. by scribe*

[1] 26 July.   [2] One of the parish churches.

[3] Richard became sacrist in 1220 (*Bury Chronicle*, p. 5). The writer's use of *tunc* suggests that he was writing after this date.

[4] i.e. the abbot elect. The petition is put forward by an advocate or proctor of the party defending Hugh's election; the objection is made by a similar representative of the opposing party.

[5] One of the judges, perhaps Richard de Morins, the most illustrious canonist of their number. The slight obscurity here is no doubt due to the writer's copying extracts verbatim from the records.

[6] *Corpus Iuris Canonici*, ii. 2, 7; R. Naz, *Dictionnaire de Droit Canonique*, ii (Paris, 1937), s.v. 'calomnie'; Sayers, *Judges Delegate*, p. 85. The plaintiff

house with the justices delegate. The judges saw that they could not proceed with the hearing that day because of the magnates; some thought that the king ought to be called, others the contrary, and they themselves were unable to take the advice of any jurist because one or the other of the parties would reject him as suspect. Consequently they would not pronounce a verdict until they had had more mature deliberation. So they appointed for the parties the day after St. James'[1] in St. Peter's church[2] at St. Albans, in the presence of the royal officials, constituted after exactly the same form as had been arranged for the earlier day.

But because it was very difficult for so many monks to make such a long journey, the next day before the delegates, the abbot elect's party appointed three proctors to act for them, with this proviso, that if necessary they could produce further witnesses, or on the other hand, if all three were unable to be present, two or one alone would suffice. The opposing party similarly elected three representatives with the same proviso. The proctors of the abbot elect's party were Peter the cellarer, Richard of Hingham and Master Nicholas of Dunstable. Those of the opposing party were Richard the precentor, Robert the sacrist, and Adam the infirmarer.

After these men had been appointed and correctly admitted by each man's vote, Richard of Newport, then subsacrist,[3] rose and knelt before the judges, humbly begging pardon for having so often transgressed the election oath taken earlier. Before the whole convent they joyfully accepted his penitence, prescribing absolution and penance, and dismissed him, now fully grounded in faith. Immediately after, it was asked on the abbot elect's behalf for those opposing his election to swear that they were not litigating against him with malicious intent. To which it was objected that he[4] was not to be answered according to the normal procedure of a trial, but as it were out of court. He[5] replied that the oath was like the oath of calumny, which was not taken until the suit had been contested, and then, if it could and ought to be taken, it should be sworn by an advocate for the whole community.[6] But because the

promised that he had not brought the case in bad faith, that he would not request unnecessary delays, corrupt the judges, produce false instruments, etc. The 'contesting of the suit' consisted of a formal accusation stated by the plaintiff and replied to by the defendant, and marked the commencement of the process proper (ibid., pp. 84–5). In this inquiry Hugh's opponents are evidently regarded as the plaintiff, even though the action arose from the appeal lodged by the defenders of his election.

uero parte, scilicet electi, contrarium asserente, eius diffinicionem questionis usque ad diem partibus datam duxerunt differendam.

Super expensis uero factis et faciendis in hac causa ita prouiderunt, quod super factis, prehabita taxacione moderata, reciperent probacionem, et de sacristia et de aliis obedientiis quas magis uiderent habundare, facerent fieri solucionem. De faciendis autem prouiderunt, quod Ricardus consacrista[1] de sacristia prouideret expensas utrique parti moderatas, scilicet duobus aduocatis hinc et duobus inde; et monachis ipsis quorum personalem presentiam instantia cause desiderat; ita quidem quod ipsemet dux sit itineris et expensarum testis; et districte preceperunt sacriste quod dictum eius officium nullo modo impediat in expensis inueniendis. Super quo sacrista appellauit, sed eius appellationi non duxerunt deferendum.

f. 182   Die itaque prefixo apud sanctum[a] | Albanum coram constitutis, ad locum accedentes utrique, presente ibidem domino Wyntoniensi episcopo, iusticiario domini regis[2] aliisque magnatibus quampluribus, cleroque magno utrique parti assidente, erexit se magister Nicholaus coram eisdem, mandatum domini pape recitando, rationibusque plurimis euidenter ostendit quod cum dominus papa uices suas tribus presentibus commisisset, eisque litteris suis mediantibus ut mandatum suum exequerentur diligenter iniunxisset, orta est questio in electionem factam, precipue[b] id quod continetur in nouella constitucione Innocentii tercii, scilicet an rex requisitus esset super assensu prestando electioni faciende.[3] Cui obiectioni magister Nicholaus ita respondit quod non erat necesse, eo quod generale mandatum regis ad eos sicut et ad alios peruenerat[4] formaque litterarum in medio perlecta est, et de plano dixit regium assensum requisitum fuisse, sed post transmissionem litterarum suarum. Tunc cantor prorupit in uerba, dicens quod antequam littere regis peruenissent ad capitulum destinatus est ipse et magister Thomas de Walsingham cum eo ad regem, ut assensum eius requirerent.[5]

---

[a] H *adds* Aedmundum, *canc. by scribe and Hand C*   [b] precepisset H

---

[1] Presumably Newport had adopted this title because the sacrist would now be frequently absent from the house in his capacity as proctor for his party. Cf. Samson as subsacrist in 1182 (*JB*, p. 19). It was evidently the custom at Bury for the subsacrist to meet the expenses of official journeys.

[2] An undated letter of Innocent III (probably February–April 1214) rebukes Peter des Roches for conduct injurious to the rights and liberties of the Church, the result of charges against him received by the pope. This letter may be

abbot elect's party asserted the contrary, a decision on this question was postponed until the day appointed for the parties.

As to expenses incurred and yet to be incurred in the course of the inquiry, the judges provided thus: those already incurred, after they had been reckoned up correctly and given approval, should be paid for out of the sacristy and the other obedientiary offices which seemed the wealthier. As for those yet to be incurred, they decided that Richard the acting-sacrist[1] should provide sufficient spending-money out of the sacristy for each party, that is, for the two advocates of each, and for those monks whose personal presence at the inquiry was necessary. He was also to be responsible for their journeys and for the expenses which they incurred; and they strictly ordered the sacrist not in any way to impede the meeting of expenses from his department. The sacrist appealed over this, but they disallowed it.

On the appointed day both parties came before the justices at St. Albans, where the bishop of Winchester, the king's justiciar,[2] was present, and a great many other lords and ecclesiastics, seated on either side. Master Nicholas rose and read the papal mandate before them, giving evidence, supported by weighty reasons, that after the pope had commissioned the three judges there present as his delegates, and had enjoined them by letter to carry out his orders responsibly, there arose a point about the election which was the subject of the recent constitution of Innocent III, namely, whether the king's consent had been required before going ahead with it.[3] In answer to this question Master Nicholas maintained that it had not been required, for the king's general mandate had come to them as to others,[4] and it had been read out to them all in its essentials, and certainly, he said, the king's assent had been required, but only after the sending of his letter. Then the precentor broke into speech, saying that before the king's letter had been received in chapter, he and Master Thomas of Walsingham had been sent to the king to ask for his assent.[5]

connected with his opposition to Hugh's election (Cheney, *Letters*, no. 967, printed in appendix). That Innocent did receive complaints about Peter's attempts to delay the course of the inquiry is known from his letter below, p. 155.

[3] See above, p. 30 n. 2.   [4] See above, p. 6.

[5] The precentor is undoubtedly right, and it is hard to see what point Master Nicholas is making when in fact the monks had not obeyed the provisions of King John's mandate, which ordered the election to be made in his presence (see above, p. 6). The precentor is not mentioned earlier (p. 5) as making the journey to obtain the king's assent.

Excepciones dilatorie*a* 1

Primo*b* querimus qui continentur nomine 'prouisorum',2 ut sciamus qui sunt qui litteras impetrauerint; et uolumus interrogari celerarium, an pape impetrauerit litteras, an suo nomine fuerint impetrate. Deinde querimus an uelint dicere potestatem fuisse collatam absolute in septem monachos, an sub modo an sub condicione. Deinde querimus quo uerbo et quo fuit consensum in eandem electionem, uel quibus. Deinde querimus de quorum monachorum machinacione intelligunt, per hoc quod dicitur 'machinantibus monachis'.2 Item dicimus quod cum electio que dicitur facta de Hugone et appellatio facta pro eadem ad dominum papam interposita, legato in capitulo sancti Aedmundi presentata*c* sit, idem legatus de consensu totius conuentus de eadem electione cepit cognoscere et inquirere et quosdam de monachis examinare. Vnde, quia non facta mencione de hac ueritate littere postea sunt impetrate; item, quia non faciunt mencionem de litteris domini legati, quarum*d* auctoritate inquisicionem facere cepit de hac electione, dicimus litteras illas nullas esse, nec aliquam esse uestram iurisdictionem.3

Ediciones*e* 4

Sciatis*f* nos intelligere nomine 'prouisorum' celerarium et alios qui stant cum eo pro electione domini H(ugonis) electi. Item celerarius constanter asserit quod per eum et per alios quos dicimus 'prouisores' littere impetrate sunt. Item dicimus quod potestas eligendi fuit collata ⟨in⟩ septem, prout continetur in decreto tocius capituli, in quo dicunt quod in illos septem communi et consona uoluntate uota sua de electione facienda contulerunt. Item consenserunt electioni, quia electum ab illis septem pronuntiata sollempniter electione in osculo pacis susceperunt, et ei omnem honorem electo debitum exhibuerunt, secundum quod ipsum arbitrati sunt esse exhibendum; scilicet assignando ei locum superiorem post abbatem, et in pane et in

---

a *Space left for rubricator, with faint pencil guide by scribe; heading provided by* Hand B   *b* *Rimo* H; *space left for rubricator; small* p *as guide in marg. by* scribe   *c* presentante H   *d* quorum H   *e* *As for n.a. above* *f* ciatis H; *space left for rubricator; small* s *as guide in marg. by scribe;* S *suppl. by* Hand C(?)

---

1 See above, p. 80 n. 5.   2 Above, p. 74.
3 The Exceptions and Statements in Reply are obviously copied or excerpted from the records of the inquiry, as are the *Acta* which follow. The Exceptions are addressed by the advocates of the anti-election party to their counterparts of the opposing faction, except for the last item, which is directed at the justices themselves. This item is in fact the 'dilatory exception' directed against the

Dilatory Exceptions[1]

First we ask who are meant by 'prudent men',[2] that we may
know who obtained the letter; and we wish the cellarer to be
questioned as to whether he obtained the papal letters or whether
they were obtained in his name. Next, we ask whether absolute
power was vested in the seven monks, or if it was under limit
or condition. Thirdly, we ask the wording and nature of the consent to the election, and who gave it. Again, we want to know who
the monks were whom they knew to be devising anything, as
referred to in the phrase 'conniving monks'.[2] Next, we say that
when the so-called election of Hugh and the appeal for it to the
pope were made known to the legate in the chapter-house at
St. Edmunds, he began to investigate and inquire about it with
the whole convent's consent, and to examine some of the monks.
Now because he made no decision as to the election's validity,
they then sought the letter. Therefore, because they do not
mention the legate's letter on the authority of which he began
his inquiry into the election, we pronounce your letter null and
void, and your jurisdiction to be invalid.[3]

Statements in Reply[4]

Know that by 'prudent men' we mean the cellarer and others
supporting with him the election of the abbot elect Hugh. Next,
the cellarer openly admits that the letter was obtained by him
and by the others whom we call 'prudent men'. Again, we say
that the power to elect was vested in the seven monks as contained in the decree of the whole chapter, in which it is said that
they have unanimously consented to the election being made by
those seven. Moreover they did so consent to the election, for
when the abbot elect was solemnly pronounced chosen by the
seven, they received him with the kiss of peace, and showed him
all the honour due to an abbot elect, as far as they thought
necessary, namely assigning him the highest seat after the

conduct of the action. The paragraph as a whole has been misnamed in the text;
it is not a set of 'exceptions', but rather of 'interrogatories' (Sayers, *Judges
Delegate*, p. 86). The aim of these and the 'responsiones' which follow were 'to
fix neatly the points on which the parties disagreed, and to expose exactly what
was to be proved'.

[4] Sayers, *Judges Delegate*, pp. 78–9. But this is not the normal 'Editio' or
'Libel'. Rather it is a set of 'responsiones' (see preceding note).

ferculis dupplicem porcionem, et alias habendo eum publice pro electo. Verbo etiam consenserunt in*a* eum electum, publice nominando, et pro eo publice in capitulo appellando. Item machinari dicimus eos, contradicendo electioni cui primo uerbo et facto consenserant, prout supradictum est.[1]

Post has excepciones et discussiones hec sunt acta apud sanctum Albanum:[2]

Dictis autem die et loco secundum formam premissam partibus in nostra presentia constitutis, presente etiam domino Wyntoniensi, domini regis iusticiario et quibusdam aliis magnatibus regni, recipimus omnes dilatorias excepciones tunc competentes a contradictoribus electi. Et cum orta esset altercatio magna super domini regis uocacione,*b* aliis ipsum uocare debere, aliis | asserentibus in contrarium, nolumus aliquid super hoc diffinire, sed secundum formam ⟨mandati⟩ domini pape decreuimus illum diligenter admonere et efficaciter inducere, ut electioni H(ugonis) suum imperciatur assensum uel, si placuerit, quare hoc nolit facere rationem nobis ostendat per responsalem ydoneum, in crastino sancti Michaelis in maiori ecclesia apud sanctum Aedmundum.[3] Ibidem eciam interlocuti sumus iusiurandum esse prestandum*c* a contradictoribus electi post litem contestatam et non ante; super quo fuit alias disputatum. Preuidimus eciam electores illos de quorum uita et debilitate timetur, secundum formam decretalis 'Quoniam frequenter',[4] sine omni preiudicio litis contestationis; predictis autem diem et locum constituimus peremptorium,*d* ut iuratorum dicta non ualeant ante litem contestatam, et post litem contestatam iterum examinabuntur super propositis a contradictoribus electioni.

His itaque hoc ordine rite gestis, tres dicti iudices dominusque Wyntoniensis magnatesque plurimi et iurisperiti existentes ibidem

f. 182ᵛ (margin)

---

a *Added over line by Hand C*   *b* uicte H, *corr. in marg. by Hand A*
c H *adds* esse   *d* H *adds* et

---

[1] The objection to the justices' jurisdiction raised in the Interrogatories is not dealt with here, since it was quashed by the judges themselves (see below, p. 111).

[2] The drawing up of written *acta* for each stage of a suit was established practice by the time of the Fourth Lateran Council, which made it obligatory (Sayers, *Judges Delegate*, p. 52).

abbot's and by a double portion of bread and other dishes, and in other ways also acknowledging him publicly as abbot elect. Furthermore they agreed verbally to his election, publicly nominating and appealing for him in the chapter-house. Finally, we say that those monks were conniving who opposed the election to which they had at first agreed in word and deed, as said above.[1]

After these objections and inquiries the following was done at St. Albans:[2]

On the day and at the place appointed by earlier arrangement, the parties met in our presence, before the bishop of Winchester, the king's justiciar and other magnates of the realm. And we heard all the dilatory exceptions put forward by the abbot elect's opponents. Then a serious argument arose about the summoning of the king, some asserting that he ought to be summoned, others the contrary. We did not want to pronounce upon this, but according to the papal mandate we determined to warn him diligently and persuade him effectually to give his assent to Hugh's election, or, if it pleased him, to give us his reason why not by a competent representative on the day after St. Michael's in the larger church at St. Edmunds.[3] At the same time we decided that the oath to be taken by the abbot elect's opponents ought to be sworn after the contesting of the suit and not before. Over this there was further argument. We also provided for the electors, fearing for their safety of life and limb, according to the decretal *Quoniam frequenter*,[4] without any prejudice to the contesting of the suit. And we appointed a time and place for the parties so that the words of those under oath should have no authority until the suit had been contested. After the contesting of the suit we will examine afresh the accusations made by the opponents of the election.

After this the three judges, the bishop of Winchester, and the large number of magnates and jurists there present advised Hugh

---

[3] 30 September. The parish church of St. James is probably meant.

[4] *Corpus Iuris Canonici*, ii. 2, 6, 5, which stated that, if the lives of the witnesses were threatened, or if any of them were liable to be absent for a long period, their testimony might be heard before the 'contesting of the suit', rather than vice versa, which was the normal procedure.

H

consul⟨u⟩erunt dominum H(ugonem) electum quatinus litteras
iudicum in propria persona domino regi nullo alio mediante defer-
ret commonitorias. Sed quoniam idem H(ugo) sine fratrum suorum
consilio tunc absentium iter illud subire sane non decreuit, respondit se illud libenter uelle subire, si tamen in hoc consilium
fratrum suorum adquiesceret. Iniunxerunt ergo magistro Nicholao
ut onus illud cum litteris suis sub hac forma subiret:

Excellentissimo domino I(ohanni) Dei gratia illustri regi
Anglorum, H(enricus) abbas de Wardune et R(icardus) prior
de Donestaple et decanus Salesberi eternam in Domino salutem,
et tam ⟨de⟩uotum quam debitum in omnibus famulatum.

Mandatum domini pape suscepimus in hec uerba, etc. (ut
supra.)[1] Huius igitur auctoritate mandati, cupientes in omnibus
et per omnia deferre regie maiestati, de consilio multorum
iurisperitorum excellentiam uestram cum omni precum instantia
qua possumus admonemus et humiliter exhoramus quatinus
electioni H(ugonis) monachi de sancto Aedmundo qui canonice,
sicut dicitur, electus est in abbatem, dignemini regium impertiri
fauorem et assensum aut, si placuerit clementie uestre, pro
reuerentia domini pape, in crastino sancti Michaelis[2] apud
maiorem ecclesiam de sancto Aedmundo per responsalem
ydoneum dignemini rationem nobis assignare et docere, quare
fauorem uestrum denegetis et assensum. Iniunctum enim est
nobis, ut si illam electionem de persona ydonea inuenerimus
celebratam, ipsam auctoritate apostolica, appellatione postposita, confirmemus. Rogamus insuper ut excellentia regia erga
paruitatem nostram non indignetur si apud eam officio nostro ex
nobis iniuncta auctoritate fungamur.

Valeat, etc.

In crastino uero[a] inuencionis sancti Stephani martyris,[3] facta
mencione in capitulo per dominum H(ugonem) electum super
itinere magistro Nicholao a iudicibus commisso, presentibus
priore et sacrista, adiecit quod dominus Wyntoniensis pariterque
iudices et magnates cum uniuerso clero apud sanctum Albanum
existentes, in hoc omnes adquieuerunt, ut ipse, sicut dictum est,
iter istud subiret. Vnde uestrum est, scilicet fratrum suorum,
consulere utrum expediat necne. Cuius consilio utpote sano cum
uniuersi fideles adquiescerent, postulauit humiliter ut sibi

---

[a] H adds as, canc. by scribe

to take the admonitory letter from the judges to the king in person. But because Hugh thought it unwise to undertake this journey without the advice of his absent brothers, he replied that he would gladly make it, but only if it was agreeable to them. So they ordered Master Nicholas to take on the task of delivering their letter, which read as follows:

To the most excellent lord John, by the grace of God illustrious king of the English, Henry abbot of Wardon, Richard prior of Dunstable, and the dean of Salisbury send perpetual greetings in the Lord, and their devoted and due obedience in all matters.

We have received a mandate from the pope in these words, etc. (as above).[1] By the authority of this mandate, therefore, desiring in and through all things to be subject to the royal majesty, we humbly advise and entreat your excellency, with the advice of many jurists and with all the urgent prayer we can muster, that you either give your royal favour and assent to the election of Hugh, monk of St. Edmunds, who, as is said, was canonically elected as abbot, or, if it please your clemency, out of reverence for the pope, deign to give us reasons why you deny your favour and assent by a competent representative in the larger church at St. Edmunds on the day after St. Michael's.[2] For it is enjoined on us that if we find that election to have been celebrated in a fit person, we are to confirm it by papal authority, appeal disallowed. We ask your royal excellency, moreover, not to be angry towards our insignificance, since it is by virtue of our duty and the authority laid upon us that we do this.

Farewell, etc.

On the day after the finding of St. Stephen the martyr,[3] the abbot elect Hugh told of the journey laid on Master Nicholas by the judges, in the chapter-house before the prior and sacrist, adding that the bishop of Winchester, the judges, magnates, and the many clerks present at St. Albans had all agreed that he also ought to make that journey, as I have said. Now it is your duty, as his brothers, to advise whether it is necessary or not! When all the faithful party had expressed their agreement with the sound advice of these men, he asked humbly for a contribution to meet

---

[1] See above, p. 74. [2] 30 September. [3] 4 August.

magistroque Nicholao in expensis fieret exhibicio, sicut paulo ante
prior et conuentus per litteras delegatorum susceperant in mandatum. Ad que sacrista hiis uerbis allocutus est, dicens: 'Quoniam
expensis infructuosis et grauamine multiplici, huius electionis
causa, obedienciam meam nullo mediante leuamine uideo onerari,
iudicesque extra iurisdictionem talia presumentes, pro ea ad legatum appello contra eorum mandatum et contra omnes homines,
ne quid per eos aut per alios innouando in sacristia siue commu-
tando constituatur; et si forte legatus non sufficiat, presenciam
domini pape appello.' Appellauit secum I(ocelinus) elemosinarius,
cui silentium impositum erat,[1] ne per eorum preceptum, scilicet
iudicum, cum nullum esset, supradictis fieret in uno denario
exhibicio. Quo facto sacrista, inito cum elemosinario post capitulum consilio,[2] in hoc adquieuit, ut domino H(ugoni) electo
alioque, quemcumque de toto conuentu uellet eligere, dummodo |
f. 183 magistrum Nicholaum non eligeret, x. marcas inueniret; alioquin
nec etiam unum denarium eidem pro aliquo inueniret. Quo tamen
fauente, accepit secum dominum Ricardum de Heingham in loco
magistri Nicholai profectusque est die sancti Oswaldi regis et
martyris[3] uersus dominum regem, tunc Pictauia existentem.[4] Illo
quidem die completus est circulus anni quo primo mandatum
domini regis super electione secundum consuetudinem Anglie
tractanda suscepimus, licet post litterarum susceptionem et
singulorum fratrum examen secundum formam electionis, non eo
die uerum etiam in crastino Transfiguracionis dominus H(ugo) a
septem electoribus in capitulo denominatus est electus et a toto
conuentu in osculo pacis susceptus.[5]

Euoluto temporis[a] curiculo annorum, uidelicet duorum et
quantum superest a Natali usque ad diem sancti Romani martiris,[6]
in tercio anno post decessum uenerabilis memorie S(amsonis)
domini[b] abbatis, tempore interdicti in pratello sepulti,[7] facta est
mencio per sacristam super ipsius remocione. Et conuenientibus
in unum priore scilicet et cantore magistroque Thoma de Walsingham aliisque magnatibus, ut in ecclesia sepeliretur causa maioris
honoris, solus sacrista resistebat, dicens quod nec ille nec alius,
eo tantum[c] potestatem habente, in ecclesia sepeliretur. Et eleuans

---

    [a] H *adds* circulo, *canc. by Hand C*   [b] dicti H   [c] tamen H

    [1] Matt. 22: 34.
    [2] A common O.T. expression; cf. above, p. 13 n. 4.

the expenses of himself and Master Nicholas, as provided in the
mandate of the judges delegate, which the prior and convent had
received a little earlier. But to this the sacrist had the following to
say: 'Because I see my department, on account of this election,
being burdened by useless expenditures and multiplied loads,
with no aid in sight, and because the judges are presuming to go
outside their jurisdiction in this matter, I appeal to the legate
against their mandate, and against all men, that neither by them
nor any others should any changes or innovations be made in the
sacristy. And if the legate is not sufficient then I appeal to the pope.'
Jocelin the almoner, on whom silence had been imposed,[1] seconded
him, saying that not a single penny ought to be offered them under
the judges' order, since it was of no force. But the sacrist, entering
into discussion[2] with the almoner after chapter, agreed to provide
ten marks for the abbot elect and one other, whomever he wished
to choose from the whole convent, provided it were not Master
Nicholas; otherwise on no account would he give a penny. The
abbot elect, agreeing to this, took Richard of Hingham instead of
Master Nicholas and set out on the day of St. Oswald king and
martyr[3] to reach the king, then in Poitou.[4] Now that day completed a whole year from the time when we first received the
king's mandate ordering the election to be carried out according
to English custom; although it was not that day but on the day
after Transfiguration, following the reception of the king's letter
and the prescribed examination of each brother, that Hugh was
chosen and nominated by the seven in the chapter-house and
received by the whole convent with the kiss of peace.[5]

With the swift passage of time, namely two years plus the period
from Christmas to the day of St. Romanus martyr,[6] being the third
year after the death of Abbot Samson of blessed memory, buried
during the interdict in the cloister garth,[7] the sacrist raised the
question of his removal. The prior, precentor, Master Thomas of
Walsingham, and others of note agreed unanimously that he ought
to be buried in the church for greater honour. Only the sacrist
resisted this, saying that neither he nor anyone else, be he never so
illustrious, ought to be buried in the church. He was disinterred

---

[3] 5 August.
[4] John had sailed for Poitou on 9 February (Wendover, ii. 98).
[5] See above, pp. 7–11.   [6] 9 August.
[7] During the interdict no one could be buried in hallowed ground.

eum a terra die Martis proxima ante Assumpcionem sancte Marie,[1] hora quasi matutinali,[2] utpote cuius iudicio omnia tunc temporis terminabantur, per totam diem super tripodes in pratello constituens inter uesperas monachorum[3] transuexit in capitulum, nullo ibidem monacho presente preter eo et Alano Walense. Et ut hec [a] eidem sacriste specialius in laudem cederent et gloriam, eo feruencius in effectum ducere festinabat propositum, quo dominum H(ugonem) electum esse remocius cognoscebat.[4]

Interiectis postmodum paucis diebus, appropinquante Sabbato quatuor temporum post exaltacionem sancte Crucis,[5] in quo, cum diuersis locis forent ordines pronuntiati, domini R(obertus), id est sacrista et R(icardus) precentor, fons et origo tocius dissencionis electionis, spiritu elacionis et superbie inflati et secundos in congregatione abbates se preferentes,[6] omnesque alios paruipendentes, maximeque sacramento electionis inclinantes in omni loco pre magnitude potentie[7] repudiantes, iniquitatem iniquitati et scandalum scandalo, ut per hoc etiam eorum intencionem omnes[b] innotescerent serenius,[c] adicere necdum desistebant.[d] Conuenerunt quidem die Lune ante Sabbatum quatuor temporum[8] in camera prioris super quatuor nouiciis coram eodem tantummodo ordinandis, magistro Thoma de Walsingham in ulcione, uidelicet eo quod cum ueritate staret eleccionis, penitus repulsam paciente.[9] Et licet dominus prior tale consilium, indiscrete conceptum et uenenose, ratione dignitatis sue et preeminencie pocius repulisse quam admisisse debuisset,[e] de facili assensum non denegauit prebere. Insuper et ad maiorem cautelam, ut ipse istius maliciosi tractatus iudicaretur inmunis, se absentauit. Sed cum, teste apostolo, 'nihil absconditum quod non reuelabitur et occultum quod non scietur',[10] dominus Albinus subprior quinta feria subsequente[11] in pleno capitulo ex parte prioris precepit sacriste ut tantummodo quatuor nouiciis ordinandis, sicut ante prolocutum erat in camera eiusdem, prouideret. Quo audito, et ⟨cum⟩ iam planum[f] fieret ad unguem quod prius latebat, factus est tumultus magnus inter filios[12] seruare ueritatem studentes et pacem. Et super hiis conuenientes in unum,[13]

---

[a] hoc H   [b] omnibus H   [c] sererenius H   [d] assistebant H
[e] debuisse H; -t added by Hand C   [f] plenum H

---

[1] 12 August.   [2] About 4 a.m.   [3] About 6 p.m.
[4] Douai, Bibliothèque de la Ville, MS. 553 (Registrum Coquinarii from the abbey), fifteenth century, f. 7ᵛ: 'Sampson sepultus est in capitulo . . . sub lapidibus marmoreis quadratis' (James, On the Abbey, p. 181). His tomb was found there early this century.
[5] 20 September.   [6] Reg. Ben., c. 65.   [7] Esth. 13: 2.
[8] 15 September.

on Tuesday before the Assumption of the blessed Mary,[1] about the hour of matins.[2] And since at that time everything was done as the sacrist decided, the coffin was placed on tripods in the garth for the day, and while the monks were at vespers,[3] he transferred it to the chapter-house, no other monks being present except Alan of Wales. And that this might contribute yet more to his praise and glory he hastened on the business enthusiastically; especially as he knew the abbot elect to be far away.[4]

A few days later Ember Saturday drew near,[5] when ordinations were to be made in various places. Robert the sacrist and Richard the precentor, the fount and origin of all the dissension over the election, became inflated with a spirit of pride and elation, considering themselves as second abbots[6] among the congregation and belittling all the others. Especially, in the magnitude of their power[7] did they utterly scorn those who inclined to the election oath. They did not cease to add iniquity to iniquity and scandal to scandal, so that their intention was clearly perceived by everyone. For on the Monday before Ember Saturday[8] they met the prior in his chamber and decided that only four novices should be ordained, obstinately and utterly rejecting Master Thomas of Walsingham in revenge for his support of the election's validity.[9] The prior, although by reason of his pre-eminent dignity he ought rather to have rejected than admitted such advice, indiscreetly and harmfully conceived as it was, readily gave it his assent. And for greater precaution, so that no one should guess that he was involved in this wicked plan, he absented himself from the house. But as the apostle testifies, 'nothing is hid which shall not be revealed, and nothing concealed which shall not be made known'.[10] For when Albinus the subprior on Thursday[11] in full chapter ordered the sacrist on the prior's behalf to prepare four novices only for ordination, as had been arranged earlier in the prior's chamber, everything which had previously been concealed came out into the open, and there was a great furore among those striving to maintain truth and peace.[12] Those who had never departed from their united stand since the election, but had remained at one in their loyalty,[13]

[9] A monk normally took orders seven years after profession (D. Knowles, *The Religious Orders in England*, ii, Cambridge, 1955, p. 23). Presumably this time had come for Master Thomas, who also happened to be eminently qualified.
[10] Matt. 10: 26; cf. above, p. 55 n. 7.   [11] 18 September.
[12] Os. 10: 14; cf. above, p. 15 n. 5.
[13] A common O.T. expression; cf. also *JB*, p. 19.

utpote qui nunquam post electionem ab unitate discordantes sed
semper in unitate fidei[1] permansere concordantes, prouido consilio
et communi litteras sub hac forma domino Eliensi destinauerunt:

Reuerendo domino et patri in Christo sanctissimo E(ustachio),
Dei gratia Elyensi episcopo, quidam monachi sui sancti Aedmundi reuerenciam[a] debitam cum salute.

Nouerit uniuersitas uestra, quod quidam de domo nostra
exfrontes, aduersarii libere electionis nostre, in | proposito
habent mittere ad uos quosdam monachos preter conscienciam
capituli hac die Sabbati a uobis ordinandos, omissis quibusdam
dignioribus et magistro Thoma de Walsingham, cuius promocio
foret pernecessaria uniuersitati, uidelicet ad uerbum Dei
dilucide predicandum; linguam enim et mentem habet ad hoc
pre ceteris expeditam. Qui etiam in ulcionem, quod stat cum
ueritate electionis ab hac promocione turpiter est repulsus.
Petimus igitur pro Deo et reuerentia sanctorum suorum Aedmundi et Aetheldrede, ut maioris mali et inuidie cesset occasio, ne
absque consciencia capituli, maxime quamdiu sumus sine pastore,
recipiatis de domo nostra aliquem ordinandum. Nos enim, salua
pace uestra, ne hoc aliqua ratione fiat in preiudicium monastici
ordinis appellamus. Clericos etiam ordinandos ad presentacio-
nem alicuius priuate persone de domo nostra, si placet, admittere
non debetis, quia qui sine capitulo beneficiare non potest, nec
sine capitulo de iure poterit presentare.

Quibus ita iam missis, Albinus supprior ex sua parte, consilio
magistri Nicholai interposito, alias litteras destinauit priori, ut
uidelicet domum uisis litteris ad tumultum sedandum uenire, seu
magistrum Thomam cum aliis ordinandis mittere festinasset.
Quod cum prior intelligeret litterasque diligenter apud Waledene[2]
inspiceret, cum omni festinacione rescripsit suppriori, ut magistrum Thomam de Walsingham pariterque Galfridum fratrem
sacriste cum aliis ordinandis misisset, idemque, ut hec sollempnius
prosequerentur, dictis die et loco occurreret; factumque est ita.
Sed antequam dominus prior cum ordinandis ibi uenisset, dominus
Elyensis litteras supradictas ex parte memoratorum susceperat
inspiciendas. Quibus diligenter inspectis, dominoque priore et
sacrista cum magistro Thoma cum aliis ordinandis iam ad eum
accedentibus, nullo modo nullaue ratione animum eiusdem ad

[a] H *adds* patri

[1] Ephes. 4: 13.
[2] Saffron Walden, Essex, twenty-five miles south-east of Bury.

met together over this[1] and with provident and unanimous counsel
sent the following letter to the bishop of Ely:

> To their reverend lord and father in Christ, the most holy
> Eustace, by the grace of God bishop of Ely, certain of his monks
> of St. Edmunds send reverent obedience and greetings.
>
> May your greatness know that some shameless members of
> our house, enemies to our right of free election, have proposed
> to send you some monks for ordination this Saturday, without
> the consent of chapter. But they have omitted some of the more
> worthy candidates, including Master Thomas of Walsingham,
> whose promotion is very necessary to the community, namely
> for the clear preaching of the word of God; for he has the
> necessary command of speech and understanding to do this
> before others. But in revenge for his support of the election as
> valid, he is dishonourably barred from this promotion. We ask
> you, therefore, out of reverence for God and His saints Edmund
> and Etheldreda, and in order to deprive them of this opportunity
> to practise further wickedness and ill will, not to receive any
> ordinand from our house without the consent of chapter,
> especially while we are without a pastor. For we appeal, saving
> your peace, against this being carried out, for whatever reason,
> in prejudice of the monastic order. You ought not to admit, if
> you please, any clerks for ordination at the presentation of any
> private person of our house, for as it is impossible to benefice
> without chapter's consent, so by law no one can present
> without it.

Shortly after this had been sent, Subprior Albinus, by the advice
of Master Nicholas, sent a further letter to the prior on behalf of
his party, asking him to return home and calm the tumult, or else
quickly send Master Thomas with the other ordinands. When the
prior, at Walden,[2] read the letter with attention and learnt of this,
he wrote back at once to the subprior, ordering Master Thomas of
Walsingham and Geoffrey the sacrist's brother to be sent with the
other ordinands; he himself would meet them at the prescribed
time and place so that they would be honourably attended. And
so it was done. But before the prior and the ordinands arrived,
the bishop of Ely received the election party's letter and read it
carefully, so that when the prior, sacrist, Master Thomas, and the
other ordinands came, they could not persuade him to proceed

gratiam ordinum prosequendam poterant inclinare, donec prior caucionem prestitisset ibi sufficientem, quod super appellatione litterarum supradictarum nullus de cetero questionem ei neque uerbum moueret. Quibus hoc ordine prosecutis, dominus Elyensis eos cum magistro Thoma admisit ad gratiam, quos eo absente intra*a* se statuerat ante omnino repellendos.

Istis siquidem secundum ordinem, licet extra seriem nostre materie plane digestis, iam nunc ad materiam recurramus. Igitur, ut superius dictum est, omnibus iam paratis et dispositis ad iter domini H(ugonis) electi ex necessario spectantibus, necdumque eo ammoto, inuidus ille sacrista, 'qui eo bonis iustius inuidet quo appetitu bone uoluntatis caret',[1] accito latenter uno de garciferis*b* suis nomine Talpa cum litteris pluribus contra insontem et eius eleccionem festinanter ad regem direxit, ut domino H(ugone) postmodum subsequente ipsum regem magnatesque regi assistentes sibi causeque sue reperiret contrarios; insuper et ut quos ibidem dominus H(ugo) sperabat amicos inuenire, exfrontes experiret aduersarios; factumque est ita. Pro dolor! quod talis fraus, talis iniquitas, tanta malicia et uersucia fraudis diabolice sub columbe specie et ouina pelle sit protracta et contexta. Non recolens sane, qui talia perpetrauit, illius Dominici prouerbium,*c* dicentis: 'Que uultis, homines, ut ego uobis faciam, hec*d* et uos aliis faciatis',[2] et: 'Qui parat proximo suo foueam, primo incidat in eam',[3] et: 'Quod sibi non uult quis fieri, aliis*e* ne faciat',[4] ne fortasse postmodum iusta Dei sententia 'conuertatur dolor eius in caput eius, et in uerticem ipsius iniquitas eius descendat*f*'.[5]

Itaque dominus H(ugo) processu temporis regi Pictauia existenti accedens, ipsum regem per suggestionem cuiusdam filii Rogeri Bigot regi familiaris[6] aliorumque magnatum curie per adquisicionem sacriste, sibi et electioni sue modis*g* omnibus inuenit resistentem. Qui tamen postea ad peticionem magistri Roberti*h* de Curtun legati Francie sedatus ⟨est⟩, atque dominum

---

a in terra H   *b* garciferos H   *c* This should probably read prouerbii, or be omitted   *d* hoc H   *e* alii H   *f* descendet H   *g* modum H
h H adds Bigot, canc. by scribe

---

[1] Abbo (*Mem.* i. 8). The printed text has *plus* where New York Pierpont Morgan Library MS. 736 (p. 155) and other Bury MSS. have *iustius*.
[2] Matt. 7: 12.
[3] Prov. 26: 27; Ecclus. 10: 8, 27: 29, conflated with one of the many biblical verses concerning behaviour towards one's neighbour.
[4] An addition to the text of Acts found in some Greek and Old Latin MSS.,

with the ordinations until the prior had provided a sufficient guarantee that it would not cause any of the others (because of the appeal contained in their letter) to raise complaint against him. When these matters had been settled the bishop of Ely admitted them with Master Thomas into his grace—those whom, before their arrival, he had firmly intended to send back.

Having related in full these matters according to the sequence, although outside the main theme of our subject, let us return to this theme. After everything necessary was disposed and prepared for the abbot elect's journey, but before his departure, that envious sacrist, 'hater of good men all the more, since he himself lacked good will',[1] secretly summoned one of his lackeys named Mole and sent him post-haste to the king armed with many letters against the innocent man and his election. His intention was that Hugh, following later, should find the king himself and the nobles around him unfavourably disposed towards him and his cause, and furthermore that those men there whom he hoped to find sympathetic he would instead find shameless adversaries. And so it was done. For shame! That such trickery, such iniquity, such malice, and crafty, devilish fraud should lie covered and concealed beneath the guise of a dove or a sheep's fleece! He who perpetrated such a deed was not reflecting wisely on the word of his Lord, who said: 'Whatsoever things you wish me to do to you, do you even so to others',[2] and: 'Whoever prepares a pit for his neighbour, may he first fall into it himself',[3] and: 'What a man does not wish to be done to him, let him not do to others',[4] lest afterwards the just sentence of God by chance 'turn his mischief upon his own head, and his violent dealing upon his own pate'.[5]

Some time later Hugh came to the king in Poitou, and found him utterly unapproachable concerning him and his election because of the inciting of one of Roger Bigod's sons, his familiar,[6] and of other magnates of the court whom the sacrist had bribed. Later, however, the king was calmed by the intercession of Master Robert de Courçon, legate of France, and received Hugh into such favour

from the latter of which it passed into some Vulgate MSS. See F. Liebermann, *Die Gesetze der Angelsachsen*, 3 vols. (Halle, 1903–16), i. 45 (section 49, 6); iii. 48, and C. Plummer, *The Life and Times of Alfred the Great* (Oxford, 1902), p. 124.

[5] Ps. 7: 16.

[6] Probably Hugh, eldest son and heir of Earl Roger, later to be one of the twenty-five barons of the Charter. He died 1224–5.

H(ugonem) in tantam suscepit gratiam, ut non solum in litteris suis
f. 184 priori et conuentui transmissis eum nominaret electum, | uerum
etiam mandaret se iam de eius promocione spem bonam concepisse.
Fuit autem hic tenor:

> I(ohannes) Dei gratia rex Anglie, etc., priori*a* et conuentui*b*
> sancti Aedmundi etc.
>
> Ad peticionem domini legati tractauimus cum electo ue-
> stro super negotio electionis sue. Sed quoniam multis perplexi
> negociis operam ad hoc dare non potuimus, efficacem execu-
> cionem huius negocii suspendimus donec uenerimus in Angliam.
> Nos autem tunc per Dei gratiam super negocio illo uobiscum
> amicabiliter tractabimus, facturi inde Domino fauente quod
> Deo erit acceptum et domui uestre fructuosum.

Alias quidem litteras tunc temporis domino Wyntoniensi scripsit
in hec uerba:

> I(ohannes) Dei gratia rex Anglie, etc., uenerabili patri in
> Christo P(etro) eiusdem gratia Wyntoniensi episcopo etc.
>
> Ad peticionem magistri R(oberti) legati Francie locuti sumus
> cum electo sancti Aedmundi super negocio electionis sue, quod
> processum bonum sortietur,*c* Deo fauente, cum in Angliam
> uenerimus; et ideo uobis mandamus, quatinus blada eiusdem
> abbatie et nemora et omnes possessiones in manu nostra*d*
> existentes in bona pace custodiri faciatis, ita quod nichil inde
> ammoueatur uel diripiatur, donec in Angliam uenerimus.

Inter hec quidem, adueniente die statuto, uidelicet die sancti
Michaelis,[1] conuenerunt partes utreque in domo hospitum: et
nitentes inimici ueritatis et ecclesie iurisdictionem delegatorum
cassare, nutu diuino iustoque Dei iudicio factum est ita, ut omnes
allegationes quas contra ueritatem electionis omni populo cognitam secum agere putabant, ad iudicium tam laicorum quam
clericorum ibi existentium contra semetipsos proponerentur.
Facta autem super obiectis et responsis altercacione, interrogatum
est decretum capituli.[2] Quod cum magister Ricardus de Derham
alta uoce coram omnibus perlegisset, erigens se a sede paulatim
Ricardus precentor ita cecinit, audientibus omnibus: 'Per os
Domini, istud decretum est falsum!' Ad cuius igitur antifonam
melius intonandam, erexit se magister Iohannes de Houtoune,[3] et

---

a prior H   *b* conuentus H   *c* sortitur H   *d* H *adds* possidentes,
canc. by Hand C

---

[1] 29 September. On 18 August the king witnessed a letter appointing Peter
des Roches his proctor in the cause (*Rot. Litt. Pat.*, p. 140).

that not only did he call him 'abbot elect' in his letter to the prior
and convent, but also ordered them to take heart as to his promotion. For these were his words:

John by the grace of God king of England etc., to the prior
and convent of St. Edmunds etc.

At the legate's request we have discussed with your abbot
elect the matter of his election. But since we were unable to give
time to it because of much pressing business, we have suspended
its effective completion until we return to England. Then, by
God's grace, we will discuss it with you amicably, doing, if the
Lord will, what is pleasing to God and fruitful for your house.

At the same time he wrote another letter to the bishop of Winchester as follows:

John by the grace of God king of England etc., to his venerable
father in Christ Peter by His grace bishop of Winchester etc.

At the request of Master Robert, legate of France, we spoke
with the abbot elect of St. Edmunds about his election, that
good results might be achieved, God willing, when we return
to England; and so we order you to see that the corn and woods
and all the possessions of his abbey which are in our hand are
kept in peace, so that nothing is taken or plundered from them
until we come to England.

Meanwhile the appointed day, St. Michael's,[1] arrived, and both
parties met together in the guest-house. And although the enemies
of truth and of the Church tried to annul the delegates' jurisdiction,
by the divine decree and just will of God all the allegations which
they advanced against the election's validity—known to everyone
present—exposed them to the adverse judgement of the clergy and
laity there. After some argument about the charges and replies,
the decree of the chapter[2] was asked for. When Master Richard of
Dereham had clearly recited it in everyone's hearing, Richard the
precentor, rising a little from his seat sang out: 'By the Lord's
face, that decree is false!' To intone his antiphon more sweetly
Master John of Houton[3] rose and demonstrated by reasoned,

---

[2] i.e. the convent's *carta de rato* (see above, p. 11).

[3] The two Masters were evidently advocates for the election-party. John of
Houton was archdeacon of Beds. by 1216–17; *Pinchbeck Register*, ed. Lord
F. Hervey (Brighton, 1926), i. 480.

euidenti ratione atque probabili ostendit ipsum cantorem per illud
contradictum litem contestasse.[1] Hiis igitur peractis et iam coram
Wyntoniensi, parti aduerse in auxilium occurrente, recitatis, cum
festinacione mandauit iudices per Matheum Mantel et Eustachium
de Faukenberge.[2] Erat autem ipse in camera abbatis cum multitudine magnatum et potentium, hac speciali de causa ut electionem
impedirent. Accedentibus ad eum iudicibus, nunc minas nunc
blandimenta nunc persuasiones ut diem illum ad alium protel-
lassent pretendit, preostenso eciam dominum regem, sicut a
quibusdam in mandatis acceperat, iam dicte electioni suum pre-
buisse assensum; rogans et consulens,[a] pro bono pacis et scandalo
inter alterutrum partem uitando, ut[b] alium diem partibus statu-
erent, ita quidem quod nichil alicui super obiectis et responsis ad
diem deperisset, promittendo[c] sub sacramento ab illo die in antea
neque per se nec[d] per alium ab eo destinatum facte electioni fieri
detrimentum, etiam si dictus electus gratiam domini regis interim
non obtinuisset. Cuius tamen uicti precibus[e] difficilime adquieuerunt, aliumque diem partibus dederunt, ut scilicet in hiis actibus
continetur:

> In crastino autem sancti Michaelis, constitutis in presentia
> nostra apud sanctum Aedmundum procuratoribus partis electi
> et procuratoribus partis contradictorum eius, presente etiam
> iusticiario cum multis magnatibus regni, disputatum est plenarie
> super quibusdam excepcionibus que iurisdictionem nostram
> cassare uidebantur. Quibus de consilio peritorum cassatis et
> articulis edicionis plenius dilucidatis, prouisis etiam expensis x.
> librarum inter aduocatos utriusque partis diuidendis, et
> H(ugoni) electo ad dominum regem profecto x. marcis prouisis,
> dedimus diem peremptorium partibus apud ecclesiam de Cruce
> Roies[4] ut iuri pareant, scilicet diem Veneris proximam ante
> festum sancti Martini;[3] hac ratione precipue moti, quod spera-
> bamus predictum electum gratiam domini regis interim impe-
f. 184ᵛ   > traturum, uel nuntium nostrum, per quem dominum | regem
> admonuimus sepedicte electioni suum impertiri assensum, infra
> dictum diem rediturum.

His igitur ordine supradicto terminatis dominoque electo circa
regem Pictauia existentem moram faciente et iam eo ad peticionem

---

    a consulans H   *b* aut H   *c* permittendo H   *d* *Added in marg.*
by Hand A   *e* precidus H

---

[1] i.e. the precentor had made a formal contradiction of Master Richard's
statement, thus beginning an action against himself, on the issue of the decree's
validity.

plausible argument that by his contradictory statement the precentor had contested the suit.[1] Afterwards these things were reported to the bishop of Winchester by the adverse party, who
ran to him for help, and with all haste he sent for the judges by
Matthew Mantel and Eustace de Fauconberg.[2] For he was in the
abbot's chamber with a great many magnates and powerful men
especially to hinder the election. When the judges had come before
him he used threats, coaxing, and persuasion in turn to make them
postpone the business to another day. His main reason was that
the king, as he understood from his mandates, had now offered
his assent to the election. So he asked and advised them, for the
sake of peace and to avoid scandal between the parties, to appoint
another day for them, for no one had suffered so far over the
charges and replies. And he promised on oath that from that day
on nothing would be done to the election's detriment by himself
or by his orders, even if the abbot elect had not in the meantime
obtained the king's favour. With great reluctance they acquiesced,
conquered by his entreaties, and gave the parties another day, as
contained in the following acts:

On the day after St. Michael's at St. Edmunds, the proctors
of the parties defending and opposing the abbot elect met before
ourselves, the justiciar and many of the magnates of the realm.
Certain exceptions which seemed to annul our jurisdiction were
fully debated, which were quashed by the advice of the jurists,
and the items making up the reply were more fully clarified.
It was provided that the sum of £10 should be divided among
each party's advocates, and that 10 marks should be paid for the
abbot elect's journey to the king. And we appointed the Friday
before St. Martin's day[3] for the parties' case, at the church of
Royston.[4] This we did mainly because we hoped that the abbot
elect would gain the king's favour in the meantime, or that our
messenger, by whom we warned the king to give the election
his assent, would return before that day.

Meanwhile the abbot elect, who was staying near the king in
Poitou, and had been admitted to his favour at the legate Robert's

[2] Both curials; the former sheriff of Herts. and Beds., the latter the king's
treasurer and later bishop of London.
[3] 7 November.
[4] The Augustinian priory of Royston, Herts.

domini*a* R(oberti) legati, ut superius habetur, in gratiam eiusdem admisso, precepit dominus rex electo ut uersus Angliam quam cicius properasset; erat enim et illum cum omni festinacione ibidem subsecuturus. Factumque est ita, ut uno eodemque tempore dominus rex et electus in Angliam uenissent, licet locis diuersis applicuissent. Applicuit enim dominus rex apud Dertesmue in crastino sancti Wilfridi episcopi,[1] et dominus H(ugo) electus eodem die apud Doure.

Inter hec autem profectus erat magister Ricardus de Derham ad dominum Wyntoniensem cum litteris domini regis prohibicionis, scilicet ne res seu nemora uel mobilia ad abbatiam pertinentia distraherentur seu destruentur. Quo inuento apud Corf,[2] ubi etiam dominus rex affuit presens, suspensum est negotium donec idem Wyntoniensis super hoc regis uoluntatem plenius percepisset. Cui cum Wyntoniensis super hoc mencionem fecisset, precepit dominus rex cum festinacione litteras in hec uerba fieri:

I(ohannes) Dei gratia rex Anglie etc., custodibus abbatie sancti Aedmundi salutem.

Ad peticionem magistri R(oberti) de Curtun legati Francie locuti fuimus cum electo sancti Aedmundi super negotio electionis sue, quod Deo fauente bonum sortietur processum; et ideo uobis mandamus quod blada eiusdem abbatie et nemora et omnes possessiones in manu nostra existentes in bona pace custodiri faciatis, ita quod nil ammoueatur uel diripiatur donec aliud mandauerimus.

Quas cum magister Ricardus apud sanctum Aedmundum detulisset, die scilicet sanctorum Romani et Seuerini,[3] statim denunciatum est balliuis abbatie quatinus in crastino apud sanctum Aedmundum apparuissent, preceptum domini regis audituri; quod utique factum est. Illa itaque die uenit dominus H(ugo) electus domum, hac speciali de causa, ut cartas et munimenta a regibus super electione libera antiquitus confirmata domino regi secum asportaret inspicienda. Dominus autem rex, dummodo Pictauia*b* existeret, ad peticionem dicti legati promiserat electo quod si carte et munimenta nostra liberam nobis testificassent electionem, in aduentu suo in Angliam facte electioni impertiretur assensum. Quo cum sacrista cognouisset, spemque aliquam de processu electionis iam concepisset, moleste tulit, et pertrahens intra se qualiter regis mutaret propositum, ne promouendo electum illud

---

a H *adds* regis, *canc. by scribe*   *b* *Twice* H; *first canc. by Hand C*

[1] 13 October. This is the only source to give John's place of landing, and the date appears to be more accurate than that in Wendover, who gives the 19th

request, as said earlier, was ordered by the king to return to England with all speed, for he would shortly follow him there. And so it happened that the king and the abbot elect arrived in England at one and the same time, although they disembarked at different places, the king at Dartmouth on the day after the feast of St. Wilfrid bishop[1] and Hugh on the same day at Dover.

Meanwhile Master Richard of Dereham had gone to the bishop of Winchester with the king's letter prohibiting the plundering or destruction of the abbey's possessions, woods, and movables.[2] But when he had found him with the king at Corfe the matter was suspended until the bishop had sounded the king's mind more fully over it. When the bishop mentioned it the king ordered a letter to be composed at once, in these words:

> John by the grace of God king of England etc., to the guardians of the abbey of St. Edmund, greetings.
>
> At the request of Master Robert de Courçon, legate of France, we spoke with the abbot elect of St. Edmunds about his election, so that, God willing, a suitable solution might be arrived at. So we order you to ensure that the corn and woods and other of his abbey's possessions which are in our hand are kept in good order, so that nothing is stolen or plundered from them, until you hear further from us.

Master Richard brought this to St. Edmunds on the feast of SS. Romanus and Severinus,[3] and it was at once announced that the abbey's bailiffs were to come to St. Edmunds the next day to hear the king's orders; and thus it was done. On the same day Hugh came to the house, his intention being to take for the king's inspection the charters and muniments confirmed by the ancient monarchs defending our right of free election. For the king, while in Poitou, at the legate's request had promised the abbot elect, that if our charters and muniments testified to our right of free election, he would give his assent to the election as made on his return to England. When the sacrist got wind of this, and realized that now there was some hope of the election's consummation, he took it badly. Pondering within himself how the king's decision could be altered (lest as well as favouring the abbot elect he should

(Wendover, ii. 111). The *Itinerary* states that he was in Dartmouth on the 15th, at Dorchester on the 17th, and at Corfe on the 18th.

[2] John was at Corfe 18–20 October (*Itinerary*).

[3] 23 October.

duceret in effectum, assumpsit secum Thomam Capram, sue
infidelitati similem, festinauitque illo die quo dominus H(ugo)
electus uenit domum de Pictauia occurrere regi, perturbando
scilicet electi promocionem.

Factoque crastino, id est Sabbato ante festum apostolorum
Simonis et Iude,[1] uenit H(ugo) electus in capitulum, et ostenso
qualiter dominum regem communi consilio Pictauia adisset, et
super negocio suo quale*a* ibidem, ut superius habetur, responsum
ab eodem recepisset, humiliter peciit, ut carte, scilicet sancti
Aedwardi gloriosique regis Henrici, liberam nobis confirmantes
electionem et protestantes, non habito ad eius personam respectu,
sed pocius ad libertatem beati patroni sui Aedmundi indemnem
conseruandam et illibatam, domino regi secum mitterentur in-
spiciende. Quibus propositis, omnes aduersarii tanquam ex uno
ore reclamabant, dicentes: 'Dominus noster rex nudius tertius
nobis per litteras suas significauit, in proximo nos uisitaturus*b*
amicabiliterque de pace inter nos tractaturus; quamobrem osten-
sionem cartarum ad presens contradicimus, donec eius presentiam
uideamus.'

His igitur hoc ordine completis, capituloque finito, et ex more
regule sedente electo cum aliis in claustro,[2] ad locucionem accessit
ad eum Iudas Scariot, pretendens ei osculum pacis, dicens: ' "Aue
rabi", et osculatus est eum.'[3] Nomen uero illius erat Adam, et non
uacat quod dicitur 'Adam', id est, 'in dolo dans aue'.[4] Hic enim
erat primus postquam idem H(ugo) electus erat, qui pretendebat
ei xenia sua in dolo, uidelicet in cogleariis argenti et culcitro ut,
sicut satis expresse habetur, eo acrius eundem postmodum infes-
f. 185   taret, quo ipse de | eius amicitia presumeret specialius. Siue potest
dici 'Adam' a 'dando aliena';[4] dedit enim quod non habuit; osculum
quidem pretendens pacem dissimulauit exterius, dum dolum et
dolorem in corde machinaretur interius. Nam in media nocte
sequenti, postquam eundem osculatus erat in die, assumptis secum
Ricardo precentore et Philippo, iter suum uersus regem propera-
uit, ut ipsi cum sacrista et Thoma Capra Ricardoque Caluo, curie
regis existentibus, facte electioni, licet contra sentenciam excommunicationis, modis omnibus et uiribus resisterent.

Igitur dominus H(ugo), consilio fidelium, cum transcripto
predictarum cartarum sub sigillo prioris incluso, die sanctorum
Crispini et Crispiniani,[5] comitantibus secum Petro celerario,

---

a qualem H   *b* uisitaturos H

[1] 25 October.
[2] *Reg. Ben.* contains no obvious reference; but see Lanfranc, *Constitutions,*
pp. 4–5, where conversation in the cloister after chapter is specifically mentioned.

consent to his election), he took Thomas the Goat, his like in disloyalty, and hurried to meet the king on the very day when the
abbot elect returned home from Poitou, hoping to throw his
promotion into disorder.

The next day, being the Saturday before the feast of the apostles
Simon and Jude,[1] Hugh entered the chapter-house and told how
by the advice of all he had approached the king in Poitou, and what
reply he had received, as already related. And he asked humbly for
the charters of St. Edward and of the glorious King Henry,
declaring and confirming our freedom of election, to be sent with
him for the king's inspection, not out of respect for his own
person, but rather to keep safe and unharmed the liberties of their
blessed patron Edmund. To this proposal all his enemies cried out
with one voice, saying: 'Our king wrote to us the day before
yesterday, saying that he would visit us shortly and negotiate an
amicable settlement with us. We oppose, therefore, the showing
of our charters until he is here in person.'

After this matter was closed and chapter over, the abbot elect
took his seat with the others in the cloister, according to the custom
of the *Rule*,[2] and Judas Iscariot came to speak with him, offering
him the kiss of peace, saying: 'Hail, rabbi', and kissing him.[3] This
was Adam, and not for nothing was this his name, since it signifies
'the giving of a treacherous greeting.'[4] For after Hugh's election
he had been the first to present him gifts—silver spoons and a
coverlet. But this was done in treachery, as became clear enough, so
that, having been especially privileged with his friendship, he
could attack him all the more keenly later. Just as 'Adam' can also
be derived from 'giving what belongs to another',[4] so he gave what
he did not possess, simulating peace outwardly by a kiss, while
harbouring treachery and resentment in his innermost heart. For
no sooner had he kissed Hugh that day, than he went quickly to
the king in the dead of the following night, accompanied by
Richard the precentor and Philip, so that, staying at the king's
court together with the sacrist, Thomas the Goat, and Richard the
Bald, they could oppose the election by all ways and means,
although in the face of the sentence of excommunication.

Hugh therefore, by his faithful friends' advice, went to the king
on the day of SS. Crispin and Crispinian[5] with copies of their

---

[3] Matt. 26: 49; Marc. 14: 45.
[4] These are not true etymologies, but verbal puns.   [5] 25 October.

Ricardo de Heingham, Roberto camerario, R(ogero) filio Drogonis, magistro Nicholao, Ricardo de Saxham, iter suum uersus regem direxit. Veniente quidem domino H(ugone) ad curiam, domino regi extra Londoniam cum dictis sociis ocurrit.[1] Quem ut sacrista, Adam infirmarius, cantor, Philippus, Ricardus de Storteford et Thomas Capra eminus intuissent, circumdantes circumde-derunt[2] regem ne electus uel socii eius ad eum haberent accessum, sicut nocte precedenti apud Wyndlesoures[3] inter eosdem fuit prolocutum, ubi et coram domino rege omnia mala contra ele-ctionem proposuerant. Quo uix accedente, et cum rege super electionis sue negocio sermocinante, tale ab eo accepit responsum: 'Accede ad Wyntoniensem; ipse enim exponet tibi uoluntatem meam.' Cui accedens, licet nichil fructuosum percipiens, reuersus est ad regem. Sicque ter[a] dominus rex, nescio quo spiritu ductus,[4] dominum H(ugonem) electum illo die, licet in uanum, transmisit ad Wyntoniensem. Mane autem facto[5] accessit electus ad regem in capella, ubi nondum missa fuit celebrata. Qua tandem finita dixit electus: 'Domine mi rex, laboraui sustinens super adquirenda gratia uestra et audire per uos seu per Wyntoniensem responsa, cum nullum adhuc penitus recepissem.'[b] Ad quem rex: 'Quid uis ut dicam tibi? Ego pocius diligo me et coronam meam quam te uel honorem tuum. Excitasti enim bellum contra me, ⟨a⟩ quo[c] nequaquam bonum consequetur effectum.' Quod cum dominus H(ugo) instanter negasset, ut decuit, adiunxit rex: 'Non utique propter te specialiter hoc dixi, sed et propter alios quosdam.'[6] Igitur dominus H(ugo), cum in adquirendam domini regis tunc gratiam non posset[d] amplius proficisci,[e] domum reuersus est die omnium sanctorum,[7] quem quidem die Martis sequenti[8] secutus est rex. Sed non est pretermittendum quod antequam dominus rex apud sanctum Aedmundum uenisset, tale mandatum in crastino omnium sanctorum[9] priori et conuentui per litteras suas destinauit:

I(ohannes) Dei gratia rex Anglie etc., priori et conuentui etc. Audiuimus quod H(ugo) de Norewalde, qui se facit electum

---

[a] tercio H   [b] recepisset H   [c] quod H   [d] H *adds* tunc
[e] proficissi H

---

[1] John was in London 28 October (*Itinerary*).
[2] Ps. 117: 11.   [3] 27 October (*Itinerary*).
[4] This phrase suggests that the writer was present at the time.
[5] Num. 22: 41; cf. above, p. 18 n. 1.
[6] Who were these 'certain others'? Other churchmen would seem to be meant, probably the archbishop of Canterbury and other bishops who supported the papal position on elections, and who favoured the baronial cause.

charters, impressed with the prior's seal, accompanied by Peter the cellarer, Richard of Hingham, Robert the chamberlain, Roger FitzDrew, Master Nicholas, and Richard of Saxham. Coming to court with these friends, then, Hugh met the king outside London.[1] When the sacrist, Adam the infirmarer, the precentor, Philip, Richard of Stortford, and Thomas the Goat saw him coming from a distance, they surrounded[2] the king, so that neither the abbot elect nor his friends could have access to him; for they had planned this the night before at Windsor,[3] where they had spoken all sorts of evil things against the election before the king. When the abbot elect did manage with great difficulty to see the king and talk with him about the election, he received this reply: 'Go to the bishop of Winchester; he will tell you my wishes.' So he went, but got nothing from him and returned to the king. And three times that day, with what motive I do not know,[4] the king sent Hugh to the bishop of Winchester, but nothing came of it. The next morning[5] the abbot elect came to the king in his chapel before mass. When it had been celebrated the abbot elect said: 'My lord king, I have worked hard to gain your favour and to obtain an answer from you or the bishop of Winchester, but so far it has got me absolutely nowhere.' To whom the king: 'What do you want me to say to you? I have to consider myself and my crown before you and your honour. You have stirred up rebellion against me from which you can expect no good result!' But when Hugh stoutly denied this as was only right, the king added: 'I did not say this with reference to you in particular, but on account of certain others as well.'[6] Hugh therefore, seeing that there was no point in continuing his attempts to gain the king's favour on this occasion, returned home on All Saints' day,[7] followed in fact by the king on the following Tuesday.[8] But you must know that before his arrival the king sent this letter to the prior and convent on the day after All Saints:[9]

John by the grace of God king of England etc., to the prior and convent etc.

We have heard that Hugh of Northwold, who calls himself

[7] 1 November.

[8] 4 November. The *Itinerary* shows that John was at Bury and Long Melford on this date, and elsewhere on the 3rd and 5th, thus supporting the author's chronology.

[9] 2 November.

uestrum, dedit uobis intelligere quod gratiam nostram habet et beniuolentiam. Sed ut rei ueritas uobis planius innotescat, uobis mandamus quod nunquam gratiam nostram promeruit, nec aliquid erga nos fecit quare illam habere debeat.

Subsecuto uero rege dicto die, id est die Martis post festum omnium sanctorum, et honorifice a conuentu ut decuit suscepto, statim denuntiauit illis se capitulum intraturum,[a] super negocio electionis, sicut ante mandauerat, tractaturum. Introeunte domino rege capitulum, nullo laico secum comitante[b] preterquam Segerio de Quenci comite Wincestrie et Philippo de Hulekotes,[1] gladium coram rege portante, factoque silentio magno,[2] sic ora resoluit:[3] 'Fratres mei, licet abutar intrare sepius capitulum monachorum, facta tamen peregrinatione mea, in corde duxi uos presentaneo uisitaturus[c] accessu. Nunc igitur, quia Domino disponente propositum duxi in effectum, rogo uos ut in processu uestre electionis minus discrete ⟨quam debuit⟩ facte seruato iure meo semper f. 185ᵛ usitato procedatis. Quod | si feceritis, et in[d] consiliis meis adquieueritis, sublato dilacionis periculo illum qui se gerit electum uel alium secundum uestram dispositionem, quemcumque de uobismetipsis elegeritis, recipiam in pastorem et gratiam. Si uero in hunc modum consiliis meis utpote sanis aures uestras non inclinaueritis, licet inuitus tria uobis pericula emergentia predico, ut illis saltem cognitis de duobus malis partem eligatis meliorem. Primum quidem est, quod domus uestra per controuersiam[e] super electione uestra siue dissensionem inter uos subortam, processu temporis in paupertatem incidet et penuriam. Secundum uero, quod fama uestra omni religione et parte repleta denigrabitur.[f] Tercia autem, quod odium principis incurretis.'[4] Hiis ideo tribus de causis a domino rege premissis, consulendo precepit electo, ut super electione in manu regis resignanda, atque appellationibus pro eadem factis resignandis, una cum suis consuleret. Cui mox dominus H(ugo) electus, ut per cuius os Spiritus aperte loquebatur Sanctus,[5] ait: 'Licet omnia nostra in manu domini nostri regis sint

---

[a] intracturum H, *which adds* gladium coram rege portante, factoque silencio magno sic ora resoluit, *canc. by scribe*   [b] comitatante H, *corr. by scribe*   [c] uisitaturos H   [d] *Added over line by Hand C*   [e] conuersiam H   [f] denigrabatur H

[1] One of John's captains, a loyal servant who was entrusted with various offices, although not of any considerable feudal position (Painter, pp. 252, 268–9, 304, 352, etc.).   [2] *Reg. Ben.*, c. 65; cf. above, p. 7 n. 7.   [3] A Virgilian tag; cf. above, p. 89 n. 2.

your abbot elect, has given you to understand that he has our favour and goodwill. But that you may know the real facts more fully, we inform you that he has never deserved our grace, nor has he done anything for us whereby he ought to have it.

On the king's arrival, being the Tuesday after All Saints, he was received by the convent with appropriate honour; at once he expressed his intention of entering their chapter-house, to discuss the business of the election, as he had notified them earlier. When he had entered the chapter-house, unaccompanied by any layman except Saer de Quency, earl of Winchester and Philip de Ulecotes,[1] who carried the sword before him, complete silence prevailed[2] and the king delivered himself as follows:[3] 'My brothers, although I am not in the habit of entering a chapter of monks very often, nevertheless I thought it a good idea, after performing my pilgrimage, to visit you here. Now therefore, as I have by God's will put my proposal into effect, I ask that in the matter of your election, which was not made discreetly enough, you proceed in obedience to my customary rights. If you do this and abide by my advice, then, without any dangerous delay, I will receive as your pastor and admit to my favour whomsoever you choose from among you, either him who calls himself abbot elect, or any other you please, just as you shall decide. But if you close your ears in this way to my counsel, although it is sound, I warn you, although against my will, of three dangers ahead, so that at least, knowing which are the two worse, you may choose the third and least evil. The first is, that your house, owing to the quarrel or dissension which has broken out amongst you over your election, is likely in course of time to fall into poverty. The second, that your reputation spread among all men of religion and in every place, will be besmirched. The third, that you will incur your ruler's hatred.'[4] For these three reasons the king advised the abbot elect to discuss with his friends the possibility of resigning his election into his hand, and of withdrawing the appeals in its defence. Then the abbot elect Hugh, as one through whose mouth the Holy Spirit clearly spoke,[5] said: 'Although all our belongings are placed in

---

[4] A conciliatory speech from John, indicating that he had no personal objection to Hugh, and testifying to the weakness of his political position. A few days later, 21 November, he granted the well-known charter bestowing the right of free election on the churches of his realm (*Councils*, pp. 38–41).

[5] Act. 1: 16.

posita, et ad ipsum spectet de iure libertates ecclesiasticas inde-
mnes seruare et illibatas, regie tamen uoluntati per omnia et in
omnibus, saluo iure ecclesiastico, libenter obediam.'[1] Quibus
premissis coram rege, seruato in omnibus iure ecclesiastico,
precepit rex consilio Pharaonis et excercitus eius,[2] ut pars a parte
separaretur. Estimabat enim, sicut a Pharaone (id est ⟨sacrista⟩)
acceperat,[a] quod in regia presentia non inueniret, pre timore regie
maiestatis, de toto conuentu vi. eius uoluntati repugnantes. Sed
res mira et ualde obstupenda,[3] quod facta diuisione inter partem
utramque, ad regis edictum hinc inde in capitulo sedentem, miro
modo repleta est pars fidelitatis in parte dextera capituli collocata,
super partem sacriste in parte sinistra capituli sedentem. Vnde pre
admiratione rei euentus et miraculo preostenso, repleta est pars
infidelis (id est sacriste) stupore et extasi,[4] necnon et ipse rex. Sed
non est pretermittendum quod Ricardus de Neuport et Iohannes
de Disce, duo scilicet apostate,[b] cognita superius transgressione
sacramenti prestiti super electione coram iudicibus in pleno
capitulo, et ab eisdem suscepta penitentia, uouentes ab illo die in
antea cum sacramento ueritatis firmiter perseuerare,[5] illo die
coram rege partem dextere excelsi[6] relinquentes, licet contra uotum
suum et sacramentum, inter discipulos antichristi sinistrum
chorum capituli tenentes se collocauerunt. Intuens quidem pars
ueritatis se, interuenientibus meritis gloriose genetricis Dei Marie,
necnon et beati patroni sui Aedmundi, pro cuius dignitatibus usque
ad effusionem sanguinis, si tamen necesse esset, audacter certarent,
iam interna recreacione uisitati,[7] abiecto timore seruili, induti[c]
sunt spiritu fortitudinis,[8] atque pre ceteris illud Dominicum
habentes: 'Cum steteritis ante reges et principes, nolite cogitare
quomodo aut quid loquamini; dabitur enim uobis in illa hora quid
loquamini',[9] erexit se unus de tribu Iuda, Robertus scilicet camerarius, et stans in medio coram rege sub breuitate uerborum
modum electionis et sacramentum in capitulo factum, necnon et
confirmaciones regum, predecessorum scilicet suorum, ut beati

---

[a] acciperat H   [b] apostati H   [c] inducti H

[1] Perhaps consciously reminiscent of Becket? See *Materials for the History of
Thomas Becket, RS* iii. 273, 279.
[2] Exod. 15: 4.
[3] Gregory, *Dialogus*, i. 10, 200: 'Res mira et uehementer stupenda. . . '.

our lord king's hand, whose rightful prerogative it is to maintain
the liberties of the Church unharmed and inviolate, I will nevertheless cheerfully obey his will in all things and on all occasions,
saving the law of the Church.'[1] After this statement, by which the
Church's rights were fully guarded, the king, on the advice of
Pharaoh and his host,[2] commanded the two parties to divide. For,
according to what Pharaoh (the sacrist) had told him, he imagined
that in his presence, from fear of the royal majesty, he would not
find half a dozen monks in the whole convent who would resist
his will. But a wonderful and quite astonishing thing happened,[3]
for when the parties divided at the king's command, taking their
seats on either side of the chapter-house, the faithful party on the
right outnumbered to a quite amazing extent the sacrist's party
seated on the left. The unfaithful sacrist's party, astonished at
such a miraculous occurrence, were struck dumb with confusion,[4]
as was the king himself. But you must know that Richard of Newport and John of Diss, the two apostates who, as mentioned
earlier, had received penance before the judges in full chapter
after confessing their transgression of the election oath, and had
promised to persevere firmly in the future in support of the oath
of truth,[5] left the party 'on the right hand of the Most High'[6] that
day before the king, contrary to their promise and oath, and
assembled with the servants of antichrist on the left side of the
chapter-house. But the party of truth, protected by the merits of
Mary, glorious mother of God, and of their blessed patron Edmund,
for whose dignities they were ready to contend bravely and, if
necessary, to shed their blood, were visited with renewed spiritual
strength.[7] Casting from them servile fear, and putting on a brave
spirit,[8] they held to these words of the Lord before their fellows:
'When you shall stand before kings and princes, take no thought
for what or how you will speak; for in that hour it will be given
you what you shall say.'[9] One of this tribe of Judah, Robert the
chamberlain, rose, and standing in the midst before the king he
described clearly and succinctly the manner of the election and the
oath taken in chapter, and also the confirmations of their freedom

---

[4] Act. 3: 10.
[5] See above, p. 91. But only Richard of Newport was mentioned.
[6] Ps. 76: 10.
[7] Cf. Abbo (*Mem.* i. 16): '. . . iam recreabatur uisione internae lucis. . . .'
[8] Is. 11: 2.
[9] Matt. 10: 18–19 (cf. Marc. 13: 9–11).

Aedwardi gloriosique Henrici patris sui, insuper et ipsius, confirmantes nobis liberam electionem, dilucide monstrauit et aperte;
rogando postmodum ut huic facto ita sollemniter et canonice
celebrato, ob amorem Dei genetricis et beati Aedwardi suum
diucius non denegaret^a impertiri assensum. Quibus ita propositis
dominus rex uertit se ad partem sinistram, dicens: 'En, audistis
quanta iste proposuit contra uos!';[1] tanquam diceret: 'O uos
contradictores parti electionis, necnon et ipsi electo, et sub
uinculo sacramenti mihi astricti electionem quamuis canonice
factam in assuetam consuetudinem meam reuocare, quid respon-
detis contra obiecta uobis?' Cui sacrista: 'Domine mi rex, proposita eius narratione falsa et intellecta, subticuit quod uerum est.
Ego quidem domino meo regi rem gestam et eorum iniquitatem in
f. 186 facto | electionis per omnia exponam. Rei quidem ueritas est, quod
tres elegerunt septem et conuentui presentauerunt. Quibus presen-
tatis, quidam stimulo superbie et inuidie agitati, contra unum
illorum septem maliciose insurgentes, pre magnitudine uirtutis
eius et scientie ammouerunt illum, et alium minus dignum in loco
eius substituerunt. Quibus tamen huius⟨modi⟩ forma (non utique
seruata) sub prestito sacramento^b erat^c suppressa, uidelicet ut
illum susciperent in pastorem qui a pluribus a conuentu nomina-
retur. Hiis igitur ita maliciose et subdole peractis, et ab illis
septem examen singulorum de conuentu in scriptum redactum,
seminator iste tocius discordie et inuentor, scilicet Thomas de
Walsingham, apprehendens scriptum, in partes reduxit multiplices
etiam sociis suis inconsultis, et hac ratione, ne dicta forma, scilicet
de persona in quem plures de conuentu consensissent, obserua-
retur. Huius igitur electionis facte hec est ueritas, et sic maliciose
et subdole et non canonice in ea per eundem processum est.'
Cumque antichristus ille (id est sacrista) coram rege quod
uerum erat et purum sicut^d in scoriam[2] reducere conaretur,
surexerunt uniuersi fideles uoce consona reclamando, dicentes:
'Quoniam ista manifeste falsa non sine magna premeditacione
coram domino nostro rege proposuisti, ecce! angelus Domini stans
in medio accepta sententia scindet^e te medio![3] Penitere ergo dum
licet, ne tunc non liceat cum^f incipias uelle penitere.'[4]

^{a} denegasset H ^{b} *Twice* H ^{c} era H ^{d} sic et H
^{e} scedet H ^{f} *Added in marg. by Hand C*

---

[1] Cf. Matt. 27: 13, and above, p. 18 n. 5.
[2] Is. 1: 22: cf. above, p. 18 n. 4.

of election made by his predecessors, the blessed Edward and the
glorious Henry his father, and by himself as well. And then he
asked that out of love for the mother of God and the blessed
Edward he might no longer deny his assent to this deed so solemnly
and canonically celebrated. At this the king turned to the party on
the left, saying: 'There; you hear how much he has brought
against you!'[1] as much as to say: 'O you opponents of the election
party and of the abbot elect, you who are bound under oath to
bring the election, even if canonically performed, into line with my
customary liberties, what have you to say to these objections?'
To whom the sacrist: 'My lord king, his story, told cunningly and
falsely, suppressed the truth. But I will explain in full to my lord
king the nature of the deed itself and the iniquitous way they
went about it. The truth of the matter is that three men chose
seven and presented them to the convent. But after they had been
presented, some men incited by pride and envy rose up wickedly
against one of those seven, and removed him because of his great
virtue and wisdom, substituting another less worthy man in his
place. In this way the procedure adopted earlier under oath,
namely that they would receive as pastor him who was named by a
majority of the convent—not kept to anyway—was quite disregarded. After these evil and malicious deeds had been perpetrated, the opinion of each member of the convent was taken down
in writing by those seven. Then that inventor and disseminator of
all discord, Thomas of Walsingham, getting hold of this document,
edited it without even consulting his friends, so that the procedure
of choosing the person in whom a majority of the convent had
consented could not be followed. Now this is the truth about the
election, that it proceeded deceitfully and maliciously, and not
canonically in one person agreed to by all.' When that antichrist
the sacrist had tried to reduce what was pure and true to dross[2]
before the king, all the faithful rose, crying with one voice:
'Because you have told the king such lies, obviously well pre-
meditated, behold! may the angel of the Lord who stands in our
midst and hears your words cut you off in our midst;[3] repent,
therefore, while you may, lest, when you later begin to desire
repentance, you are refused.'[4]

[3] Dan. 13: 55.
[4] Cf. New York Pierpont Morgan Library MS. 736, pp. 55–6: 'Quapropter
dum licet iniustam sententiam corrige, ut forte cum uolueris, minime liceat.'

Erigens se quidem Ricardus precentor cepit balbuciendo confirmare quod sacrista proposuerat. Interrumpens quidem H(ugo)
de Thefford eius sermonem coram rege, ait: 'Si ad regis domini
nostri sederit uoluntatem, ut huius rei ueritas coram eo serenius
patefiat, suscitetur a precentore nobis, domino nostro suggerenti,
utrum ipse una nobiscum presente corpore Dominico iurauerit[a] se
suscepturum illum in pastorem, quem post examinacionem singulorum nobis septem donassent.' Cui precentor, utpote cuius
spiritus totus sistit in naribus, sine deliberatione sui ait: 'Quoniam
ueritati uniuersis notorie difficillimum est repugnare, fateor plane
uerum esse quod proposuisti, quod iam penitet me fecisse.' Ad
que H(ugo) de Thefford: 'Nunc igitur, domine rex, super huius
delicto publice confesso uestrum est penitentiam iniungere.'
Quibus dictis, et pre magna confusione responsionis precentoris
pars aduersa retro abeuntes, accesserunt magister Thomas de
Walsingham et Ricardus de Saxham ad regem, acriter et uerbis
asperis exhortantes ut ipse secundum confirmaciones predecessorum suorum, necnon et ipsius, tractare non[b] dedignaretur
conuentum in electione canonice et secundum Deum et canones
facta. Quibus dominus rex: 'Fratres, carta inusitata[1] nullius
ualoris est; et quoniam hucusque ista subticuistis, ita ut in nullo
tempore per aliquem libertatibus meis usitatis sint obiecta in
contrarium, uana reputanda sunt et friuola.' Quidam autem reuche[2]
de parte aduersa cognomento Taillehaste — utinam bonus
emulator[3] — regiam plus studens captare beniuolentiam[4] quam
libertatibus ecclesie sue saluandis (si tamen necesse esset occum-
bere!), plane coram rege, cunctis audientibus, priuilegiis nostris
nobis a regibus confirmatis contradixit. Post quem subsecutus est
alter, eidem malicie nequaquam ⟨carens⟩, Henricus cognomento
scilicet Rufus, dicens: 'Adorande rex et tremende, ego iam in
senio positus numerum iam sub hac forma religionis compleui
quinquagenarium. Nunc igitur, quoniam pro libertatibus uestris
domini nostri regis usitatis una cum uiris omni religione pro-
batis steti decertans, et in hoc quibusdam nouiciis repugnans,
affectus iniuriis, lacessitus opprobriis, minisque innumeris incus-
sus sum sepius et diuersis. Ob quam causam domini mei regis

---

[a] iurauerunt H   [b] *Added in marg. by Hand B*

---

[1] Alternatively, *inusitata* could be translated 'unheard-of'.
[2] Not *renche*, as Arnold transliterated it. In Middle English *reuthe* was

Now rising to his feet Richard the precentor began, stammering, to confirm the sacrist's words. But Hugh of Thetford, interrupting him, said to the king: 'If our lord king wishes to know the true facts more clearly, let us challenge the precentor, at your bidding, as to whether he swore on the sacrament with the rest of us to receive as pastor him whom the seven named, after they had examined everyone individually.' To this the precentor, his heart in his mouth, replied unthinkingly: 'Since it is very difficult to deny what is known to the whole community, I fully admit that what you said is correct, and I wish now that I had not done it.' Upon which Hugh of Thetford said: 'Now therefore, lord king, it is your right to prescribe penance for this wrong which has been publicly confessed!' At these words, much confused by the precentor's reply, the adverse party were put to rout. Master Thomas of Walsingham and Richard of Saxham went to the king and urged him with sharp and reproachful words not to disdain to negotiate with the convent over the election in the spirit of his own and his predecessors' confirmations, for it was lawful according to God and the canons. To this the king replied: 'Brothers, an unused[1] charter is valueless; and because until now you have remained silent about these things, so that they have not been raised at any time in opposition to any of my customary liberties, they must be thought vain and frivolous.' Now a certain grievous fellow[2] of the opposing party named Taillehaste—would he were an emulator of good—[3] striving to gain the royal goodwill[4] rather than to save his church's liberties (if only it had been necessary to die for them!), utterly contradicted the privileges which the kings had confirmed to us before the king while all sat listening. After him followed another of similar wickedness, Henry surnamed Rufus, who said: 'O king to be adored and feared, I am now an old man, having completed fifty years in the religious life. Because I have stood shoulder to shoulder with men of deep and proven religion in defence of our lord king's liberties, opposing in this certain novices, I have been afflicted with wrongs, scandalously provoked, and threatened countless times in diverse manners. For this reason I, unhappy as I am, ask mercy of my lord king, that

normally an abstract noun meaning repentance, sorrow, grief, etc.; see *Stratmann's Middle-English Dictionary*, ed. H. Bradley (Oxford, 1891), s.v. Here, presumably, 'one who causes sorrow'.

[3] 1 Pet. 3: 13; cf. above, p. 86 n. 3.

[4] See above, p. 4 n. 3.

misericordiam miser efflagito, ut ad eorum ardua pericula eui-
tanda uestra saltem pax in me requiescat, atque regia maiestas contra aduersarios dignitatibus suis repugnantes furorem suum
"in manu potenti et brachio extento"[1] exardescat.' Cui ⟨cum⟩ domi-
f. 186ᵛ nus | rex, tanquam dedignando responsa reddere, seu cuius mole-
stiam uel tranquillitatem pro indifferenti sustinens, obmutuisset,
ait Philippus de Hulekotes: 'O homo, regia pace undique consti-
patus ne pertimescas.'

Dominus quidem rex, pre admiratione uisa, immo pre ostenso
miraculo in multitudine monachorum sibi inᵃ facie resistentium,
non modicum paruipendens nec immediate sustinens, minas
eisdem pretendendo sic a capitulo recessit. Cumque de
egressu capituli ad cimbalum[2] peruenisset, accedens ad eum
Thomas Capra — qui uere loquebatur ut capra — ut in eo quod
regi cupiebat placere displicuit, procedensque dominum regem
benedixit in faciem,[3] dicens: 'Letetur cor dominiᵇ nostri regis
super auditis, et etiam non obstupescat. Habet enim hic intus
uiros ualidos et robustos ad regiam per omnia libertatem strenue
protegendam.' Qui et bene dicebatur Thomas, id est 'totus male
sonans'.[4] Hic itaque uersipellis alter erat Iudas, quoniam cum
dominus H(ugo) electus pre magna cordis dileccione et fiducia
secum associasset, et in cameram suam collocasset, sibique priuata
sua denudasset, protraxit intra se quomodo electum more Iude
traderet Iudeis et excercitui, id est, Pharaoni eius, quibus omnia
secreta electi latenter communicauit. Pro quo etiam delicto postmodum cognito a secretis electi separatus est, et ad claustrum
quod dicitur infernus girauagorum siue miserorum[5] repulsus est.
Non sine merito, quia cum prius in honore esset non intellexit,
comparatus est infidelibus, et similis factus est illis.[6]

Superueniente quidem mane, cum uenerabilis H(ugo) domino
regi ob ipsius honorem et reuerentiam preberet extra uillam
conductum, ecce repente uentus uehemens a regione aquilonari,
immo, ut uerius dicam, ipse aquilo, in spiritu fauoris et superbie
taliter domum alterius Iob, id est Hugonis, humilitatis scilicet
gratia ortam,ᶜ impingereᵈ conatus est,[7] dicens: 'Domine mi rex,

---

ᵃ H *adds* fine, *canc. by scribe*   ᵇ dominum H, *corr. by scribe*
ᶜ ortatam H   ᵈ impegere H

---

[1] Deut. 7: 19, etc.
[2] The *cimbalum* was a bell or gong hanging in the cloister near the refectory,
to sound the meal-times. Lanfranc, *Constitutions*, p. 6 n. 2. Alternatively, it
could also refer to the Norman gate-tower of the abbey, which was (and is)
the belfry for the parish church (now cathedral) of St. James.
[3] Iob 1: 11, 2: 5.   [4] See above, p. 115 n. 4.

I may escape their harsh threats, that your peace may at last be in me, and that the royal majesty may flame out in anger "with powerful arm and mighty hand"[1] against the adversaries opposing his dignities.' The king remained silent, disdaining so much as to answer, as if indifferent to his peril or peace, but Philip de Ulecotes said: 'O fellow, fenced in as you are on every side with the king's peace, you need not be afraid.'

Now the king, having seen with astonishment the miraculous number of monks resisting him to his face, took it very ill, nor would he bear it for a moment, but left the chapter-house breathing threats. And when, after leaving the chapter-house, he had come as far as the refectory-bell in the cloister,[2] Thomas the Goat, appropriately named, went to him, desiring to placate his displeasure. Greeting the king to his face[3] he said: 'May our lord king rejoice and not be astonished at what you have heard. For within this house you have strong and brave men ready to protect the royal liberties vigorously and in every way possible.' Thomas was a fitting name for him, as it signifies '*to*tally *ma*levolent in *s*ound',[4] for he had acted like the sly Judas of old. When Hugh, trusting him in the magnanimity of his nature, had made him his confidant, employing him in his chamber and laying bare to him his private affairs, he, Judas-like, was planning how he could deliver up the abbot elect to the Jews and their army, that is, to his Pharaoh, to whom he secretly made known all the abbot elect's private affairs. Once his wickedness became known he was kept from the abbot elect's secrets and banished to the cloister named the 'Inferno of the Gyrovagi' or 'Miserable'.[5] Serve him right! For not appreciating the honour in which he had earlier been held he was numbered with the unfaithful, and made in their likeness.[6]

In the morning Hugh offered to conduct the king out of the vill, to do him honour and reverence, but behold! there came a great wind from the north, or rather, more accurately, the north wind himself, full of pride and partiality, who strove to batter the grace and humility of Hugh like another house of Job,[7] saying: 'My lord

[5] Many monasteries had a chamber named 'inferno' or something similar, for the confinement of recalcitrant monks. There seems to be no other known reference to a chamber of this name at Bury.

[6] Ps. 48: 12, 20.

[7] Iob 1: 19. See Gregory, *Moralia in Iob* (*PL*, lxxv, cols. 520, 525–6, 592), for the spiritual interpretation of Job, the wind, and the house.

iste homo qui se gerit electum uobis assistens, modis omnibus et uiribus coronam regiam nititur a uobis auferre. Et nisi regia prouidentia idem ab hoc malicioso proposito celerius choerceatur recedere, timendum est ne huius rei exordium, hucusque contra regiam dignitatem ab eodem prosecutum, in breui sortiatur effectum.'[1] Quibus in hunc modum coram rege, adiuncto sacramento, a sacrista[a] prosecutis, dictus H(ugo) qui more angelico pius semper experiebatur et modestus, in spiritu lenitatis[2] absque omni fastu superbie, modesta in instanti eidem sacriste reddere festinauit responsa, dicens: 'Omnis fraus et mendacium in se reuersum eo acrius suum ledit amatorem proprium, quo ex percussione peruerse intencionis idem leditur inestimacius. Ne igitur tibi surrepat ut alii alias dolum moliaris, honorando proximum, quantum ad te, manifeste[b] falso, cum in hoc ledaris, incidendo quo impedire nitebaris, sicut et nunc? Sciasque subinde me temporis processu ipsi regi in omnibus suis agendis regnoque suo te utiliorem experiri, neque omnimode uoluntati tue me die hodierna uelle consentire.'

His igitur tali ordine prosecutis subsecutus est dies partibus prefixus apud Crucem Roies,[3] ubi etiam dominus H(ugo) cum procuratoribus cause sue, licet inanibus sumptibus, accessit, sicut in hiis actis euidenter continetur:

Dictis uero die et loco utraque parte constituta, nobis etiam secundum mandatum nobis iniunctum procedere uolentibus, uir uenerabilis dominus W(illelmus) electus Couentrensis[4] nobis in consistorio consistentibus litteras domini regis presentauit, quibus nos duxit erogandos, ut dictis die et loco dicte cause subsederemus, et alium diem competentem daremus, cui peracta peregrinacione sua inchoata posset personaliter interesse, uel procuratorem destinare. Ad eciam efficacius impetrandum, litteras domini Cantuariensis archiepiscopi et suffraganeorum eius nobis in communi porrexit, quarum[c] transcripta penes nos retinemus. Que plenius intuentes, pariterque cum circumstanciis suis, diligenter considerauimus, et de sano quorundam consilio, prehabito ad hoc consensu electi sancti Aedmundi, preces domini regis et aliorum pro se supplicantium duximus admittendas, predicto electo et eius contradictoribus statuentes diem peremptorium, diem Martis proximum post festum sancti

---

[a] sacristia H, *corr. by scribe*   [b] manifesto H   [c] quorum H

---

[1] Was Hugh having dealings with the rebel barons? The famous meeting of the barons at St. Edmunds seems to have taken place at about this time, probably 20 November, the feast of St. Edmund. See Appendix IV.

king, this man assisting you and conducting himself as abbot elect, is working with might and main to deprive you of your royal crown. And unless he is quickly persuaded by the royal provision to abandon this wicked idea, it is to be feared that within a short time he will accomplish what he has even now set in motion against the royal dignity.'[1] To this kind of talk, put forward on oath by the sacrist before the king, Hugh, always of an angelic nature, pious and modest, mild in spirit,[2] and without any arrogant pride, quickly made answer: 'All cunning and falsity turned in upon itself harms its own lover dreadfully with the blows of its perverse intention. Do you not realize how many others you harm by treating one as near you as your own self with manifest falsehood? For in this you are only wounding yourself, aggravating what you are trying to prevent, just as you are right now. And know this, that over the years I have repeatedly been of more use in all the king's business and realm than you; and I have no intention of letting you get your own way today.'

After this the day appointed for the parties at Royston arrived,[3] and Hugh, accompanied by the proctors of his cause attended, although put to useless expense, as is clearly shown in these acts:

On the set day and at the appointed place, both parties came before us. To us, who wished to proceed according to the mandate laid on us, the worthy William, bishop elect of Coventry[4] presented letters from the king while we were sitting in council, which entreated us to postpone the cause from that day and place, and to appoint another day so that, after his unfinished pilgrimage was over, he might attend personally or send a proctor. To add weight to his appeal, moreover, he sent letters addressed to the three of us from the archbishop of Canterbury and his suffragans, of which we retain copies. Diligently considering and examining these in the light of the circumstances, taking the advice of various people, and obtaining the consent of the abbot elect of St. Edmunds, we decided to grant the prayers of the king and those who appealed on his behalf, appointing as a set date for the abbot elect and his

---

[2] Gal. 6: 1.

[3] 7 November.

[4] William of Cornhill, consecrated bishop of Coventry by Stephen Langton, 25 January 1215. A faithful servant of the king, whom he had served for many years on the Exchequer.

f. 187   Nicholai[1] apud ecclesiam sancti Aedmundi, fir|miterque in animo concepimus quod huiusmodi precum obtentu principale negocium de cetero non prorogemus, et hoc idem domino regi litteris nostris communibus[a] significauimus.

Igitur die partibus dato et in hoc utraque[b] adquiescente, peruentum est ad diem statutum. Cumque pars utraque iudicibus in consistorio considentibus ibidem se opponeret, atque super litis[c] contestacione facta seu facienda, propter quod precentor dixerat superius, facta est discussio non modica. Data interlocucione pronuntiatum est a iudicibus in publico, litem non esse contestatam; prestito quidem prius sacramento a precentore, quod uerba sibi imposita non proposuit animo litem contestandi. Hec igitur et alia ad diem illum facta uel proposita in actis subsequentibus habentur expresse. Ne igitur supersticiose uidear pluries idem repetere, acta illius diei, textum rei geste per ordinem explanando, me habent excusatum.

Dictis igitur die et loco partibus in presentia nostra constitutis, proposuit precentor pro parte contradictorum electi, se ob quasdam[d] iniurias sedem apostolicam appellasse, et illi appellationi se uelle firmiter inherere. Nos autem super hoc auditis hinc inde propositis, pensatis etiam iniuriis, et habito cum iurisperitis consilio, predictam appellacionem non admisimus, quia partibus fuit appellatio inhibita, nec appellauit in casu in lege indulto. Subsequenter pars electi proposuit coram nobis litem esse contestatam per quedam uerba a precentore proposita, et testes sollemniter admittendos. Sed super hoc quibusdam hinc inde propositis, pronuntiauimus contestationem factam non esse; delato tamen prius iureiurando precentori, quod uerba sibi imposita non proposuit animo litem contestandi. Postea, cum pars electi suam constanter proponeret intencionem, exhibuit coram nobis H(enricus) de Ver[2] litteras domini regis patentes, quibus idem rex constituerat eundem H(enricum) procuratorem in causa quam dicebat uentilari inter ipsum et dictum electum, licet per nos non esset ad causam uocatus, sed tantum admonitus ut electioni suum preberet assensum, uel quare nollet nobis ostenderet rationem. Super hoc quidem exhorta est questio, an dominus rex uocandus sit in hac causa,

_____

[a] communicauimus H, *corr. by Hand A*   [b] utroque H
[c] litteris H, *corr. by scribe*   [d] quasdas H

_____

[1] 9 December.
[2] A minor scion of the house of Vere, owning lands in Suffolk, and one of the

adversaries the Tuesday after the feast of St. Nicholas,[1] at the church of St. Edmunds. And we firmly determined that we would not prolong the main business again because of such a request, and we informed the king of this by a joint letter.

This day appointed for the parties and agreed to by them soon arrived. And when both parties came before the judges in solemn session, there was much discussion about whether the law had been challenged by the precentor's earlier statement. After discussion, the judges publicly pronounced that the law had not been challenged, for the precentor had earlier taken oath that he did not intend to defend in law the words which he had used. These and other matters dealt with that day are expressed in the following acts. By providing their text, which explains the course of the action, I am excused from seeming overscrupulous in repeating the same sort of thing many times.

On the day and at the place appointed, the parties assembled before us, and the precentor, on behalf of the party opposing the abbot elect, informed us that because of certain injuries he had appealed to the apostolic see, and he intended to abide firmly by this appeal. But after hearing the views of both sides, and evaluating the extent of the injuries, we disallowed the appeal by the jurists' advice, for appeal was forbidden the parties, nor was his appeal a lawful exception to this. Subsequently the abbot elect's party suggested to us that the precentor's words had challenged the law, and that witnesses ought to be duly summoned; but we declared that no challenge had occurred, after hearing the views of both sides, for the precentor had already taken oath that he had not intended to challenge the law by what he had said. Later, when the abbot elect's party firmly declared its intention, Henry de Vere[2] showed us the king's letters patent appointing him his proctor in the case which he said was between him and the abbot elect, although we had not called him to the inquiry, but rather had asked him to assent to the election, or else give us reason why he did not wish to do so. And out of this rose the question of whether the king ought to be summoned to the case, seeing that his proctor was present,

king's household clerks (*Magna Carta*, p. 248). His letter of appointment, in which Hugh is referred to as 'qui se gerit electum', is in *Rot. Litt. Pat.*, p. 124b, dated 2 December.

precipue cum presens sit eius procurator, et nil contra electum proponat. Insuper, an causa regis et monachorum simul tractari debeant, uel separatim, precipue cum procurator eius appellaret ne cause eorum separatim agerentur.

Hiis igitur ita propositis et indecisis, de assensu parcium testes admisimus, tres uidelicet electores; et adhibitis nobis de consensu parcium accessoribus, domino Wygorniense episcopo[1] et magistro Willelmo eius clerico, eos diligenter examinauimus, quamuis non esset lis contestata,[2] tum pro consensu parcium, tum quia causa eleccionis agebatur, tum quia ex alia rationabili causa continebatur moram fore periculosam si tunc producti non essent; et facta est hec*a* productio absque preiudicio litis contestate, ita quod attestaciones suo tempore ualeant, salua etiam exceptione contradictoribus.*b* In tempore disputationis, si contra personam magistri Thome aliquid iustum duxerint opponendum, et de earundem parcium assensu, dedimus diem peremptorium tam procuratoribus quam eius contradictoribus, scilicet diem Lune proximum post Epiphaniam Domini, apud ecclesiam sancti Iacobi de Redinges,[3] precise ad contestationem litis faciendam, omni excepcione tunc competente remota. Conuenit eciam inter nos ibidem, quod si uiderimus relationem esse faciendam, non faciemus eam ante plenam cause instruccionem, nisi pars alterutra instructionem suam nimium protelauerit. Eisdem die et loco recepimus probaciones electi taxacione premissa super expensis factis ante litis ingressum, usque ad xxx. libras, et de expensis factis post litis ingressum, ultra summam receptam a sacrista, usque ad xvii. libras et vi. solidos et viii. denarios; et sic pronuntiauimus sacristam debere reddere predictas summas electo infra xv. dies | sequentes, et singulis aduocatis ii. marcas; et hoc precepimus sub pena excommunicationis obseruanda, ut si infra dictum terminum non soluerit, ab omnibus excommunicatus habeatur.

f. 187ᵛ

Inter hec autem Ricardus de Marisco cancellarius regis[4] et

---

a hoc H   *b* H *adds* scilicet diem lune proximum post epiphaniam, *canc. by scribe*

---

[1] Walter de Gray (1214–15), consecrated 5 October. From late 1205 until that date he had been John's chancellor, for which office he paid 5,000 marks. He was nephew of John's favourite John de Gray, bishop of Norwich (Painter, pp. 64–5).

but said nothing against the abbot elect; furthermore, whether the king's and monks' cases ought to be dealt with together or separately, especially as his proctor appealed against them being taken separately.

After these issues had been raised and left undecided, with the parties' consent we summoned witnesses, namely the three electors; and having admitted some assistants with the parties' consent, the bishop of Worcester[1] and Master William his clerk, we examined the electors carefully, although the suit had not been contested;[2] firstly, because we had the parties' consent; secondly, to find out more about the election; and thirdly, because there could be a dangerous delay arising from other obvious reasons if they were not examined then. So this examination was made without prejudice to the contesting of the case, in order that their attestations might be assessed later, allowing for exceptions by their opponents. With the parties' assent a firm date, the Monday after Epiphany at St. James's church, Reading,[3] was appointed for both proctors and contradictors, for the contesting of the suit, and in case anyone during the course of the dispute wished to lodge a just accusation against Master Thomas, all exceptions denied. We also decided among ourselves that if a further delay seemed necessary, we should not allow it until given a full explanation of the legal reason, unless one or the other of the parties greatly delayed its explanation. At the same time we received an estimate of expenses from the abbot elect: of those incurred before entering on the suit, £30; of those incurred after the suit had begun (apart from a sum received from the sacrist), £17. 6s. 8d.; and we declared that the sacrist was to pay these amounts to the abbot elect within a fortnight, as well as two marks for each advocate. This we ordered to be carried out under threat of excommunication if he did not pay up within this time.

Meanwhile Richard Marsh, the king's chancellor,[4] Walter

---

[2] The examination of witnesses normally followed the contesting of the suit, but had been brought forward for the various reasons mentioned in the text (see above, p. 90 n. 6). The examination of witnesses and their attestations, or sworn statements, constituted one of the main methods of proof in such an inquiry (Sayers, *Judges Delegate*, pp. 87–9). The attestations were later published and disputed (ibid., p. 89; see below, p. 151).

[3] 12 January 1215, in the parish church.

[4] The king's most trusted financial agent, notorious for his ability to extort

⟨Walterus⟩ id est episcopus Wygorniensis et Henricus de Ver
procurator eiusdem, ab eodem ad diem destinati ⟨sunt⟩, partis
scilicet contradicentis electioni in subsidium, ut saltem illum diem
auctoritate regia protelarent. Cognito se tandem non posse in
proposito proficere, pretendit Ricardus de Marisco litteras domini
regis tribus iudicibus, in quibus continebatur ipsum regem gratum
habere et ratum quod per illos tres ad illum diem fieret. Alias
autem misit priori et conuentui ex parte eiusdem in capitulo
legendas, in quibus postulauit cartam conuentus super relaxacione pecunie tempore interdicti ab eisdem quocumque modo
extorte.ᵃ¹ Quibus in capitulo presente priore perlectis, exurgentes
Ricardus de Saxham et Hugo de Theford magisterque Alanus de
Walsingham, appellauerunt contra, ne quis per sigillum conuentus,
dummodo fuissent acephali, confirmare uel infirmare alicui contra
preceptum apostolicum accemptaret. Quod ut dictis nuntiis regis
panderetur per ordinem, moleste tulerunt. In se tandem reuersi,²
et iam per sacristam et eius partem spe iterum concepta de negocio
perficiendo, ad capitulum die sequenti facie presentanea accesserunt; ea tamen intencione, ut compescendo sue uoluntati repugnantes sic demum compellerent eos ad concedenda prius denegata.
Quibus peruentis, ostensoque per Ricardum de Marisco aduentus
sui negocio, sacrista eiusque complices, ueritati et iuri ecclesiastico
sedentes in insidiis³ contra Deum et sacramentum ueritatis, regis
fauorem per omnia captare studentes, uoce consona exclamauerunt,
dicentes: 'Cum nos et omnia nostra in manu domini regis sint
posita, non possumus nec uolumus nec de iure debemus aliquid ab
eo repetere. Quamobrem, si placet, uestra uelit discrecio subtilius
inuestigare, qui et quot sint regie pacis perturbatores eiusque
uoluntati repugnantes.' Illis autem sic loqui siue garrire cessanti-
bus, erexit se magister Nicholaus, sicut ante inter filios unitatis
erat prolocutus,ᵇ et dixit: 'Viri laudabiles et per omnia strenui,⁴
uobis quedam ex parte claustralium Deum timentium⁵ atque pro
libertatibus ecclesiasticis tanquam pro iure hereditario se opponen-
cium, auribus excellentie uestre habeo proponere. Cum simus uiri
religiosi, et secundum regulam patris nostri Benedicti omnia

ᵃ exorte H   ᵇ prolocutum H

money from religious houses during the interdict. In 1214 he was sent to aid
Peter des Roches and William Brewer in governing England while John was in
Poitou. He exercised the offices of chamberlain, chancellor, and treasurer, and
held lucrative ecclesiastical sinecures. He was on the king's side in the civil war.

¹ For John's letter see *Rot. Litt. Pat.*, p. 140b, dated 2 December. One of
Innocent's conditions for the relaxation of the interdict, which took place on
2 July 1214, was that John abandon his device of obtaining ostensibly voluntary

bishop of Worcester, and Henry de Vere the royal proctor were sent that day by the king to support the party opposing the election and to have that day postponed by the royal authority. But finding that it was impossible to gain assent to this proposal, Richard Marsh delivered a letter from the king to the three judges, which intimated that he held as acceptable and pleasing what those three had done that day. But he sent another to the prior and convent for reading in chapter, in which he demanded a charter from them releasing him from repayment of the money which he had extorted from them in various ways during the interdict.[1] When this had been read before the prior in chapter, Richard of Saxham, Hugh of Thetford, and Master Alan of Walsingham, rising to their feet, appealed against it, saying that as long as they were leaderless, no one should employ the convent seal to confirm or release anything contrary to the papal precept. When this speech was reported to the king's messengers, they were very annoyed. Curbing their anger,[2] however, and hoping to obtain their object through the sacrist and his party, they entered the chapter-house the next day in person. Their intention was to put pressure on those opposing the king's will, and so force them to concede what they had earlier denied. When they had come, Richard Marsh made known the purpose of their arrival. The sacrist and his followers, sitting in ambush[3] for truth and the rights of the Church, against God and their oath, and constantly striving to gain the king's favour, cried out with one voice, saying: 'Since we and all our possessions are in the king's hands, we are unable, nor do we wish, nor ought we by law to demand anything back from him. May we suggest, therefore, most discreet men, that you ascertain accurately who and how many are these disturbers of the royal peace and opposers of his will.' When these men had ceased their speech (or rather empty chatter), Master Nicholas rose, as on previous occasions he had spoken out from among the sons of unity, saying: 'Renowned men and responsible in all your actions,[4] I have something for your excellencies' ears on behalf of those cloister monks who fear God[5] and who are fighting for their church's liberties as though for their hereditary rights. Because we are religious, all of

charters from religious houses excusing him from repayment of his extortions during the interdict. On the above evidence, John was apparently undeterred.

[2] Cf. Luc. 15: 17, and Abbo (*Mem.* i. 22).   [3] Ps. 10: 8; cf. above, p. 19 n. 8.

[4] Cf. Abbo (*Mem.* i. 10): 'per omnia . . . strenuus'.

[5] *Reg. Ben.*, c. 65; cf. above, p. 7 n. 7.

nostra debeant fieri, non uidetur pretermittendum quod idem
hortatur in regula, dicens: "Omnia fac cum consilio, et post factum
non penitebis."[1] Huic igitur sententie tanti patris nos[a] inclinantes,
petimus xv. dierum inducias, ut super his, habito cum uiris peritis
consilio, secundum beneplacitum uestrum possimus ad diem
reddere responsa. Ne igitur super induciis postulatis exirascamini,[b]
inter plurimas una est ratio, uidelicet quod sacrista et eius pars —
utinam bona — non uobis solummodo sed et domino nostro regi
dederunt intelligere, nos esse iuuenes etate et sapientia; ideoque,
cum tales simus, presumpcioni maxime deputaretur et iuuentuti,
si in tam arduis absque consilio uirorum prudentium et sine
deliberacione aliquid fecissemus.' Cui Ricardus de Marisco, extol-
lendo se supra se,[2] ait: 'Inducias huius rei omnino tibi et aliis dare
negamus. Et quoniam prior et magnates de domo, ut supprior,
sacrista, subsacrista, elemosinarius, custodes maneriorum aliique
consimiles quibus spectat specialiter repetere ista uel relaxare, iam
ad factam relaxacionem suum prebuerunt assensum, fateor plane
tuam repeticionem uel contradiccionem, si qua fuerit, uanam et
infructuosam esse.' Deinde uertens se ad priorem et ad omnes
magnates sacriste inclinantes, singillatim interrogabat, utrum in
sententiam magistri Nicholai sociorumque suorum stetissent |
f. 188 fouendam. Quibus prior, supprior, sacrista omnesque parti
sacriste inclinantes, reclamando dixerunt: 'Nos omnes,[c] quantum
in nobis est, domino nostro regi quicquid tempore interdicti uel ante
quocumque modo perceperit, absque omni repeticione nunc et in
eternum plane remittimus; et inde omnem securitatem per sigillum nostrum, si tamen inimici regis inter nos latentes ad hoc suum
prebuerint assensum, parati sumus eidem conferre.' Quo audito,
Ricardoque de Marisco contra partem iura ecclesiastica repeten-
tem se extollente supra se,[2] magister Thomas de Walsingham et
magister Nicholaus exurgentes, sigillum conuentus sub prote-
ctione[d] apostolici, ad eum appellando, posuerunt. Post quorum
appellacionem adauxit suum Radulphus de Londonia, dicens: 'Nos
utique bonis patroni nostri Aedmundi sustentati tanquam eius filii
uel executores repetimus pro eo preciosum annulum cum rubi
quod tibi, Marisce, inconsulto conuentu et contradicente, dedit
noster sacrista.' Quod quidem cum plures de conuentu instanter ita esse testificarent coram Ricardo, presentibus episcopo

---

[a] non H   [b] exiremini H   [c] H *adds* in   [d] peticione et H

---

[1] *Reg. Ben.*, c. 3. A quotation from Ecclus. 32: 24.

whose actions are supposed to be in accordance with the *Rule* of
our father Benedict, it seems unwise to ignore what he exhorts in
it, namely: "Do everything with advice, and afterwards you will
not have to repent."[1] Heeding therefore this statement from so
great a father, we ask a fortnight's amnesty, so that, after consulting
learned men over this matter, we shall be able to give you an
answer on that day according to your good pleasure. In case you
should be angered by our seeking this delay, we will give you one
of many possible reasons why we do so, namely, that the sacrist
and his party—would they were upright—have given both yourselves and the king to understand that we are immature in age and
wisdom; if this were so, it would indeed be thought great pre-
sumption and immaturity if we acted in such a difficult matter
without deliberation or the advice of prudent men.' Richard
Marsh answered him in an overbearing manner:[2] 'We absolutely
refuse to grant a delay in this matter to you or anyone else. And
because the prior and officials of the house, that is, the subprior,
sacrist, subsacrist, almoner, guardians of the manors, and the like
whose special province it is to demand or cancel repayment have
now agreed to grant its release, I declare your countermand and
opposition or whatever to be utterly invalid and a waste of time.'
Then, turning to the prior and those officials who supported the
sacrist he asked each of them whether he supported the position
of Master Nicholas and his friends. With a shout the prior, subprior, sacrist, and all his party replied: 'All of us, as far as in us
lies, fully remit now and forever whatever the king took, however
it was done, before or during the interdict, without demanding
repayment; and for maximum security we are prepared to grant
this under the convent seal, if the king's enemies hidden among
us agree.' Hereupon, and because Richard Marsh was trying to
frighten[2] the party demanding payment according to the Church's
law, Master Thomas of Walsingham and Master Nicholas, rising
to their feet, placed the convent seal under papal protection by
appeal. After their appeal, Ralph of London added his own,
saying: 'What's more, we who are sustained by the goods of our
patron Edmund, claim for him as his sons and executors the
precious ruby ring which our sacrist gave you, Marsh, without
consulting and in opposition to the convent.' After many of the
convent had straightaway testified to this in Richard's presence,

[2] Cf. Seneca, *N. Q.*iii.25; but a catch-phrase, found in other medieval writers.

Wygornensi et Henrico de Ver, pre confusione et ira late exprobra-
cionis, coram eisdem in pleno capitulo monstrauit anulum circa
collum pendentem.

Quibus tali ordine peractis, Walterus[a] Wygornensis episcopus
et Henricus de Wer, in regio negocio cupientes procedere, seorsum
extra capitulum super hoc cum magistro Thoma de Walsingham et
magistro Nicholao et R(icardo) de Saxham, non modicam fecerunt
interlocutionem; qua finita redierunt in capitulum, ubi ipse
Ricardus erat cum monachis expectans; recitatisque inter illos
tres auditis superius et obiectis, dederunt diem deliberacionis
superius postulatam, scilicet diem sancti Thome apostoli.[1]

Suscepto itaque communi assensu partis ueritatis, omnem plane
extorsionem tempore interdicti factam repetentis, statim miserunt
magistrum Nicholaum et Ricardum de Saxham ad dominum
Eliensem, ut super factis et faciendis consilium eius reportassent.
Cognita quidem Elyense ab illis rei geste ueritate, prohibuit ne
huiusmodi relaxacioni aliquando consentirent, que plane symoniam
sapere uidebatur; significando subinde priori, quod si quos de suo
conuentu haberet ordinandos, uigilia sancti Thome apostoli ad se
transmitteret.[2]

Igitur illis domum reuersis, et iam priori partique ueritatis que
sibi in peregrinatione sua fuerant dicta et responsa patefactis,
gauisi sunt uniuersi, tamen diuersis de causis. Gauisi enim sunt
fideles de tanti uiri constantia, qui (regiam subaudis) iram[b] tempo-
ralem pro tuendis libertatibus ecclesiasticis malebat incurrere,
quam eas subdole consulendo fallere. Gaudebant et alii, quia
prior[c] et sacrista, audito domini Elyensis mandato, concipiebant
se posse[d] promouere quos uellent, et quos nollent pro uoluntate
repellere. Igitur prior et sacrista, habito super his consilio, quendam
habuerunt monachum promouendum, nomine Philippum, quem
speciali dileccione amplectebantur pre aliis; et nitentes eum promouere, aliquosque qui cum electione steterant repellere, solum
conuentui ordinandum in capitulo presentauerunt. Quorum intencionem intuentes fideles, id est, pars sacramentum electionis
fouentes, contristati sunt et conturbati: super quo etiam, finito
capitulo, inierunt consilium.[3] In hoc tandem adquiescebant, ut
contra[e] Philippi promocionem precipue, perturbatoris pacis nostre
et ecclesie, per magistrum Nicholaum, Ricardum de Saxham et

---

[a] Iohannes H; *perhaps an error from an* id est *sign in the scribe's exemplar?*
[b] *Added in marg. by Hand C*   [c] priore H
[d] H *adds* -se, *corr. by Hand C*   [e] *Added in marg. by scribe*

and in front of the bishop of Worcester and Henry de Vere, he, confused and angry at this open accusation, showed the whole chapter the ring hanging around his neck.

After this Walter bishop of Worcester and Henry de Vere, desiring to proceed with the royal business, discussed the matter for a long time with Master Thomas of Walsingham, Master Nicholas, and Richard of Saxham privately, outside the chapter-house. When they had finished, they returned to the chapter-house, where Richard himself was waiting with the monks, and after the three curials had heard the various charges and replies, they granted them the day for which they had asked, that of St. Thomas the Apostle.[1]

The party of truth, agreeing together in their demand for full repayment of what was extorted from them during the interdict, at once sent Master Nicholas and Richard of Saxham to the bishop of Ely, to obtain his advice over what had been and what had yet to be done. When the bishop of Ely learnt the true facts from these men, he forbade them to agree at all to such a release, which plainly smacked of simony. At the same time he notified the prior that if he had any ordinands in his convent, he should send them to him on the vigil of St. Thomas.[2]

The men returned therefore to the house and told the prior and the party of truth what they had said to the bishop in the course of their pilgrimage, and his reply. Everyone rejoiced, although for different reasons. The faithful rejoiced in the firmness of such a man, who preferred to incur the anger of the world (that is, of the king), in defence of the Church's liberties, rather than deceive them with cunning advice. Others were happy because the prior and sacrist, on hearing the bishop of Ely's message, thought that they would be able to promote or reject at will whomsoever they wished. The prior and sacrist, discussing this together, decided to promote a monk named Philip, whom they especially favoured above the others, and intending to promote him and to repel any of those who supported the election, they presented him to the convent in chapter as the sole ordinand. The faithful, that is, the party holding to the election-oath, guessing their intention, were disturbed and saddened. After chapter they had a discussion about it,[3] and at length agreed that Master Nicholas, Richard of Saxham, and

[1] 21 December. [2] 20 December.
[3] A common O.T. expression; cf. above, p. 13 n. 4.

Symonem de Walsingham coram priore fieret appellatio, ne illum quem de periurio parati fuerunt conuincere ad sacros ordines promoueret; quod ita factum est, presente eciam electo. Sed quia f. 188ᵛ prior et sacrista tunc temporis ratione potestatis sue quoad | interius et exterius omnia sibi credebant inclinare, appellationem supradictorum et repugnantiam, utpote claustralium, pro minimo reportabant, neque eorum appellationem admittere iudicabant. Vnde dominus prior consilio antiqui hostis, omissa appellatione et neglecta,ᵃ assumpto secum Iohanne de Disce et Osberno capellano et consiliario, insuper et precentore illis precedente, licet ob aliam causam se profectum simulante, dictum Philippum ad gradum diaconatus domino Elyensi presentauit in crastino. Sed antequam prior cum dictis sociis ibidem peruenisset, littere dictorum claustralium Philippo ⟨contra⟩dicentium, attestantes appellacionem factam contra Philippi promocionem ob causam superius dictam, et illam per litteras dictas renouantes, coram domino Eliense fuerant recitate. Subsecuto quidem priore ad dictum P(hilippum) presentandum, pretendit ei dominus Eliensis litteras prememoratas; atque super hoc habito cum uiris peritis consilio, utrum uidelicet appellationi esset deferendum, an prioris presentationi condescendendum, responsum est ab illis non posse dictum presentatum ad quosuisᵇ ordines promouere, nisi appellatione premissa prius renuntiata. Igitur dato priori huiusmodi perᶜ episcopum responso, non sine magna confusione, infecto negocio, domum cum sociis suis rediit, die sancti Thome apostoli,¹ quo supramemorati regis nuntii diem deliberacionis repetentibus pecuniam a domo sua tempore interdicti extorsam prefixerant.ᵈ

Existentibus quidem illis in uestiario, scilicet Wygornensiᵉ episcopo et Ricardo de Marisco cancelario regis et H(enrico) de Ver, una cum priore et sacrista aliisque sibi inclinantibus, super eleccioneᶠ precipue et relaxacione districte consulentibus, ex parte prioris et sacriste et aduersariorum talia presentabantur electo per dictos nuntios regis, ut ipse quidem renunciasset electioni pro bono pacis, tali tamen pactoᵍ interposito, quod prior prioratui, sacrista sacristie, precentor precentorie, infirmarius, pitantiarius, singulique alii de parte sua qualemcumque obedientiam habentes illis plane ab illo dieʰ in antea renuntiarent, ut nec de cetero per eam aut per aliquam aliam transitum facerent. Hec autem oblacio facta fuit per dictos nuntios regis, ex parte prioris, sacriste et

---

ᵃ neclecta H   ᵇ quouis H   ᶜ post H   ᵈ prefigerant H
ᵉ Wygornensis H
ᶠ super eleccione *added in marg. by Hand A*
ᵍ pacis tali tamen pacto *added in marg. by Hand A*
ʰ illis plane ab illo die *added in marg. by Hand A*

Simon of Walsingham should appeal before the prior against the raising of Philip, disturber of our church and peace, to holy orders, since they could prove him guilty of perjury; and it was done, the abbot elect also being present. But because the prior and sacrist believed that everyone inside and outside the house would support them on this occasion because of their position, they considered the appeal and opposition of these mere cloister monks as of little account, and determined not to grant it. Instead the prior, by the advice of the Old Enemy, disregarding and neglecting the appeal, took with him John of Diss and Osbern his chaplain and counsellor, and the next day, preceded by the precentor, who pretended to be going for some other reason, he presented Philip to the bishop of Ely for ordination to the rank of deacon. But before the prior and his friends arrived there, a letter from the cloister monks was read to the bishop of Ely, opposing Philip's ordination, and recording and renewing the appeal made against his promotion for the reasons given. Soon after, the prior presented Philip, on which the bishop showed him this letter; and when he asked the advice of his learned men as to which should be granted, the appeal or the prior's presentation, they replied that it was impossible to ordain the man presented to any orders unless the earlier appeal were renounced. The bishop answered accordingly, and the prior and his followers returned home on the day of St. Thomas the Apostle[1] in great confusion, their business unaccomplished. Now this was the day appointed by the king's messengers to discuss compensation for the money which had been extorted from the house during the interdict.

After serious discussion in the vestry between the bishop of Worcester, Richard Marsh the king's chancellor, and Henry de Vere, and the prior, sacrist, and others of their party, specifically over the election and release, the royal officials suggested this course to the abbot elect, on behalf of the prior, sacrist, and his adversaries generally; namely, that for the sake of peace he should renounce his election, but on this condition, that the prior, sacrist, precentor, infirmarer, pittancer, and every member of their party holding an obedientiary office should wholly renounce their own positions for the future, so that no changes might be made by them through their present positions or any other. The royal officials made this offer on behalf of the prior, sacrist, and their friends who

[1] 21 December.

sociorum suorum electioni contradicentium.*a* Quod ut dicto electo
nuntiatum esset, intrauit capellam sancti Sabe,¹ ibique in*b* quid
super hoc responderet diligenter cum suis tractauit. Recreati
tandem uisitacione interna spirituali,² in Eum 'a quo iusta sunt
opera et recta consilia'³ fixerunt consilium. Tandem exeuntes ad
dictos nuntios representauerunt similia similibus; uidelicet, quod
celerarius celerarie, ⟨camerarius⟩ camerarie, custosque maneriorum sue custodie, omnesque alii electionem fouentes et obedientiam quamuis magnam seu minimam habentes, illis et omnibus
aliis perpetualiter renuntiarent,*c* si tamen in electum et eius
electionem canonice celebratam suum ⟨rex⟩ impertiret*d* assensum.

Quibus cum relatum esset ex parte electi et suorum, seque
minime in hac parte conspicerent profecturos, ad relaxacionem
petendam, de qua superius facta est mencio, fecere descensum.*e*
Et committentes uices suas priori et sacriste ad istud negocium
explendum, licet posse ⟨sine⟩ omnimodo interposito, tandem ad
dictos nuntios infecto redierunt neg⟨ot⟩io, atque responsum
monachorum electionem fouentium et relaxationi penitus contradicentium per ordinem exposuerunt. Quod cum audissent et
uidissent,⁴ non sine graui dolore id pertulerunt. Aestimantes
quidem in aliquo posse sibi contradicentes et relaxacioni deuincere,
fecerunt conuocari ad se in uestiario omnes illos, nullo alio
mediante. Qui numero usque ad xxxiii. accedentes, quid ⟨et⟩
quantum repetebant ibidem per magistrum Nicholaum coram illis
tribus proponebant modeste. Erat autem numerus repetitionis
quater mille marcarum, ut idem Nicholaus coram Ricardo de
Marisco et aliis duobus regis nuntiis de singulis receptis, quo et
ubi, aperte monstrauit ad unguem. Quo facto, idem Nicholaus |
f. 189 subiunxit: 'Viri prudentes et omni discrecione repleti, non latet
uos quod cum ista mater ecclesia per filios degeneres diu sit
infirmata et orbata,⁵ et ab eisdem a iure proprio alienata, iam
tanquam a graui lectulo doloris conualescens atque uires recuperata
pristinas, dispersa congregat, ablata restituit, rapta reuocat et, ut
apercius dicam, quicquid tempore siue causa sue inualescentie
Caldei a quouis fideli extra iuris ordinem hucusque rapiebant, iam
non in parte sed in toto uniuersa restaurare clamitat in plateis.⁶

---

a *Added in marg. by Hand A*   *b* *Added over line by Hand C*   *c* perpetualiter renuntiarent *added in marg. by Hand A*   *d* impertiretur H
e decensum H

---

¹ See above, p. 10 n. 2.
² Iudith 13: 30.
³ *Oratio* from the Mass for Peace; J. W. Legge, *The Sarum Missal* (Oxford,
1916), p. 395.

opposed the election. When it was told the abbot elect, he went into the chapel of St. Sabas,[1] and there discussed carefully with his friends what answer he should give. Eventually, refreshed inwardly by divine inspiration,[2] they placed their trust in Him 'from whom all good counsels and all just works do proceed',[3] and coming out they presented a similar proposal to the king's officials, as follows: that if assent were given to the abbot elect and his canonically celebrated election, the cellarer, chamberlain, guardian of the manors, and all the others supporting the election and holding an obedientiary office, great or small, would renounce their present positions and any others for ever.

When this proposal had been made on behalf of the abbot elect and his party, and it was seen that little would be accomplished along these lines, the question of the release was brought up again. But the prior and sacrist, to whom the royal officials had committed the task of explaining the matter—although they could easily have done this themselves—returned to them at last having accomplished nothing, and recounted, blow by blow, the reply of the monks who favoured the election, utterly opposing the release. When they had seen and heard these things,[4] the officials became very vexed. Thinking that they must be able in some way to conquer those who opposed them and the release, they had all of this opinion summoned to a private conference with them in the vestry. When they had arrived, to the number of thirty-three, they set forth with moderation, through Master Nicholas, the amount of their claim. Now this claim, accurately and openly calculated before Richard Marsh and the two other officials by Nicholas, who gave the place and date of each receipt, totalled 4,000 marks. When this had been done, Master Nicholas continued: 'Men of prudence and full of all discretion, you know very well that when Mother Church has long been weakened and deprived by degenerate sons,[5] and when they have alienated what she possesses by right, at length, recovering her former strength, arising as from a bed of heavy sickness, she gathers together what was dispersed, restores what was lost, regains what was plundered, and, to speak plainly, cries through every street[6] to be returned not in part, but fully,

---

[4] A common biblical phrase; cf. above, p. 22 n. 1.
[5] Cf. *Epistola Petri Pictaviensis*, in Kritzeck, *Peter the Venerable*, p. 216: '. . . matrem aecclesiam non ita orbatam uel desolatam bonis filiis ostendistis. . . '.
[6] Esth. 4: 1.

Vnde, cum sitis filii ecclesie fideles, super relaxacione a nobis postulata nobis orphanis et pastore orbatis taliter uelitis consulere, ut illud in facie ecclesie pos⟨s⟩itis sine dispendio representare.' Quibus auditis Ricardus de Marisco, uultu ferocitatis demisso, ait: 'Viri fratres, non credimus a laudabili memoria excidisse causam nostri accessus, quia, ut superius habetur, ad relaxacionem specialiter uenimus petendam.ᵃ Nunc igitur super hoc taliter nobis uestra prouideat discrecio respondere, super quo etiam dominus rex uestram prudentiam posset commendare et discrecionem, eundemque in agendis uestris magis propicium inuenire debeatis.' Cui omnes tanquam ex uno ore uoce consona dederunt responsum: 'Scias, cancellarie, nos posse de iure et uelle petita sine capite repetere, ⟨sed⟩ nequaquam relaxare, cum et relaxacio ad abbatem spectet specialiter. Vnde ne quid fraudis uel doli per sigillum nostrum nobis inconsultis fiat et contradicentibus, iterato coram domino Wygornensi et H(enrico) de Ver pro eo appellamus, et pro hominibus nostris, qui sunt bona ecclesie nostre.'

Quod ut sacrista cum parte sua, quia regiam per omnia studebant captare beniuolentiam,¹ uiderent nonᵇ posse in hac parte penetrare uel superare partem ueritatis pre nimia sui constantia, moleste tulerunt; tandemque in unum super hoc conuenientes fecerunt cartam communi consilio, priore eciam consentiente, sub nomine eiusdem et Albini supprioris, sacriste et precentoris singularumque personarum sibi contra eleccionem inclinancium. Erat autem hec forma, quod omnes hanc cartam inspicientes scirent priorem et alios superius dictos plenam fecisse relaxacionem domino regi de omnibus rebus tempore interdicti perceptis ab illis, qualiter-cumque percepisset, per suos uel per alios; et ad istud firmius roborandum dominus prior sigillo suo confirmauit.² Quo facto tradiderunt Ricardo de Marisco domino regi deferendam, et hac intentione, scilicet ⟨ut⟩ inspecto numero multitudinis sibi fauentis, eo acrius contra electum et electi fautores, ei in hac parte contra-dicentes, exardesceret. Expletis istis hoc ordine a sacrista et eius parte, et omnibus per ipsum Ricardum de Marisco in uestiario existentem parti electionis plane intimatis, exurgentes magister Thomas de Walsingham et magister Nicholaus appellauerunt coram dictis nunciis, sicut superius fecerant, pro sigillo conuentus, pariterque pro hominibus suis qui sunt bona ecclesie et eorum

---

ᵃ petenda H   ᵇ nos H

¹ See above, p. 4 n. 3.
² Evidently the writer had access to the actual text.

whatever the Infidel earlier snatched away from the faithful unlawfully, whether because of the times, or the Church's weakness. Now you are faithful sons of the Church, and we orphans bereft of a pastor; your advice about the release claimed from us, therefore, should be that the money be returned to the church without loss.' Richard Marsh, assuming a ferocious look at this, replied: 'Men and brothers, we did not believe that on our arrival you would act contrary to your praiseworthy reputation; for as you know, the sole purpose of our coming was to ask for the release. If you are sensible you will answer us in such a way that the king may commend your wisdom and prudence and that your deeds may bring you into greater favour with him.' To which they replied with one voice: 'Know, chancellor, that without a head we both wish, and are able by law, to lodge a claim, but not to grant a release, for this is the abbot's responsibility. Thus, so that no fraud or guile can be committed under our seal and without our knowledge or consent, we appeal for it again before the bishop of Worcester and Henry de Vere, and for our men who are the property of our church.'

When the sacrist and his party, who were constantly striving to gain the royal goodwill,[1] saw that nothing was being accomplished in this fashion, and that the party of truth could not be scattered or subdued because of their unshakeable firmness, they were very annoyed. After discussing the matter among themselves, they drew up a charter by common agreement and with the prior's consent, in his name and that of Albinus the subprior, the sacrist, precentor, and each person inclining to them against the election. It took this form: that all the viewers of this charter should know that the prior and the others just mentioned had granted the king full release of everything taken from them during the interdict, however it was done, whether by his men or by others; and to strengthen it more firmly, the prior confirmed it with his seal.[2] It was then given to Richard Marsh to take to the king, so that, seeing the number of his supporters, he might be aroused to greater hostility against those who opposed his will in this matter, the abbot elect and his followers. When the sacrist and his party had arranged this, Richard Marsh announced it to the election party in the vestry, upon which Master Thomas of Walsingham and Master Nicholas, rising to their feet, appealed before the officials, as they had done earlier, for the convent seal, and for their men, the property and

sustentamentum, in hunc modum: uidelicet ne ⟨quid⟩ per illud fraudis uel doli ad derogacionem eleccionis canonice facte fieret, inconsulto conuentu et inscio, per aliquem; insuper et ne homines abbatie, qui sunt bona sua, ad huius⟨modi⟩ relaxacionem faciendam per regiam aliquatenus compellerentur*a* potestatem.

Quorum appellationem non admittentes deflexerunt uersus Kateshil,[1] ubi omnes, tam sokemanni quam burgenses et milites de abbacia, erant summoniti illo die contra eosdem*b* apparere. Subsequentibus quidem causam sui aduentus, responsum est ab omnibus: 'Nos hic et in eternum plane remittimus domino regi quicquid a nobis tempore aliquo seu quocunque modo perceperit, quantum ad nos siue ad posteros nostros, nulla omnino reseruata nobis reclamacione aut repeticione ab isto die in antea.' Et ad expressionem maioris securitatis et testimonii, quidam ex illis qui inter alios reputabantur maiores tanquam pro se et pro aliis illud idem scripto et sigillorum impressione confirmauerunt. Inter hec f. 189ᵛ quidem | magister Thomas de Walsingham ibidem adueniens coram omnibus, tam laicis quam clericis, appellationem factam ex parte conuentus renouauit. Cui tamen appellationi Ricardus de Marisco et H(enricus) de Ver necdum deferentes sic processerunt.

Subsecuto postmodum die partibus apud Radinges prefixo,[2] facta est ibidem sollempniter litis contestatio; regem tamen abiudicatum non debere cause interesse, presente H(enrico) de Ver procuratore eiusdem, ut in his actis plenius scribitur:

Dictis die et loco procuratoribus electi et contradicentium*c* sibi cominus constitutis,*d* facta est litis contestatio sollempniter et in scriptis; ita quod edicioni facte a procuratoribus electi et responsioni*e* partis alterius sigilla apposuimus. Formam eciam prescriptam electoribus, ut utraque pars fatebatur, sigillis nostris signatam custodie sacriste commisimus, et electores alia uice examinatos, scilicet Robertum camerarium et Iocelinum de Altari, iterum iuratos de nouo super nouis articulis examinauimus. Dicto uero die et loco admissa est plenarie disputacio, an rex ad hanc causam uocandus esset necne, presente H(enrico) de Ver procuratore eiusdem; et cum consilio iurisperitorum interlocuti sumus ipsum non esse uocandum, precipue cum qualibet die litis presens fuit in lite domini regis procurator generalis,

---

a compellerent H   *b* contra eosdem H, *possibly for* coram eisdem
c contradicentibus H   *d* constituti H   *e* responsionem H

sustenance of the church, in this manner: that no one should use it to perpetrate fraud or trickery in prejudice of the canonically made election, without consulting the convent or letting them know; and further, that the royal power should not be used in any way to compel the men of the abbey, who were its property, to make a release of this kind.

But, disregarding this appeal, they journeyed to Catshill,[1] where all the abbey's sokemen, burgesses, and knights had been summoned to appear before them that day. After being told the cause of their arrival, everyone replied: 'We fully remit to the king now and for ever whatever he took from us at any time or in any manner, reserving nothing for reclaim by us or our descendants in the future.' And for greater security and testimony, some reputed the greater of their number confirmed this in writing and with their seals, on behalf of themselves and the rest. In the meantime, however, Master Thomas of Walsingham, coming to that place, renewed the appeal on the convent's behalf before them all, both clergy and laity. But since Richard Marsh and Henry de Vere would not grant it, they proceeded as above.

Shortly after, the day appointed for the parties at Reading arrived,[2] and there the suit was appropriately contested. It was decided that the king need not be present seeing that his proctor, Henry de Vere, was there, as is explained more fully in these acts:

On the day and at the place appointed for the proctor of the abbot elect and his opponents, the lawsuit was duly contested and the proceedings taken down in writing. We impressed with our seals the statements of the abbot elect's proctors and the other party's replies. We also impressed with our seals the form which had been prescribed for the electors as acknowledged by both parties, committing it to the care of the sacrist. Then we caused to be sworn in again the electors whom we had examined earlier, Robert the chamberlain and Jocelin of the Altar, and re-examined them about the new statements. At the same time and place full discussion was allowed as to whether the king ought to be called to the hearing or not, his proctor, Henry de Vere, being present. And with the advice of skilled jurists we decided that it was unnecessary to call him, since his general

---

[1] Not far from Bury itself; where the abbot's court was normally held.
[2] 12 January 1215.

uel etiam ad hanc causam specialem, qui nichil electo uel electioni obiciens tantum dilacionem flagitabat. Et statuimus diem*a* peremptorium, diem scilicet Iouis proximam ante festum sancti Valentini apud sanctum Aedmundum,[1] ad testes recipiendos super crimine falsi, periurii, inobedientie et scandali*b* et in contencione conuentus super quibusdam articulis in iudicio editis, si interim tale consilium a peritis habuerimus, quod debeant admitti; et eundem diem statuimus ad apercionem pristinarum attestacionum et disputacionem audiendam. Et prouidimus aduocatis utriusque partis quatuor marcas pro salario.

Igitur sub hac*c* forma die partibus constituta apud sanctum*d* Aedmundum apparuerunt illo die communiter contradictores electi, tam claustrales quam obedientiarii, ut confirmarent sacramento quod ea que a sacrista et Adam infirmario, procuratoribus eorum, interposito sacramento erant superius apud Radinges proposita, non erant maliciose obiecta.[2] Et accedens Albinus supprior ad sacramentum, nihil excepit nisi periurium; Henricus Ruffus excepit periurium; Walterus primus similiter; W. de Bosco similiter; R(icardus) Taillehaste excepit formam; H. de Bradefeld similiter; I(ocelinus) elemosinarius periurium; I(ohannes) Disce nihil excepit; Petrus de Tifteshale nihil; Thomas Capra nihil; G(alfridus) de Graveley nihil; R(icardus) de Stertesford nihil; Philippus excepit formam; H(enricus) de Londonia nihil; Salomon periurium; R(ogerus) de Stanham formam; W. de hospitali formam; Gregorius nihil; Willelmus Mothes formam; Henricus de Len formam; A. Scot formam; A(damus) nutritus*e* Hugonis formam; P(etrus) de Wridewelle formam; Willelmus de Stanhoue subcamerarius totum excepit.[3] Super hiis itaque premissis admissa est illo die disputacio plenarie; insuper et quodam peremptorio[4] a contradictoribus electi proposito, sicut in hiis actis comprehenditur:

Superius[5] autem sic fuerunt obiecta a contradictoribus electi in iure exposita: quod cum septem electores recepissent formam electionis a conuentu, et recedere inceperunt a capitulo,

---

a H *adds* eundem ad apercionem pristinarum attestationum, *canc. by scribe*
b scandalo H   *c* *Twice* H   *d* secundum H, *corr. by scribe*
e *Twice* H

[1] 12 February.
[2] This is the 'Oath of Calumny'. See above, p. 90 n. 6.
[3] The writer is evidently copying a record.

proctor had been present at the suit on every day of its prosecu-
tion, and more particularly because he had pressed for so much
delay, although not lodging any objection against the abbot elect
or his election. We appointed a definite date, the Thursday
before the feast of St. Valentine[1] at St. Edmunds to hear witnesses concerning the crimes of forgery, perjury, disobedience,
and scandal, and for the dissension in the convent over certain
statements made during the trial, providing, however, that we
decided in the meantime, with the jurists' advice, that they
ought to be admitted. We appointed the same day both for the
opening of the earlier attestations and for the hearing of the
dispute. And we provided four marks as pay for the advocates
of each party.

After this manner, therefore, on the day appointed for the
parties at St. Edmunds, the abbot elect's opponents appeared in
a body, both cloister monks and obedientiaries, to confirm on
oath that what their proctors, the sacrist and Adam the infirmarer,
had declared on oath earlier at Reading was not inspired by
malice.[2] And Albinus the subprior, taking oath, answered nothing
if not perjury; Henry Rufus perjured himself; the first Walter
likewise; W. du Bois likewise; Richard Taillehaste likewise; H. of
Bradfield likewise; Jocelin the almoner perjury; John of Diss
nothing; Peter of Tivetshall nothing; Thomas the Goat nothing;
Geoffrey of Graveley nothing; Richard of Stortford nothing;
Philip took the oath; Henry of London nothing; Solomon perjury;
Roger of Stanham likewise; W. of the hospital likewise; Gregory
nothing; William Mothes likewise; Henry of Lynn likewise;
A. Scot likewise; Adam foster-son of Hugh likewise; Peter of
Wordwell likewise; William of Stanhope the subchamberlain the
same.[3] And so a full disputation over this was permitted that day,
and a peremptory exception[4] was lodged by the abbot elect's
opponents, as contained in these acts:

The following objections were earlier[5] lodged in law by the
abbot elect's opponents: that when the seven electors had
received the form of the election from the convent and had

---

[4] A more serious form of the 'dilatory exception' which could decide the suit
in the plaintiff's favour (Sayers, *Judges Delegate*, p. 80).

[5] This use of *superius*, unless the word has been interpolated by the author,
suggests that the proceedings were being recorded on a single roll.

iniunctum fuit eis a priore sub districtione iuramenti, prestiti de
forma seruanda, quod ante electionem consumatam diuisim et
secreto non colloquerentur. Et ex hoc facto dixerunt eum
incurrisse crimen inobedientie et crimen periurii, quia pro-
hibicioni non obediuit. Item crimen falsi exponunt sic: cum
prior scripsisset archiepiscopo sub hac forma, 'Cantuariensi
archiepiscopo prior et conuentus sancti Aedmundi salutem', et
quedam alia uerba,[1] subscripsit idem prior litteris suis, et sub
sigillo suo signauit. Ex eo quod dictas litteras fecit irrequisito
conuentu et inscio, dicunt litteras fuisse falsas, et electum, quia
eis usus est inscio | conuentu, in falsi crimen incidisse.

f. 190

Postmodum uero dictis die et loco partibus in nostra presentia
constitutis, decano Salesberi absentiam suam excusante, a
parte[a] electi confessa est quod post prohibicionem predictam
colloquium habuit cum quibusdam superuenientibus ad domum
panis, cuius custodiam tunc habebat,[2] de principali negocio
nulla habita mencione. Litteris etiam sic usus est, quod unus ex
procuratoribus partis sue earum exemplar tradidit iudicibus
inter gesta cause. Confessa est autem scandalum ortum inter
fratres occasione electionis ipsius, sed non culpa sua.

Quia igitur superflua esset probacio ubi reus confitetur
factum, ideo, notatis confessionibus et auditis disputacionibus
super obiectis, attestationes aperuimus super principali negocio.
Et licet ante publicacionem contradictores electi proponerent
ipsum electum in manu regis omne ius suum resignasse, et
per hanc excepcionem uelud peremptoriam silencium electo
imponendum, nos tamen, attendentes quod multi dies peremp-
torii erant eis dati ad obiciendum in electionem, uel in personam
electi, quia infra dictos dies hoc non proposuerunt, imminente
ipsa publicatione, eam non credidimus admittendam; tum quia
uehementer presumpsimus eam ad solam dilacionem malitiose
propositam; tum quia dominus legatus Francie, qui electum in
Pictauia domino regi presentauit, per litteras suas nobis patentes
scripsit, quod dictus electus noluit resignare, licet super hoc

[a] *for* a parte, pars H

---

[1] This was probably a letter requesting the archbishop to write to the pope in
support of Hugh's election, as he did in January 1214 (see below, Appendix I).
[2] Part of his duties as subcellarer.

begun to retire from the chapter-house, they were strictly
enjoined by the prior that, according to the prescribed form,
they should not speak together secretly and apart before the
fulfilment of the election. Because of this they said that the
abbot elect had committed the crimes of disobedience and
perjury, for he had disobeyed the prohibition. Likewise they
explained the crime of forgery thus: because the prior had
written to the archbishop in this way, 'To the archbishop of
Canterbury the prior and convent of St. Edmunds send greeting', and so on,[1] the prior witnessing this letter and signing it
with his own seal. Because he wrote unsought-of and unknown
to the convent, they say it was invalid, and that the abbot elect,
because he made use of it unknown to the convent, was guilty
of forgery.

Shortly after, at the same time and place, with the parties
gathered in our presence, the dean of Salisbury excusing his
absence, the abbot elect's party confessed that after the prohibition he had held a discussion with some men who came by
chance to the bake-house, of which he had charge at the time,[2]
but no mention was made of the principal business. And he
admitted that he had made use of the letter as described, for
one of the proctors of his party had delivered a copy of it to
the judges during the course of the action. Furthermore, he
confessed that scandals had arisen among the brothers as a
result of his election, but that he was not to blame for them.

Therefore, proof being unnecessary when the defendant
admits the deed, having noted the confessions and heard dis-
putations over the accusations, we published the attestations
over the principal matter. And although before the publication
the abbot elect's opponents declared that he had resigned all
his rights into the king's hands, as if by this peremptory exception to impose silence on him, we nevertheless, noting that they
had been given many days for objections to the abbot elect or
the election, but that within this time they had not come up
with anything, being nearly ready to publish the attestations,
believed it unnecessary to admit their exception: firstly, because
we very much suspected that it had been put forward solely from
a malicious desire to promote delay; secondly, because the French
legate, who had presented the abbot elect to the king in Poitou,
wrote to us in his letters patent that the abbot elect did not wish

sepius esset requisitus, sed causam suam commisit Deo et
iudicibus suis; tum quia post reuersionem domini regis in
Angliam ipse rex litteris suis quas inspeximus uocauit eum
electum, et eciam in aliis litteris scriptis, electum nichil fecisse
quare ipsius gratiam promereri debuisset,[1] et ob quedam alia
que nos ad idem mouebant. Et quamuis contradictores electi
super hoc appellauerunt, eorum tamen appellationi non duximus
deferendum, sed statuimus diem peremptorium partibus,
scilicet diem Martis proximam ante festum sancti Gregorii apud
sanctum Aedmundum,[2] ad disputationem consummandam et
audiendam sententiam diffinitiuam.

Prouidimus etiam aduocatis partis electi pro salario c. solidos,
iniungentes[a] sacriste et subsacriste quod infra viii. dies eis
numerent predictam pecuniam, alioquin ab eo die habeantur a
priore et conuentu excommunicati.

Adueniente quidem die partibus constituto, iudicibusque pariter
cum electo et eius parte loco prefixo expectantibus per moram non
modicam procuratores partis aduerse, cum necdum apparuissent,
miserunt ad eos per duos religiosos ut coram eis iuri parerent ad
disputandum super attestationes, si eis placeret, et ad sententiam
diffinitiuam secundum mandatum domini pape audiendam. Set
post trinam sub hac forma citationem, per diuersos religiosos
scilicet factam, inuiti comparuerunt, cum magistro Roberto de
Areines et domino Pagano Longobardense et magistro A. de
Redgraue.[3] Quibus accessis, surrexit magister R(obertus) de
Areines, et omnimoda disputacione omissa appellauit pro sacrista
et eius parte ad dominum papam, ne iudices procederent ad
sententiam proferendam, et appellando fecit sacristam recedere.
Quam quidem appellationem maliciose propositam iudices uolentes
subtilius et apercius inquirere, accesserunt ad capitulum ubi omnes
erant adunati, et incipientes ad suppriorem, ceperunt interrogare
singulos partis sacriste, utrum illi appellationi superius a sacrista
et Adam infirmario facte uellent inherere uel non. Quibus in
instanti per suppriorem et per singulos alios responsum est: 'Nos
appellationi sacriste nunc facte et aliis omnibus contra electionem

---

[a] iniungestes H, *corr. by scribe*

---

[1] See above, pp. 113, 117–19. They do not appear to quote the second letter
correctly; in it John called Hugh 'he who calls himself your abbot elect'. Did the
election-party alter the wording of its contents before making them known
to the judges? The statement of the judges suggests that they did not actually
view this letter themselves.
[2] 10 March.

to resign, although often urged to do so, rather committing his cause to God and his judges; thirdly, because after the king had returned to England, he himself in a letter of his which we have inspected called him 'abbot elect', and also in another letter, saying that the 'abbot elect' had done nothing to merit his favour;[1] and there were other reasons also which influenced our decision. Although the abbot elect's opponents appealed against this, we would not grant it, but appointed as a definite date the Tuesday before the feast of St. Gregory[2] at St. Edmunds to finish the disputation and pronounce judgement.

We also provided that the abbot elect's advocates were to be paid 100 shillings, ordering the sacrist and subsacrist to pay this amount to them within a week, or else from that day on be treated as excommunicate by the prior and convent.

When the appointed day arrived, the judges and the abbot elect and his party waited for a long time at the prescribed place for the proctors of the adverse party, and when at length they had not appeared, they sent two religious to them, ordering them to appear before them, to submit in law to the disputing of the testimony given by the witnesses, if they pleased, and to hear the final verdict, according to the papal mandate. After the third summons of this kind, that is, by various religious, they came reluctantly, bringing with them Master Robert de Areines, the lord Pagan of Lombardy and Master A. of Redgrave.[3] When they had arrived, Robert de Areines rose, and foregoing any attack on the testimony of the witnesses, appealed to the pope on behalf of the sacrist and his party against the judges' proceeding to a verdict; and he made the sacrist retire while he appealed. But the judges, wishing to ascertain by careful and public inquiry to what extent the appeal was made maliciously, entered the chapter-house where everyone was gathered. Beginning with the subprior, they proceeded to interrogate each of the sacrist's party as to whether they wished to abide by the appeal made by him and Adam the infirmarer or not. To this the subprior and each of the rest at once replied: 'We adhere firmly to the appeal made just now by the sacrist and others

---

[3] In a final bid to delay proceedings, the anti-election party had apparently added a third, probably Pagan of Lombardy, to their two original advocates. His title of *dominus*, together with his surname, suggests that he had taught at Bologna, where this title was more usual than *magister*. *Rashdall's Medieval Universities*, ed. F. M. Powicke and A. B. Emden (Oxford, 1936), i. 19.

H(ugonis) dicti electi factis firmiter inheremus.' Quibus auditis, reuersi sunt iudices ad locum protribunalem, et sedentes in consistorio ceperunt diligenter inter eos tractare, quomodo melius et securius, secundum mandatum apostolicum eodem die iterato illis directum, possent procedere. Erat quidem hic tenor mandati:[a]

f. 190[v]

Innocentius episcopus, seruus seruorum Dei etc.,[b] dilectis filiis abbati de Wardone et priori de Donestaple | Lincolniensis dioceseos et decano Salesberi, salutem et apostolicam benedictionem.

Significauit nobis dilectus filius H(ugo) electus ad regimen monasterii sancti Aedmundi, quod cum examinacionem electionis sue uobis duximus committendam, uos propter impedimentum quod opposuit uenerabilis frater noster Wyntoniensis episcopus, et cauillaciones sacriste ac quorundam monachorum eiusdem ecclesie, contra factum et iuramentum proprium temere uenientium, finem eiusdem negocii plus debito prorogastis. Quia uero ex hoc posset monasterio imminere periculum, per iterata scripta precipiendo mandamus, quatinus friuolis et inutilibus excepcionibus non obstantibus[c] negocium ipsum iuxta precedentis mandati nostri tenorem ratione preuia[d] terminetis, preceptum apostolicum taliter impleturi, quod de negligentia uel contemptu argui non possitis.

Tu denique, fili abbas, etc. Datum Laterani vii. kal. Februarii, pontificatus nostri anno xvii.[1]

Huius igitur increpacione apostolici mandati iam secundi taliter correpti, diucius ueritatem omnibus liquidam protelare formidantes, Deumque pre oculis[2] et iusticiam cause perscrutate habentes, armauerunt se signaculo crucis, et reuertentes de interlocucione ad locum consistorii, ceperunt audacter coram omni populo ibi assistente recitare a gemino ouo[e3] per priorem de[f] Donestapel quicquid actum erat a primo die delegationis eorum secundum mandatum apostolicum in hac causa usque ad illum diem. Intuens quidem magister Robertus de Areines sententiam contra sacristam 'in ianuis'[4] iam fore pronuntiandam, nitebatur uiribus omnibus uerborum intricacione et tumultu impedire eam. Et quoniam iudicibus idem Robertus[g] debitam in sententia pronuntianda non exhibebat[h] reuerentiam, dictus prior eidem R(oberto) consensu coniudicum ex parte summi pontificis, cuius uicem in hac parte

---

[a] *Here begins the extract in* C, *with* Littera dompni Innocentii pape iii. pro supramemorato electo   [b] et H; *om.* C   [c] non obstantibus C; *om.* H
[d] prima C   [e] euo C   [f] *om.* C   [g] .R. H; Robertus C
[h] exibeat H, *corr. over line by Hand* C(?)

against the election of Hugh called "abbot elect".' Hearing this, the judges returned to the place of trial, and sitting in solemn assembly, they began carefully to discuss between themselves how they could proceed better and more securely, in the light of a new papal mandate sent them that day. Now this is what the mandate said:

Innocent bishop, servant of the servants of God etc., to his dear sons the abbot of Wardon, the prior of Dunstable, both in the diocese of Lincoln, and the dean of Salisbury, greetings and the apostolic blessing.

Our dear son Hugh, elected to the rule of the monastery of St. Edmunds, has made known to us that after we had committed to you the examination of his election, you protracted the termination of the business more than you ought, because of impediments imposed by our worthy brother the bishop of Winchester and the cavils of the sacrist and some monks of his church, heedlessly contradicting their own deed and oath. Since from this danger could threaten the monastery, we order you by this second letter to finish the business according to the tenor of our earlier mandate and by the guidance of reason, disallowing frivolous and useless exceptions, and so to satisfy the papal order, that you will not be accused of negligence or contempt.

You lastly, son abbot etc. Given at the Lateran, 26 January, in the seventeenth year of our pontificate.[1]

Spurred on, therefore, by the rebuke of this second mandate, dreading to delay longer in making the truth clear to all, having God and the justice of the cause before their eyes,[2] they armed themselves with the sign of the cross and returned from their private discussion to the place of counsel. There the prior of Dunstable as spokesman proceeded to recount boldly to all present all they had done 'from the twin egg',[3] that is, from the first day of their delegation laid on them in this cause by the papal mandate, up to that very day. But Master Robert de Areines, guessing that a judgement against the sacrist was now imminent,[4] tried with all his might to impede this by a flood of cunning words. But because he did not show appropriate reverence for the judges and the pronouncing of the sentence, the prior of Dunstable with

---

[1] 26 January 1215. Cheney, *Letters*, no. 990.
[2] A formula common in the texts of canon-law judgements, probably suggested by Rom. 3: 18.
[3] Hor., *Ars Poet.*, 147.   [4] Matt. 24: 33.

gerebat, imposuit silentium. Sed cum per hoc necdum siluisset, adauxit penam excommunicationis coram omnibus, et sic demum pronuntiauit sententiam confirmacionis. Quam quidem sententiam dicti iudices cum in capitulo coram conuentu recitassent, tam sacrista quam precentor et alii contradictores electi ibidem, appellationibus suis renunciantes, in eius oscula irruerunt, promittendo coram eisdem ab illo die in antea eidem canonicam obedientiam, ut in hac carta continetur:

Omnibus Christi fidelibus ad quos presens scriptum peruenerit, frater H(enricus) dictus abbas de Wardone et R(icardus) prior de Donestaple et*a* A(dam) decanus ⟨de⟩ Salesberi,[1] salutem in Domino.*b*

Nouerit uniuersitas uestra nos mandatum domini pape suscepisse in hec*c* uerba: 'Innocentius etc.'[2] Huius igitur auctoritate mandati ad instantiam predictorum prouisorum ad dictum monasterium corporaliter accedentes,*d* uocari fecimus sacristam et monachos alios, predicti electi contradictores, quatinus coram nobis comparerent secundum formam mandati apostolici iuri parituri,*e* et in electi personam uel electionis formam, si uellent, aliquid obiecturi. Partibus igitur coram nobis in*f* iudicio constitutis, post plures uocationes,*g* et excepciones dilatorias in lite propositas lis tandem coram nobis fuit solempniter*h* contestata. Electores etiam, per quos plena negocii fieri debuit instructio, cum debita fuerunt sollempnitate et diligencia examinati, et eorum dicta congruo tempore publicata. Expletis postmodum secundum ordinem iuris solempnibus, decretum electionis, acta et confessiones in iure factas, et attestationes ipsas cum sollempni deliberacione et discussione iudiciali inspeximus diligenter. Omnibus igitur de more iudiciorum rite peractis, et sepedicti electi persona*i* a nobis arcius examinata,*j* cum nobis sufficienter liqueret eius*k* electionem regulariter et de persona ydonea canonice celebratam, uirorum prudentium et utriusque iuris peritorum consilio,*l* reiectis et reprobatis hiis que uel in electi personam uel in electionis formam minus probabiliter fuerunt obiecta, solum*m* Deum pre oculis habentes,[3]

a *Added over line by scribe* H   *b* in Domino *om.* C   *c* hoc H
d accedentes corporaliter C   *e* periti C   *f* hiis C   *g* notaciones C
h solempniter fuit C   *i* personam HC   *j* examinatam HC   *k* eis C
l consilioque C   *m* non solum C

[1] Adam succeeded Richard Poore as dean after the latter's election as bishop of Chichester, 9 January, and consecration on 25 January 1215.
[2] See above, p. 75.
[3] See above, p. 155 n. 2.

the consent of the other judges, imposed silence on him in accordance with the judgement of the pope, whose deputy he was in this matter. But as he was still not silenced by this, he threatened him in front of everyone with excommunication; and so at last they pronounced sentence in favour of confirmation. Now when the judges declared the verdict to the convent in the chapter-house, the sacrist, precentor and the other opponents of the abbot elect who were present, renouncing their appeal, rushed forward to give him the kiss of peace, promising him their canonical obedience from that day on, as contained in this charter:

To all the faithful in Christ to whom this writing comes, brother Henry abbot of Wardon, Richard prior of Dunstable, and Adam dean of Salisbury[1] send greetings in the Lord.

May you all know that we received a mandate from the pope in these words: 'Innocent etc.'[2] By the authority of this mandate, therefore, sent at the instance of the aforesaid 'prudent men', we went in person to the monastery and caused the sacrist and other monks, who opposed the abbot elect, to be summoned and to submit to the law in our presence, according to the form of the papal mandate, and, if they wished, to present any objections to the abbot elect's character or the form of his election. The parties gathered before us in court, therefore, and after many summonings and dilatory exceptions put forward in law, the suit was duly contested in our presence. The electors, by whose testimony a full reconstruction of the matter had to be made, were duly and diligently examined as was appropriate, and their statements made public at the same time. Shortly after, having completed this according to solemn law, we carefully examined the election decree, records and confessions made during the case, and the attestations themselves, with appropriate delibera-tion and judicial discussion. After everything had been carried out according to the rules of law, we closely examined the abbot elect's character, and when it seemed sufficiently clear to us that his election had been regularly and canonically celebrated in a fit person, with the advice of prudent men and of experts in both canon and civil law, we rejected and reproved those who had with little credibility objected to the abbot elect's character or the form of his election. Then, having God alone before our eyes,[3] and afire with the love of justice, we confirmed his election

et amore iusticie accensi, eandem, auctoritate nobis in hac
causa commissa, per sententiam diffinitiuam confirmauimus,
contradictoribus silentium perpetuum imponentes. Huic autem
diffinitioni nostre, cum eam in capitulo recitaremus, tam
sacrista quam precentor et ceteri contradictores electi adquiescentes in eius amplexus irruerunt, et eum ut canonice
f. 191   electum et rationabiliter confirmatum | osculati sunt; et una cum
aliis fautoribus eiusdem ibidem coram nobis canonicam ei
obedientiam promiserunt. Vt igitur hec a nobis tam sollempniter
acta robur perpetue firmitatis optineant, ea huius scripti serie et
sigillorum nostrorum appositione duximus roboranda.

Valeat uniuersitas uestra in Domino.

Igitur, licet in hac sententia contineatur quod, facta huius-
⟨modi⟩ᵃ recitacione a iudicibus in capitulo, sacrista et alii in
amplexus electi irruerunt, in sequentibus tamenᵇ euidentius
habetur qualiter et quando et sub qua districtione, tanquam inuiti
et quodammodo coacti¹ id fecerunt. Nam, sicut habetur superius,
postquam sacrista pro certo didicissetᶜ sententiam contra eundem
fore denunciandam,ᵈ recessit inde appellando; atque non eo
minus, prolata postmodum sententia, iudices duxerunt electum in
capitulum ut coram conuentu rei diffinicionem recitarent. Ad
illam itaque recitacionem audiendam absentauerunt se tam sacrista
quam precentor et Adam infirmarius et alii partis eorum. Quo
tamen itaᵉ facto, iudices duxerunt inde electum ad magnum
altare, cum ymno sollempniter a monachis et clero decantato;
atqueᶠ subsecuta ibidem a priore de Donestaple oratione, re-
duxerunt eum in chorum, et collocauerunt in sedem abbatis; ubi
sui et quidam, licet pauci, de parte aduersa in eius oscula irruerunt,
non tamen sacrista, neque precentor, neque Henricus Ruffus,
neque Walterus, neque Iohannes de Disce, neque Adam infirmarius, neque Gregorius, neque Willelmusᵍ pitantiarius cum aliis
pluribus, se subtrahentes. Quod cum iudices uidissent, iterato cum
electo intrantes capitulum, adunauerunt conuentum, sequente
populo non modico. Mox autem illis coadunatis, iudices mandauerunt sacristam et precentorem etʰ Adam infirmarium atque
alios absentes, per priorem scilicet et duos alios monachos,
quatinus auctoritate sibi indulta apparuissent ibidem coram eis
mandatum apostolicum audire. Quibus, licet inuite, tunc primo

---

ᵃ huius H; huius facta C   ᵇ tam H, *corr. over line by Hand* C
ᶜ didicisset H, *corr. over line by scribe*   ᵈ pronunciandam C   ᵉ *Om.* C
ᶠ at C   ᵍ .W. H; Willelmus C   ʰ at C

in a definitive judgement, by the authority committed to us in this case, imposing perpetual silence on his opponents. Now the sacrist, precentor, and the rest of the abbot elect's opponents, acquiescing in this our verdict when we pronounced it in the chapter-house, rushed forward to embrace him, kissing him in token of his being canonically elected and rationally confirmed; and they promised him their canonical obedience in our presence, together with the others. That these our solemn acts may abide in perpetual firmness, therefore, we have caused them to be written down in their due order, strengthening them with our seals.

Farewell to you all in the Lord.

Now although, according to this statement, the sacrist and others rushed to embrace the abbot elect after the verdict had been pronounced by the judges in the chapter-house, nevertheless the following information will make clear to what extent they did so under compulsion, as though unwilling and constrained to do so.[1] As I said before, after the sacrist became certain that the verdict was going to be pronounced against him, he withdrew to lodge an appeal. Nonetheless the verdict was given soon after and the judges then led the abbot elect into the chapter-house, to declare their decision to the whole convent. So the sacrist, precentor, Adam the infirmarer, and others of their party absented themselves from that pronouncement. After it the judges led the abbot elect from there to the high altar, while a hymn was sung by the monks and clerks; and when the prior of Dunstable had offered prayers there, they led him back to the choir and placed him in the abbot's seat, where his own and some of the adverse party, although few, hastened to give him the kiss of peace, but not the sacrist or the precentor, or Henry Rufus, or Walter, or John of Diss, or Adam the infirmarer, or Gregory, or William the pittancer, or many others who had slipped away. When the judges perceived this, they re-entered the chapter-house with the abbot elect and called the convent together, many other people also being present. As soon as they were all there, the judges ordered the sacrist, precentor, Adam the infirmarer, and other absentees by the authority committed to them, through the agency of the prior and two other monks, to appear before them to hear the papal mandate. When

---

[1] Cf. *JB*, p. 73: 'quasi inuiti et coacti'.

apparentibus, recapitulauit prior de Donestaple processum facti
secundum apostolicum mandatum sibi et sociis^a superius directum,
non pretermittendo quod in fine illius continetur mandati,
uidelicet quod, cognita ueritate electionis et confirmata, com-
pescerent ecclesiastica censura contradictores auctoritate predicta.
'Igitur hoc ordine secundum mandatum nobis iniunctum processi,
uolumus scire a te, sacrista, et ab aliis alias eleccioni contradicentibus, utrum sententie nostre diffinitiue, et domino H(ugoni) electo
per eandem a nobis confirmato, adquiescere uultis aut contradi-
cere.' Sacrista quidem, super hac^b responsione in arto iam positus,[1]
et precauens tamen ne contradicendo sententie diffinitiue aut
electioni incurreret sententiam quam iudices erant parati contradictoribus inferre, ait illis: 'Si uos, quos nulla ueritatis latet
circumstantia, protestaueritis in periculo anime uestre hic coram
nobis, eleccionem sine fraude secundum Deum processam, fateor
me plane sententie uestre et electioni de cetero assentire.' Mox-
que omnes eiusdem partis idem promiserunt. Quibus abbas de
Wardone, coram multitudine tam laicorum quam clericorum,
taliter satisfecit: 'Confiteor coram Deo et sanctis eius et uobis,
atque in periculo anime mee pro me et sociis^c meis protestor,^{d} quod
electio facta de H(ugone) de Norwolde, secundum quod intelligi-
mus et examinacione diligenti perscrutati sumus, et ueraciter^e
scimus, a Deo est, et uera et^f canonica.' Quibus auditis sacrista
atque alii singuli, tunc demum in eius amplexus irruentes promiserunt ei^g canonicam obedienciam.

Sopita itaque hoc ordine quoad iudicium populi et suffocata
omni malicia contra electum superius proposita, statim subsecutus
est dominus abbas suum officium. Nam in secunda die sequenti,
quod est sancti Gregorii,[2] post eius confirmacionem, eo capitulum
tenente atque in omnibus quoad spiritualia uices abbatis^h gerente,
constituit Ricardum de Stertesforde custodem criptarum, atque
postmodum die sequente commisit eidem Ricardo pariterque
magistro Alano, curam super confessionibus priuatis excercendam.
Quo facto, prior atque supprior et seniores in ordine tulerunt
indigne, eo quod duos nouicios pares illis fecerat, qui diu ante eos

^{a} consociis C ^{b} Om. C ^{c} consociis C ^{d} contestor C
^{e} ueracitates C ^{f} et C; om. H ^{g} Om. C ^{h} C adds plenarie

[1] Cf. *JB*, p. 86: 'in arto positus'.
[2] 12 March. His confirmation, then, would have been on the 10th. The *Bury Chronicle* (p. 2) and *Cronica Buriensis* (*Mem.* iii. 11) both give the date of Hugh's

they had at last appeared, although reluctantly, the prior of
Dunstable recapitulated the course of their action according to the
papal mandate sent earlier to him and his associates, not omitting
what was contained at the end of it: that when the truth about the
election was known and confirmed, they were to threaten the
opponents of their authority with papal censure. 'So, having
carried out this business enjoined upon us by the mandate, we
want to know from you, sacrist, and from the other opponents of
the election, whether you intend to obey or oppose our final
verdict, and the abbot elect Hugh whom we have confirmed by it.'
The sacrist was put on the spot[1] as to how he should reply, but
taking care not to deny the final verdict, and so incur the punishment which the judges were prepared to mete out to those who
disregarded it, he said to them: 'If you, before whom no particle
of truth remains hidden, will state here in our presence, in peril of
your souls, that the election was carried out without trickery,
according to the will of God, I will give my full assent to your
verdict and to the election.' And simultaneously all of his party
made the same promise. To whom the abbot of Wardon, amid a
crowd of clerks and laymen made profession: 'I acknowledge in
the presence of God and His saints and yourselves, on behalf of
myself and my associates, in peril of my soul, that we truly know
the election of Hugh of Northwold, according to what we have
learnt and carefully weighed by diligent scrutiny, to be of God,
and truly canonical.' Thereupon the sacrist and each of the others
ran at last to embrace him, promising him canonical obedience.

In this way, by popular judgement, all the evil which had earlier
been directed against the abbot elect was suppressed and ex-
tinguished. At once the abbot entered upon his office. On the
second day after his confirmation, St. Gregory's,[2] he held chapter
and took charge of everything pertaining to the spiritual duties of
an abbot, making Richard of Stortford guardian of the crypts, and
on the following day appointing him and Master Alan to take
charge of private confessions. But the prior, subprior, and the
senior monks greeted this arrangement with indignation, for he had
made two novices their equals, although they had borne the 'heat

confirmation as 11 March, both perhaps drawing on the lost portion of the
Annales. In the list of abbots contained in Brit. Mus. Harl. MS. 743, f. 52
(*Registrum Lakenhethe*, late fourteenth century; *Monasticon*, iii. 155), the date
of Hugh's confirmation and blessing is given as 8 March, which must be wrong.

pondus diei sustinuerant et estus;[1] et illis ita[a] murmurantibus
peruentum est hoc ad aures electi per illum qui hec uiderat et
f. 191[v] audierat.[2] Dominus autem | electus, cupiens per omnia priori tunc
et senioribus placere, absoluit dictos a confessione superius iniuncta, uerum etiam cum unus ex illis, magister scilicet Alanus,
sepius in capitulo coram electo prostratus, absolutionem super
iniuncto petiuisset officio.

In hac igitur parte[b] domino H(ugone) electo per dies aliquot
post confirmacionem eius[c] commorante, de assensu conuentus et
domini Cantuariensis archiepiscopi, curiam adiit, comitantibus
secum priore, celerario, precentore, Adam infirmario, Ricardo de
Hengham magistro⟨que⟩ Nicholao ad supplicandum uidelicet[d]
domino regi ex parte conuentus, ut dictum H(ugonem) ab eis
canonice electum et iam confirmatum in eius gratiam susciperet et
amorem. Qui cum uenissent extra Notingham, uidelicet in
Schyrewode,[3] dominumque regem a longe uenientem intuiti
essent, descenderunt ab equis suis, ut scilicet pedibus regi occur-
rendo ipsius gratiam perinde facilius adquirerent; et eo cominus
accedente corruerunt ante eum, genibus flexis, regiam beniuolentiam flagitando et gratiam. Eapropter, humilitate tali coram eo
preostensa, miro modo placatus[e] est rex; atque non permittens[f]
electum humo diucius iacere,[g] erexit eum, et sic demum in hiis
uerbis ora resoluit:[4] 'Bene uenias, domine electe, saluo iure regni
mei.'[5] Et pergentes pariter longo tempore secretius adinuicem
loquebantur, nullo mediante alio.[h] Cumque dominus electus illo
die super negocio[i] a domino rege plenum non posset habere
responsum, accessit[j] in crastino in capella, ubi ipse rex[k] missam
erat auditurus. Qua finita, dixit rex electo:[l] 'Vade ad Willelmum
Brewere;[6] ipse enim uoluntatem meam tibi plenius exponet.' Quo
accedente, et inter plurima a quodam priore et Pagano Longobardense[7] obiecta electo et responsa, dixit ei Willelmus[m] Brewere:
'Dominus noster rex hac die Lune, que est secunda[n] post festum

---

  [a] itaque C   [b] potestate C   [c] eius confirmacionem C   [d] uidelicet
ad supplicandum C   [e] C adds factus   [f] permittentem HC
[g] iacentem H   [h] alio mediante C   [i] C adds suo   [j] accessit C;
accepit H   [k] rex ipse C   [l] electo rex C   [m] .W. H; Willelmus C
[n] C adds dies

---

  [1] Matt. 20: 12.
  [2] Ier. 23: 18; cf. above, p. 22 n. 1. Perhaps the author himself?

and burden of the day'[1] long before them. And their murmuring was brought to the abbot elect's ears by one who saw and heard it.[2] So, wanting to please the prior and seniors in all things, he absolved these men from the confessions earlier laid on them, especially as one of them, Master Alan, had knelt many times before the abbot elect in chapter, asking to be released from the duty laid on him.

After Hugh had been with them for several days after his confirmation, he went to court with the assent of the convent and the archbishop of Canterbury, accompanied by the prior, cellarer, precentor, Adam the infirmarer, Richard of Hingham, and Master Nicholas, to ask the king on the convent's behalf to receive him into his favour and love, seeing that he had been canonically elected by them, and was now confirmed. When they had arrived outside Nottingham, in Sherwood forest,[3] and saw the king coming in the distance, they dismounted from their horses so that, meeting him on foot, they might gain his favour more readily. And when he had come up to them, they went down on their knees, beseeching his favour and grace. Because of such humility displayed before him, the king was wonderfully appeased; and not permitting the abbot elect any longer to lie on the ground he raised him, and then addressed him in these words:[4] 'Welcome, lord abbot elect— saving the rights of my realm!'[5] And continuing together for a long time they talked with one another apart and in private. But the abbot-elect was unable to obtain a full answer from the king that day over his business, so he came the next day to the chapel, where the king himself was about to hear mass. When it was over, the king said to the abbot elect: 'Go to William Brewer,[6] for he will fully explain my wishes to you.' So they went to him, and after many objections lodged against the abbot elect by a certain prior and Pagan of Lombardy had been answered,[7] William Brewer said to them: 'Our lord the king is to hold a council this coming Monday, that is the second day after the feast of the blessed

[3] John was at Nottingham 24–31 March, and from 26–28 stayed at Clipstone, near Sherwood, where there was a royal hunting-lodge (*Itinerary*).

[4] A Virgilian tag; cf. above, p. 89 n. 2.

[5] See above, p. 121.

[6] John's most faithful servant, grown rich in the royal service, and active as an Exchequer baron. Painter, pp. 71–8, and *passim*.

[7] Since Pagan was earlier an advocate of the anti-election party (see above, p. 153), his opposition here suggests that they had not yet lost all hope of quashing Hugh's election, in spite of the judges-delegate's decision.

beati*a* Ambrosii,[1] cum baronibus et magnatibus suis*b* Anglie super quibusdam arduis regni sui apud Oxhoniam habiturus est consilium.[2] Verum igitur, quoniam negocii uestri processus eius usitatis uidetur libertatibus derogare, consilio baronum suorum fidelium ad illum diem plenius uobis super hoc respondebit.'*c*

Igitur dominus H(ugo) electus, sub hac spe consolacionis, ad diem apud Oxhoniam prefixam accedens, tam archiepiscopus quam comes Salesberi pariter cum Wyntoniense et Ricardo de Marisco atque Willelmo Brewere et aliis magnatibus ibidem presentibus, effectualiter pro eo regiam interpellando maiestatem efflagitabant. Sed quoniam rex intra se statuerat dicto H(ugoni) electo nullatenus assentire, nisi precederet certa quantitas nummorum, licet etiam ad id*d* consentiendum a regis consiliariis pluries admonitus, sed, domini Cantuariensis consilio, minime adquiescens, post magnas tandem expensas et dierum dilaciones,*e* post uerborum etiam*f* palliaciones*g* et fatuas magnatum promissiones, super dicti H(ugonis) electi negocio, tale a domino rege egressum est responsum: 'Quoniam fidelium meorum consilio super uniuersis Anglie electionibus iam*h* ad derogacionem libertatum mearum factis dominum papam per nuncios meos conueni, suspendo ad presens negocium electionis tue, donec per eosdem mandatum illius super hiis plenius habuero.'[3]

Suscepto itaque tali responso a rege, reuersus est domum cum magistro Thoma de Walsingham et magistro Nicholao, die parascheue ante Pascha,[4] nondum*i* tamen benedictus; quo etiam die dominus Lucas episcopus*j* de Euerous uenit ad*k* sanctum Aedmundum atque ad peticionem electi confecit illo die crisma et oleum, et in uigilia Pasche ordines consecrauit. Subsequente autem die sancti Iuonis archiepiscopi,[5] accessit dominus H(ugo) electus ad capitulum, atque de consilio prioris, supprioris, sacriste, I(ocelini) elemosinarii, R(icardi) precentoris, constituit Iohannem de Disce et Adam tunc infirmarium*l* custodes omnium maneriorum ad celerariam pertinentium, necnon et Bradefeld, Pakeham,

a sancti C   *b* suos C; sue H   *c* respondebit C; respondit H   *d* ad id *om.* C   *e* C *adds* et   *f* *Om.* C   *g* pollicitaciones C   *h* tam C   *i* non C   *j* *Om.* C   *k* apud C   *l* H *adds* atque Rogerum filium Drogonis, *canc. by scribe*

[1] 6 April.
[2] The *Electio* is the only source to mention this council, which was probably the occasion when the barons hoped to receive the satisfaction promised them at London in January (Painter, p. 301). On 30 March, probably only a few days after his meeting with Hugh, the king sent a letter to him ('Rex *abbati* et conuentui...') concerning the repayment of a loan made by the prior and convent of 250 marks to the earl of Salisbury and Savary de Mauleon 'ad negocia nostra

Ambrose,[1] with his barons and magnates of England at Oxford,[2] to discuss some problems of his realm. Because the way you have gone about your business seems to show contempt for his customary liberties, he will give you a full reply over it then, with the advice of his loyal barons.'

The abbot elect Hugh, therefore, with this hope of consolation, went on the appointed day to Oxford, where the archbishop and the earl of Salisbury, the bishop of Winchester, Richard Marsh, William Brewer, and other great lords entreated as best they could for him. But the king had determined to withhold his assent to Hugh's election until he had first received a specified sum of money. Hugh was much admonished by the royal advisers to agree to this, but, by the advice of the archbishop of Canterbury, he would not. At length, after great expenses and after days of delaying, after soothing words and empty promises from the magnates, the abbot elect received the following answer from the king about his business: 'Because by the advice of those loyal to me I have sent my messengers to the pope to negotiate over the elections which are now being made all over England, in contempt of my liberties, I suspend for the present the matter of your election, until I have a clearer directive from him respecting these others.'[3]

After receiving this reply from the king, Hugh returned home with Master Thomas of Walsingham and Master Nicholas on Good Friday;[4] now he had not yet been blessed. That day Luke bishop of Evreux came to St. Edmunds, and at the abbot elect's request prepared oil and chrism, and on the vigil of Easter Sunday consecrated some monks to holy orders. A little later, on the day of St. Ivo the archbishop,[5] the abbot elect came into the chapter-house, and with the advice of the prior, subprior, sacrist, Jocelin the almoner, and Richard the precentor, appointed John of Diss and Adam the (then) infirmarer guardians of all the cellary manors, as well as Bradfield, Pakenham, Barton, Rougham,

facienda' (*Rot. Litt. Pat.*, p. 173). Part of the repayment was to be made 'per manum Roberti sacriste', who no doubt had had some say in the making of the loan, which was probably to pay for soldiers. Early in the year de Mauleon was summoned to England with a force of Poitevin mercenaries and in May the earl was in command of a similar force (Painter, pp. 299, 306).

[3] Although John had granted freedom of election to the churches of his realm on 21 November 1214 (see above, p. 119 n. 4), he was still apparently trying to negotiate a way around this concession.

[4] 17 April.   [5] 24 April.

Bertone, Rutham, Herningeswelle, Horningesheth et Werketone, ut^a illi duo nomine celerarii curam habentes extrinsecam, per manus Petri de Thifteshale et Roberti de hospitali curam intrinsecam sub illis habentium, quoad uictum monachorum et hospitum

f. 192 suffi|cientes inuenissent expensas. Petrum quidem celerarium posuit super hospitale, Walterum autem Galle super infirmarium atque Rogerum filium Drogonis super hostilariam forensem. Quibus ita^b dispositis, precepit magistro Thome^c de Walsingham et Philippo, ut cum dictis duobus[1] pergentes karucas et stauramentum singulorum maneriorum, necnon et terras nostras^d tam seminatas quam non seminatas, in scriptum redigerent. Illud idem statuit fieri per omnes obedientias de rebus tam mobilibus quam immobilibus, ne quis inde processu temporis aliquam posset facere fraudacionem. Factumque^e est^f in^g hoc anno secundo, die sancti Iouini,^{h}[2] post electionem eiusdem.

Euolutis postmodum paucis diebus, facta est commotio inter dominum regem et barones Anglie, eo scilicet quod dominus rex cartam eorundem ab illustri rege Henrico patre suo iam olim^i super maioribus libertatibus confirmatam, adnichilare pro uiribus nitebatur.[3] In huius⟨modi⟩ igitur commocione regis et regni, dominus S(tephanus) Cantuariensis archiepiscopus, qui circa negocium domini H(ugonis) abbatis terminandum partes sedulas uigilanter interponebat, dominum H(ugonem) abbatem, nondum tamen benedictum, neque ad regiam gratiam admissum, litteris suis ad se mandauit uenire^j festinanter. Quo ueniente, consuluit ne diucius propter casus fortuitos et euentus rerum^k dubios eius benedictionem aliquatenus protellasset.^{l} Cuius consilio, utpote sano, adquiescente, perrexit ad episcopum Rouensem, nomine scilicet magistrum Benedictum;[4] suscepit^m ab eo^n benedictionem apud^o uillam eiusdem episcopi que uocatur Hallinge,[5] xiv.^{p} kal. Iunii feria iii.,^{q} littera e.^{r}[6] Atque post benedictionem eius, cum^s in eodem loco in scandailles et mitra et anulo et omni sollempnitate celebrasset,[7] rei nouitas auribus presencium

---

^{a} et C ^{b} itaque C ^{c} .T. H; Thome C ^{d} Om. C
^{e} Factum C ^{f} C adds quoque ^{g} Om. C ^{h} Ieronimi C
^{i} Om. C ^{j} uenire mandauit C ^{k} rerum euentus C ^{l} protelallasset C ^{m} suscepitque C ^{n} ab eo om. C ^{o} C adds ab eo
^{p} xvi. C ^{q} ii. C ^{r} Om. C ^{s} eum C

---

[1] i.e. John of Diss and Adam.

[2] 25 April. The C reading gives 30 September, which must, of course, be wrong.

Herringswell, Horningsheath, and Warkton. They were to take charge of external business on the cellarer's behalf, while Peter of Tivetshall and Robert of the hospital had care of interior business under them, namely the provision of adequate funds for the monks' sustenance and hospitality. Peter the cellarer was set over the hospital, Walter Gale over the infirmary and Roger FitzDrew over the buying of food for the guest-house. After these people were so appointed he ordered Master Thomas of Walsingham and Philip to travel around with the other two,[1] and write down the number of ploughs and amount of stock in each manor, and also which of our lands were sown or unsown. This he ordered to be done in the offices of all the obedientiaries, together with all their property, movable or immovable, so that no one in the future would be able to defraud them. This was done on St. Jovinus' day,[2] in the second year after his election.

A few days later a dispute arose between the king and the English barons because the king was at that time trying to annul by force their charter of greater liberties, confirmed to them by his father the illustrious king Henry.[3] On account of this dispute between ruler and ruled, Archbishop Stephen of Canterbury, who was diligently using his good offices to seek an end to Hugh's business, wrote ordering him to come at once, as he was not yet blessed or admitted into the king's favour. When he had arrived he advised him that because of the chance happenings and doubtful events taking place, he ought not to delay any longer to be blessed. Agreeing to this sensible advice, he went to Master Benedict, bishop of Rochester,[4] receiving the blessing from him at the bishop's vill called Halling,[5] on Tuesday 19 May, letter E.[6] After his blessing, when he had celebrated solemn mass there in sandals and mitre and ring,[7] the news of the capture of London by the

---

[3] The Coronation Charter of Henry I; ed. H. W. C. Davis, *Stubbs' Select Charters* (9th edn., Oxford, 1913), pp. 117–19.

[4] Benedict of Sawston (1214/15–1226); he had taught at Paris and was a friend of Langton, who had recommended him for the see (Gibbs, *Bishops*, pp. 27–8).

[5] Five miles from Rochester, where the bishops had a palace before the Conquest. The abbots of Bury enjoyed the papal privilege of consecration by whichever bishop they wished (*PUE*, iii. no. 8). See also *Bury Chronicle*, p. 2.

[6] On 4 May John ordered the knights of St. Edmunds to come to Bury to hear the orders of John de Cornard regarding the custody of the abbey lands. *Rot. Litt. Pat.*, p. 135. The letter should be F.

[7] The episcopal regalia allowed the abbots of Bury by papal privilege. *PUE*, iii. nos. 186, 197, etc.

insonuit,[1] uidelicet super capcione Londonie a baronibus Anglie. Erat autem hec captio facta xvii. kal. Iunii, die Dominica, hora quasi matutinali, littera d, anno regni regis Iohannis xvi.[2] Hiis itaque hoc ordine prosecutis, dominus abbas domum rediit, celebrauitque magnum conuiuium omnibus ad illud ingredi uolentibus.

Quo facto, habito cum suis consilio, misit dominum Ricardum de Saxham apud Londoniam, ut mediante consilio baronum[a] sane perquireret utrum domini regis gratiam, tociens et tociens rescriptam,[b] rebus se habentibus ut tunc,[c] expediret efflagitare. Cui quidem dominus Cantuariensis omnesque magnates in hoc concurrerunt, ut domini sui regis gratiam non solum bis uel ter,[3] sed ⟨usque⟩ quo eam obtinuisset,[d] efflagitaret incessanter. Quo audito Ricardus profectus est[e] ad regem apud Stanes, ubi etiam inuenit comitem Warennie et comitem de Pembroc[f] et Robertum de Burgate.[4] Cumque causam sui aduentus in conspectu domini regis ex parte domini abbatis et conuentus humiliter perfudisset, respondit rex blando[g] uultu et benigno: 'Frater, reuertere quam cicius ad domum, electoque uestro ex parte mea[h] iniungas, ut ad me sine omni dilatione[i] uenire festinet.[j] Ego quidem Dei gratia faciam tantum in[k] eius presentia, ut domui uestre[l] cuncteque ecclesie Anglicane cedet in laudem et honorem.' Idem etiam in litteris suis per eundem Ricardum domino abbati destinatis,[m] licet in eisdem non nominasset,[n] abbatem significauit.

Quod cum dominus abbas cognouisset, postposita omni negocio terreno, iter arripuit in crastino uersus dominum regem post eiusdem mandati suscepcionem, die scilicet sancti Bonefacii, quod est none Iunii,[5] comitantibus secum H(erberto) priore, R(icardo) precentore, R(oberto) sacrista, Ricardo de Hengham et magistro Nicholao; inuenitque dominum regem apud Wyndlesoure, die Martis proxima post diem Pentecostes.[6] Cumque super negocio suo[o] cum domino Cantuariensi ibidem presente tractasset, affuit dominus rex per eosdem transiturus. Cui dominus Cantuariensis

[a] barones H; baronum C [b] requisitam C [c] nunc C
[d] opertinuisset H; optinuisse C [e] Om. C [f] Fenbroc C
[g] placido C [h] mea parte C [i] Om. C; blank space left
[j] festinet uenire C [k] modo C [l] Om. C [m] destinatas H, corr.; destinatas C [n] nominasse C [o] suo negocio C

[1] Cf. Augustine, De Gen. ad Litt. (PL, xxxiv, col. 469): '. . . quod autem nouum insonuit auribus . . .'
[2] The writer actually gives the correct day of the week, but the wrong day of the month, which should be the 17th. This may, however, be a scribal error.
[3] 4 Reg. 6: 10; Iob 33: 29.
[4] Supporters of the royal cause; the last-named would be particularly well known to the Bury monks since he held lands in Suffolk (Kalendar, pp. 66, 148). The date must have been about 30 May, since Richard arrived back at the house

English barons reached the ears of those present.[1] This capture
was made on 16 May, being a Sunday, letter D, about the hour of
matins, in the 16th year of King John.[2] After these events the
abbot returned home and gave a great feast to all who cared to
come.

Next, taking counsel with his friends, he sent Richard of
Saxham to London, to ask the barons' advice as to whether it was
any use entreating the king's oft-sought favour, things being then
in such a state. The archbishop of Canterbury and all the magnates
agreed that he should entreat the king's favour not merely twice
or thrice,[3] but unceasingly, until he got what he wanted. Thereupon Richard went to the king at Staines, finding there the earls
of Warenne and Pembroke and Robert of Burgate as well.[4] And
when he had humbly made known the cause of his arrival on
behalf of the abbot and convent to the king in person, the latter
replied with an unruffled and pleasant expression: 'Brother, return
home at once, and order your abbot elect in my name to hasten
to me without delay. For by God's grace I will do something in
his presence which will redound to the praise and honour of your
house and of the whole English church.' Moreover, in a letter to
Hugh which he entrusted to Richard, although he was not so
named, he let him know that he was going to make him abbot.

When the abbot received this news, forsaking all temporal
matters, he began his journey to the king, on the day after receipt
of his letter, St. Boniface's, 5 June,[5] accompanied by Prior Herbert,
Richard the precentor, Robert the sacrist, Richard of Hingham,
and Master Nicholas; and he came to the king at Windsor, on the
Tuesday after Whitsun.[6] And when he had discussed his business
with the archbishop of Canterbury there present, the king came
up, about to pass between them. To whom the archbishop of

on 4 June, and Hugh took from the 5th to the 9th to travel from Bury to the
king at the same place.

[5] On 2 June the king ordered the transference of the abbey estates to the
custody of Thomas of Barrow, perhaps because John de Cornard had joined the
baronial party (*Rot. Litt. Pat.*, p. 142b). On 3 June a great fire destroyed a
large part of the vill of St. Edmunds (*Bury Chronicle*, p. 2; *Cronica Buriensis*,
Mem. iii. 11, both probably drawing on the lost portion of the *Annales*). It
illustrates the writer's restricted interest that there is no mention of this in the
Electio.

[6] 9 June. According to the *Itinerary*, John was at Winchester on this day, and
did not reach Windsor until the 10th, the date on which he finally gave his assent
to Hugh's election. The *Itinerary* must be right, and the solution probably is
that John arrived at Windsor late in the day on the 9th.

premissa salutacione ait: 'Domine mi rex, ecce abbas de sancto
Aedmundo, qui gratiam domini regis nostri efflagitare per nos non
desistit.' Cui rex: 'Accedat ad me in crastino in prato de Stanes,
ibidemque gratia Dei et meritis uestris interpositis eius negocium
expedire attemptabimus.' Quo adueniente, atque in prato sito
⟨inter Wyndlesoure et Stanes⟩ moram diucinam faciente, post
f. 192ᵛ interlocutiones^a non modicas et internuncios nobilium | hinc inde
super hoc a domino rege sepius destinatos, tandem osculo medi-
ante abbatem admisit in gratiam; dilata tamen fidelitate ab eodem
regi debenda usque in crastinum. Quo facto subsecutus^b est rex,
et ait: 'Abba pater,¹ nunc mea restat unica peticio postulanda,
tuaque benignitate^c supplenda, quatinus, quem in meam diuina
hodie miseracio reformauit gratiam, a mense ne priuemur partici-
pacione, assit tua oratio.' Quo fauente, comederunt simul illo die
apud Wyndlesoure.

Qui quidem cum sederent post prandium super lectum regium,
alternatim super pluribus confabulantes in camera erexit^d sacrista
cunctis uidentibus, et procidens coram rege flexis^e genibus
adorauit eum, dicens: 'Benedictus Deus et pater Domini nostri
Ihesu Christi,² qui cor domini nostri regis sic uisitauit, ut non
solum dominum abbatem^f in suam admitteret gratiam, uerum
etiam preterite discordie non recordaretur.' Cui rex, audiente tam
abbate quam aliis, tanquam in furore spiritus, adiuncto sacramento
respondit: 'Per pedes Domini,³ dimidium annum transactum^g est
ex quo eum in meam suscepissem gratiam et amorem nisi tu
esses!' Et conuersus ad abbatem adiunxit dicens: 'Iste sacrista,
O abbas, multos tibi adquisiuit inimicos in curia mea. Nam cum a
partibus rediissem transmarinis, ob peticionem legati Francie in
animo disposui in meam gratiam te^h suscepisse. Sed mei, qui huius
sacriste partes contra te fouere nitebantur, pro uiribus non solum
⟨non⟩ permittebant, uerumⁱ ⟨etiam⟩ propositum meum subuertendo
ad maiorem contra te indignationem accendebant.' Quibus coram
abbate in presentia sacriste recitatis, dominus rex cepit secretius
recitare a gemino ouo⁴ quicquid in eius curia contra dominum
abbatem idem sacrista inuestigauerat. Quo uiso, miro modo
erubuit sacrista, et pre confusione non sustinens uultum regium
diucius, clam non petita a rege licentia inde se subtraxit.

---

^a locutiones inter C   ^b subsecutusque C   ^c beningnitate H
^d Om. C   ^e nexis H, corr. in marg. by Hand C   ^f Om. C
^g dimidium annum transactum H; dimidius annus transactus C   ^h Om. C
ⁱ utrum H, corr. in marg. by Hand C

---

¹ Reg. Ben., c. 2; from Rom. 8: 15, etc.
² I Pet. 1: 3.

Canterbury, after first greeting him, said: 'My lord king, here is the abbot of St. Edmunds, who has unceasingly entreated the king's favour through us.' The king answered: 'Let him come to me tomorrow in Staines meadow, where by God's grace and the aid of your merits we will attempt to settle his business.' And when he had come and waited for a long time in the meadow which is between Windsor and Staines, after much discussion and the frequent sending of messengers to and fro between the nobles and the king over the matter, the abbot was at length admitted into favour, and the king gave him the kiss of peace, postponing, however, the fealty due from him until the next day. After this was done, the king followed him and said: 'Father abbot,[1] I have now just one final request for your kindness to fulfil; let us not be without your company at table, since the divine mercy has this day restored you to my favour.' Which granted, they dined together at Windsor that day.

After dinner, while they sat together on the royal couch, conversing privately about many things, the sacrist rose before them all, and throwing himself before the king on bended knees, he did obeisance to him, saying: 'Blessed be the God and Father of our Lord Jesus Christ,[2] who has so visited our king's heart, that not only does he admit the abbot into his grace, but also puts out of his mind the earlier discord.' To whom the king, in the hearing of the abbot and others replied as in a rage, saying with an oath: 'By the Lord's feet,[3] but for you I would have received him into my favour and love six months ago!' And turning to the abbot he continued: 'This sacrist, O abbot, has won you many enemies in my court. For when I had returned from overseas I was disposed, because of the petition of the French legate, to receive you into my favour. But those around me, who were working with all their might against you on this sacrist's behalf, not only prevented and overthrew my purpose, but even caused my anger against you to grow.' And having told the abbot this in the sacrist's presence, the king began to disclose to him more privately, and 'from the twin egg'[4] whatever the sacrist had ferreted out in his court to use against the abbot. Observing this, the sacrist became amazingly red, and unable in his confusion to bear the royal look any longer, he retired secretly, without the king's leave.

[3] Similar oaths are recorded of the king by Wendover (ii. 46, etc.)
[4] Hor., *Ars Poet.*, 147; cf. above, p. 155 n. 3.

Quibus ita peractis et repetitis coram tot et tantis nobilibus, dominus quidem abbas, facta fidelitate regi in crastino, redire festinauit ad propria.[1] Qui licet adeo ab aduersariis Dei et ecclesie superius infestatus, ut nomen eius dignitatis suppeditarent, et ad gratiam regiam promerendam impedirent, ab illo die in antea non tamen ab illis, sed ab ipso rege 'Abba pater'[2] et 'sanctus' uocabatur, cum honore et reuerentia. Hac igitur felicitate, uenerabilis H(ugo) dictus abbas diuina perornans[a] dispositione, ualidi[b] tamen maris tempestate[c3] contra eum seuiente uiriliter repressa, scandalis, et mortis periculis diuersis sibi sepius protensis[d] probabiliter reiectis et reprobatis, periuriis eciam et falsis testimoniis obiectis plane et dilucide[e] conculcatis, sic se gerebat ad omnes, ut non solum ad fidei domesticos,[4] qui pro causa sua honesta pondus diei pertulerant et estus,[5] se redderet amabilem, uerum etiam alios, ne dicam inimicos sed utinam amicos, prelatia et dignitate omni studio[f] illis studeret proferre.[g]

Facta est autem huius rei diffinitio anno regni regis Iohannis xvi., a passione sancti Aedmundi cccxlvi., a passione beati Thome martiris xlv., anno solaris cicli decennouennalis[h] xix., lunaris vi., indictione iii., anno a bisexto iii., concurrente iii., regulari iii., Dominicali[i] littera d, epacta xviii.,[6] prestante Domino nostro et adiuuante, qui non solum suum sed etiam suos a manibus inimicorum taliter eruit potentum,[j7] et nos ab eorundem defendit 'labiis iniquis et lingua dolosa',[8] amen, ne eum obcecent quoad rigorem iusticie excercendum et ad cuiuslibet meritum remunerandum donis interpositis, que etiam oculos sapientum obcecant.[9] 'Dignus est enim operarius mercede sua.'[10]

---

[a] perornatus C   [b] ualida C   [c] tempestate maris C   [d] pretensis C
[e] uilucide H, *corr. in marg. by Hand C*   [f] studeo C   [g] preferre C
[h] decem nouellalis C   [i] dominicali C; dominica H   [j] *End of extract in* C

After all these things had been done before so many great nobles, the abbot did homage to the king the next day, and hastened home.[1] And although previously much assailed by the enemies of God and the Church, who tried to undermine his good name and to hinder him from winning the royal favour, from that day on he was called, not indeed by them, but by the king himself, 'father abbot'[2] and 'holy' in honour and reverence. By this good fortune, therefore, the worthy abbot Hugh, adorning his office by the divine will, manfully subdued the tempest of the mighty sea[3] raging against him, vigorously met and overcame the various scandals and deadly perils threatening him, and openly and thoroughly trampled underfoot the perjury and false witness employed against him. And he so bore himself towards everybody, as not only to show his gratitude to those of the 'household of faith',[4] who for his sake had honourably borne 'the heat and burden of the day',[5] but even in the case of others—whom I will not call his enemies although I wish I could say they were his friends—he laboured assiduously to promote them to high office and dignity in the Church.

The end of this dispute came in the 16th year of King John, the 346th after the passion of St. Edmund, the 45th after the passion of the blessed martyr Thomas, the 19th of the 19-year solar cycle, the 6th of the lunar cycle, the third indiction, bissextile year 3, concurrent number 3, regular number 3, dominical letter D, epact 18,[6] by the help and undertaking of our Lord, who saved not only his cause but also his friends from the hands of their powerful enemies,[7] and defended us from their 'lying lips and deceitful tongue',[8] amen; may they not, by the use of bribery, blind him as to the distribution of strict justice, or the rewarding of merit— such people who 'even blind the eyes of the wise';[9] 'for the labourer is worthy of his hire.'[10]

---

[1] On 11 June John notified the custodians of the abbey that he had confirmed Hugh's election, and ordered them to hand back the abbey estates to the abbot and convent (*Rot. Litt. Pat.*, p. 142b). On the same date he issued a general mandate to the same effect (ibid.).

[2] *Reg. Ben.*, c. 2; cf. above, p. 170 n. 1.

[3] Act. 27: 18; cf. Abbo (*Mem.* i. 19): 'ualida tempestate persecutionis'.

[4] Gal. 6: 10.

[5] Matt. 20: 12; cf. above, p. 162 n. 1.

[6] For a similar list of dates, probably this author's source, see Hermann, *De Miraculis Sancti Edmundi* (*Mem.* i. 88).

[7] Iud. 8: 34, etc.   [8] Ps. 119: 2.

[9] Deut. 16: 19.   [10] Luc. 10 : 7.

APPENDIX I

The texts of the following letters are in C ff. 29ᵛ–30ᵛ; all three are printed in Mem. iii. 14–16, no. 2 also in Major, Acta, pp. 13–14.

1. *See above*, p. 11[1]

f. 29ᵛ Omnibus Christi fidelibus ad quos presens scriptum peruenerit, H(erbertus) prior sancti Edmundi et conuentus eiusdem loci eternam in Domino salutem.

Nouerit uniuersitas uestra nos ratam habere electionem factam in abbatem de fratre Hugone de Norwolde per fratres nostros, scilicet Robertum camerarium, magistrum Henricum de Ely,

f. 30 Gocelinum de Altari, Iohannem de Laueham, Hugonem | subcelerarium,[2] Thomam tercium priorem, Thomam de Walsingham, in quos uota nostra unanimiter contulimus de eligendo nobis abbate. Et ut hec nostra electio, per predictos fratres nostros facta, stabilis et rata permaneat, eam presenti scripto commendauimus et sigilli nostri appositione corroborauimus.

Valeat uniuersis.

2. *See above*, p. 37

Clementissimo patri et domino Innocentio Dei gratia summo pontifici S(tephanus) permissione diuina Cantuariensis ecclesie minister humilis salutem et deuotissime obedientie[a] famulatum.

Quia uestre sanctitatis auribus multa suggeruntur, tam uera quam falsa, ne uos circumueniat falsitas ueritatis inimica,[b] quod de electione ecclesie sancti Edmundi pro certo didici, pietati uestre pro certo significare dignum duxi. Cum post decessum uenerabilis abbatis ipsius ecclesie prior et conuentus de electione pastoris sibi preficiendi de more tractassent, tandem, sicut pro certo didici, et

f. 30ᵛ sicut littere pri|oris ⟨et⟩ capituli patentes, quas post electionem factam mihi transmiserunt, in media custodia tam maioris[c]

---

[a] obedientiam C   [b] inimita C   [c] C *adds* securita

---

[1] The *Cronica Buriensis* (*Mem.* iii. 14) erroneously describes this text as the actual *littere de rato* demanded of the chapter by the seven electors before they made known their choice. If this were so, Hugh's name would hardly appear in it as it does. This version, in fact, is the *carta de rato* mentioned so often in the

Letters relating to the election dispute contained in the Cronica Buriensis *but not in the* Electio Hugonis.

1. *The convent's charter of ratification, 7 August 1213*[1]

To all those faithful in Christ to whom this writing comes, Herbert prior of St. Edmunds and the convent there send perpetual greetings in the Lord.

Let all know that we have ratified the election to the abbacy of brother Hugh of Northwold, made by our brothers Robert the chamberlain, Master Henry of Ely, Jocelin of the Altar, John of Lavenham, Hugh the subcellarer,[2] Thomas the third prior and Thomas of Walsingham, in whom, by our unanimous vote, we vested the power to elect us an abbot. And that this our election, made by these brothers, may abide secure and approved, we have commended it by the present writing and confirmed it by the affixing of our seal.

Farewell to you all.

2. *Archbishop Stephen Langton to Innocent III, January 1214*

To his most clement father and lord, Innocent, pope by the grace of God, Stephen by the divine permission humble servant of the church of Canterbury sends greetings and the servitude of his devoted obedience.

Since many things, both true and false, are brought to your holiness's ears, lest you be deceived by falsity, truth's enemy, I have thought good to make known to your piety with certainty what I have received for certain concerning the election at the church of St. Edmunds. After the death of the worthy abbot of that church, the prior and convent proceeded, according to custom, to the election of a pastor. At length, as I have learned for certain, and as the letters patent which the prior and chapter sent me after

---

Electio (see above, pp. 51, 95, 109, 157), drawn up immediately following the announcement of Hugh's election by the seven, and his acceptance by the convent. The fact that two such similar charters were drawn up, probably within an hour of each other, illustrates the extreme caution exercised in this election. Trouble was evidently expected.

[2] This is Hugh of Northwold, according to the *Cronica Buriensis* (*Mem.* iii. 12).

securitatis permansuras, quarum fidele transcriptum sanctitati
uestre transmitto presentibus litteris inclusum, testantur, fratrem
Hugonem de Norewolde eiusdem ecclesie monachum, uirum boni
testimonii, et, ut dicitur, per omnia ydoneum, sibi communiter et
concorditer in abbatem elegerunt. Supplico igitur pie paternitati
uestre, quatenus super negocio illo quod maliciose impediri
creditur consummando uestra uelit pietas facere quod rationi
uiderit conuenire; ita, si ei placet, prouisura quod ecclesie Anglicane libertas in exemplo facti huius⟨modi⟩ robur suscipiat et
incrementum.
Valeat, etc.

3. *See above*, p. 37

Innocentio Dei gratia summo pontifici E(ustachius) Eliensis
ecclesie minister humilis salutem.

In conspectu beatitudinis uestre, sicut audeo, supplices preces
et attentas effundo, quatenus ob reuerenciam gloriosi et incliti regis
et martyris electionem de pastore monasterii eiusdem factam,[a] que,
sicut publice dicitur et certissime creditur, canonice et de persona
ydonea facta est, uestre discrecionis eximia prudentia diligenter
intendere dignum ducat, ne emulatorum et libertatis ecclesiastice
iugulatorum astucia apud sedem iustitie, in qua, Domino nostro
Ihesu Christo, cuius locum tenetis in terris, disponente, sedetis,
ualeat quod sincerum est incassari, et quod ad conseruandum
electionum libertatem prouido et salubri consilio prouisum est,
cuiuscunque commercio et suggestione composita immutari.
Valeat, etc.

[a] facti C

the election for secure safekeeping testify (I send your holiness a faithful copy enclosed with this letter), they elected unanimously as abbot brother Hugh of Northwold. This man is a monk of their church, of good report, and, as is said, worthy in all respects. Therefore I beseech you, pious father, that in this matter, whose finalization is being maliciously impeded, it is believed, you will do what seems consistent with reason; thus providing, if you please, in such a way that the liberty of the English church shall gain strength and encouragement from the example of your action.

Farewell, etc.

3. *Eustace bishop of Ely to Innocent III; same occasion as no. 2*

To Innocent, pope by the grace of God, Eustace, humble servant of the church of Ely sends greetings.

Before your blessedness I dare to pour forth suppliant and diligent prayers, that out of your great prudence and discretion, and from reverence for the glorious and noble king and martyr, you will deign to give your attention to the election of a pastor for his monastery, which was made, as is said publicly and believed as most certain, canonically and in a fit person. Let not the trickery of deceivers and chokers of ecclesiastical liberty gathered around the seat of justice in which, by the will of our Lord Jesus Christ, you sit holding His place on earth, destroy what is right, or change by bribery and chicanery what was provided by mature and healthy counsel for the conservation of the liberty of elections.

Farewell, etc.

APPENDIX II

A descriptive list of documents relating to the Bury election dispute, used by the authors of the Electio Hugonis *and* Cronica Buriensis

(Documents mentioned but not quoted by them are excluded.)

1. p. 7
Mandate of King John to the prior and convent, ordering them to send a delegation to him to choose an abbot 'according to English custom'. Dated 25 July 1213. Received 5 August. Given in full, H.

2. p. 9
Oath sworn by the three electors; clearly copied nearly verbatim, although not acknowledged. Possibly a fixed formula rather than an actual document in the dispute. 7 August 1213. H.

3. p. 11
Oath sworn by the seven electors. Details as above.

4. p. 11, and Appendix I.
The convent's charter of ratification, addressed to all the faithful from the prior and convent, testifying to Hugh's election. 7 August 1213. Text in full, except for farewell and dating clauses, C.

5. p. 13
Letters patent of prior and convent to Archbishop Stephen Langton, appealing in defence of Hugh's election. 7–19 August 1213. Full text C; slightly less complete H.

6. p. 17
Letter of 'officials and wise men' of the abbey to the abbot-elect, ordering him to return to the house. Presented to the convent for ratification, but refused; subsequently sent under the prior's seal. 20 August 1213. Gist only given, H.

7. p. 23
Two mandates of King John to the prior and sacrist, ordering them to appear before him to explain why his dues from the abbey were delayed. Received at the abbey 22 November 1213. Gist of first mandate, paraphrase of second supplied, H.

8. pp. 29–31
List of supporters of the sacrist. 23 December 1213. H.

9. p. 33
Letter of Stephen Langton to Cardinal Nicholas of Tusculum, papal legate, maintaining the validity of Hugh's election, and asking him to give it his approval. Received at the abbey 24 December 1213. Detailed description of contents, H. Noted by Major, *Acta*, p. 154.

10. p. 37, and Appendix I.
Letter of Stephen Langton to Innocent III, in defence of Hugh's election. January 1214. Text, complete except for formal and dating clauses, C. Ed. Major, *Acta*, pp. 13–14.

11. p. 37, and Appendix I.
Letter of Eustace, bishop of Ely to Innocent III; details as above.

12. p. 51
Letter from Nicholas, legate of England, to Robert, legate of France, in answer to his petition on behalf of Hugh's election. Late March 1214. Paraphrase, H.

13. p. 65
Letter from Robert, legate of France, to the prior and convent, condemning the opponents of Hugh's election. Received 19 April 1214. Lacuna in MS; what remains a paraphrase, H.

14. p. 69
Writ of Stephen Langton to the prior, ordering him to restrain those of his monks who are opposing the election, lest further discord arise between regnum and sacerdotium. Received 6 May 1214. Gist given, H. Noted by Major, *Acta*, p. 154.

15. p. 75
Letters of commission from Innocent III to Henry abbot of Wardon, Richard prior of Dunstable and Richard dean of Salisbury, constituting them papal judges delegate in the election dispute. March(?) 1214. Received in England 18 May. Complete text, except for formal and dating clauses, H. Cheney, *Letters*, no. 970.

16. p. 77
Letter from the judges delegate to the prior and convent, admonishing them to prepare for their arrival. Received 31 May 1214. Detailed paraphrase, H.

17. p. 77

Sentence of excommunication pronounced at Bury by the judges delegate, 4 June 1214. Paraphrase, H.

18. p. 79

Mandate from Innocent III to the judges delegate, ordering them to correct corrupt customs at St. Edmunds. 24 March 1214. Received 5 June. Text complete except for formal clauses, H. Not in Cheney, *Letters*.

19. pp. 81–3

Mandate from Peter des Roches, the king's justiciar, to Philip de Burnham and John de Cornard, ordering them to take the abbey estates into the king's custody. Probably 3 May 1214. Received 8 June. Full text, except for greeting and dating clauses; formal clauses abbreviated, H.

20. pp. 85–7

Record of the division made in the chapter-house at Bury, written down at the command of the magnates there present. 28 June 1214. In full, H.

21. pp. 91–9

Extracts from the records of the inquiry made by the papal judges delegate. Exceptions and Replies, followed by *Acta*, 26 July 1214, at St. Albans. Obviously the full text of the inquiry records was available to the writer. Even when not quoting directly, as here, he follows their legal jargon closely; cf. earlier, pp. 79–81 (5–8 June), 81 (28 June), although much of this is based on personal observation, as are his introductory remarks to the documents from the St. Albans sitting. H.

22. p. 99

Letters of the judges delegate to King John, ordering him to assent to Hugh's election, or else give his reasons why not by a fit representative. Shortly after 26 July 1214. Full text, H.

23. p. 105

Letter of certain Bury monks to Eustace bishop of Ely, appealing against the omission of Master Thomas of Walsingham from the number of the ordinands being sent to him by the prior. 19 September 1214. Complete text, omitting formal clauses, H.

24. p. 109

Letter of King John to the prior and convent, notifying them that he will discuss Hugh's election with them on his return to England.

Received late September 1214. Complete text, omitting dating and abbreviating formal clauses, H.

25. p. 109
Mandate of King John to Peter des Roches, notifying him of the above, and ordering him to keep the abbey lands in good order. Received 18–20 October 1214. Details as above.

26. p. 111
Acta of the inquiry at Bury, 29 September 1214. Possibly complete, in which case the writer has greatly rounded out his description from personal knowledge, H.

27. p. 113
Mandate of King John to the guardians of the abbey estates, notifying them that he has held discussions with Hugh, and that they are to keep the abbey estates in good order, until his return to England. 18–20 October 1214. Received at Bury 23 October. Complete text, except for dating clause, H.

28. pp. 117–19
Letter of King John to the prior and convent, notifying them that Hugh has done nothing to merit his favour. Received 2 November 1214. Complete text, except for dating clause; greeting abbreviated, H.

29. pp. 129–31
Acta of the inquiry at Royston, 7 November 1214. Probably complete; the writer's account draws on other sources, possibly eyewitnesses if not firsthand knowledge, H.

30. pp. 131–3
Acta of the inquiry at Bury, 9 December 1214. The writer adds little to the text, which seems complete, H.

31. p. 145
Charter of the prior and certain monks of Bury, granting the king release from repayment of a sum extorted by him from their house during the interdict. 21 December 1214. Detailed paraphrase, H.

32. pp. 147–9
Acta of the inquiry at Reading, 13 January 1215. Probably complete; the writer adds nothing to the text, H.

33. pp. 149–53
Records of the inquiry at Bury, 13 February 1215. List of those opponents of Hugh who swore that their proctors were not moved by

malice, followed by *Acta*, probably complete; the author adds nothing to the text, H.

34. p. 155
Mandate of Innocent III to the judges delegate, ordering them to reach a decision in the inquiry without further delay. 26 January 1215. Received 10 March. Complete text, formal clauses abbreviated, H; slightly better version, C. Cheney, *Letters*, no. 990.

35. pp. 157–9
Charter of the judges delegate to all the faithful, announcing their decision in favour of Hugh's election, 10 March 1215. Complete text, HC.

Of the documents listed above, nos. 1–14 are concerned with the election process and its defence; the first five of these would figure in any similar election at the time, while the remaining nine result from the king's refusal to give it his consent. The rest of the documents fall into two main groups and one smaller one: letters and records relating to the inquiry of the judges delegate; royal letters and records, including the division-lists made in the Bury chapter-house by order of the curials; and finally two letters relating to domestic disputes within the convent.

The *Electio* demonstrates that at Bury the documents relating to an abbatial election were systematically filed even before the Lateran Council of 1215, by its decrees on election-procedure, made the keeping of such records particularly desirable. Yet the Council was probably the main inspiration behind both the composition of the *Electio* and the writer's concern to document his account extensively. The author's use of documents in his account of the election process (excluding the dispute which followed), ought to be compared with their employment in the *Processus Electionis Domini Symonis Abbatis* of 1257, and the *Electio Thomae de Totyngton* of 1301–2, both election accounts of Bury abbots.[1] The latter opens with the sending of messengers to the king for permission to elect, together with the text of the letter which accompanied them.[2] No such letter is mentioned by the writer of the *Electio Hugonis*, although it probably existed, just as there may have been a written reply from the king, like that given in the *Electio Thomae*.[3] The monks of Bury did not seek the permission of Henry III for the election of Simon de Luton, nor his confirmation after it; the *Electio Symonis* opens with a letter of the prior and convent to all the faithful announcing the death of Abbot Walpole and notifying the procedure to be adopted for the election of a successor.[4] A letter to the same effect

---

[1] *Mem.* ii. 253–9, 299–323.   [2] Ibid., p. 300.   [3] Ibid., p. 301.
[4] Ibid., p. 253.

appears in the *Electio Thomae*,[1] after the king's permission had been obtained, and there probably existed such a letter in the case of Hugh, although it passes unmentioned in the *Electio*. All three elections proceeded according to the *via compromissi*, and in the two later accounts appear letters of commission to those monks who were chosen by the chapter as electors. In 1257 seven monks were chosen, who elected the abbot directly,[2] but in 1301 these seven themselves issued letters of commission to the cellarer, who was to make formal election of the candidate whom they had chosen.[3] The writer of the *Electio Hugonis* mentions an oath taken by the chapter, whose words are similar to the letter of commission in the *Electio Symonis*.[4] Very probably it existed in a written form also. After this the two later accounts give the text of the formal announcement of the election of the abbot elect,[5] and then the convent's charter of ratification.[6] Neither of these appears in the *Electio Hugonis*, but the last at least certainly existed, since it is given in the *Cronica Buriensis*.[7] After this all similarity between the *Electio Hugonis* and the other accounts ceases, since they proceed relatively smoothly. The rest of the documents which they cite concern the seeking and final obtaining of papal consent to the elections.

Unlike the *Electio Hugonis* the two later accounts give the texts of all documents in the process; their purpose, more closely bound up with the Lateran decrees than the *Electio*'s, is purely legal, to exemplify the canonicity of the procedure. Hence there is only a minimum of narrative; they are little more than highly specialized cartularies. The author of the *Electio Hugonis*, however, is presenting not so much a case as a moral tale, and has selected documents from a larger collection to illustrate it. His chronicle is polemical rather than legal; it is confessedly for the edification of later generations of monks, to dissuade them from the course adopted by Hugh's opponents. Hence documents are cited to give credence to his statements, rather than to exemplify the election-procedure at every stage.

[1] Ibid., pp. 302–3.   [2] Ibid., p. 254.   [3] Ibid., p. 305.
[4] See above, p. 11, and *Mem.* ii. 254.
[5] Ibid., pp. 254, 305–6.
[6] Ibid., pp. 254–5, 306–7.
[7] *Mem.* iii. 14; see above, Appendix I, no. 1 and n. 1.

APPENDIX III

A list of monks of St. Edmunds mentioned in the text, with biographical information relevant to the inquiry pursued in the introduction.

Footnotes are to sources other than the text of the *Electio*. Surnames referring to places of birth have been normalized according to the *Concise Oxford Dictionary of English Place-Names*, ed. E. Ekwall (Oxford, 3rd edn., 1947).

A. *The Opposing Party*

A. Scot; born Scotland or Ireland? But perhaps local.[1]

Adam foster-child of Hugh.

Adam, infirmarer from *c.* 1189–1200,[2] until 24 April 1215. Possibly also abbot's chaplain *c.* 1182–1200.[3] Guardian of cellary manors from 24 April 1215. Subprior some time between 1217 and 1220.[4] Son of John of the infirmary, who held land at Rougham, Suffolk.[5]

Alan of Wales.

Albinus, subprior. Dead before *c.* 1217–20?[6]

Edmund.

Geoffrey of Graveley; born Cambs. or Herts. Brother of Robert of Graveley (see below). Ordained 1213.

Gregory, succentor by 28 June 1214; precentor 1217–*c.* 1230,[7] then sacrist, *c.* 1230–4,[8] and finally prior until his death in 1242.[9] Born Herts., near St. Albans.[10]

H. of Bradfield; born Norfolk or Suffolk.

Henry of London; a priest.

---

[1] Cf. *Kalendar*, pp. 6, 27, 43, where this surname appears.

[2] Ibid., pp. 124, 141, 168.

[3] Ibid., p. 88.

[4] He witnesses a charter of Abbot Hugh in that capacity along with Prior Herbert and Richard (de L'isle), sacrist; B.M. MS. Add. 34689, ff. 18ᵛ–19.

[5] *Kalendar*, pp. 18, 167, 168.

[6] Since he was succeeded in office during that period by Adam; Oxford Bodleian Library Charter Suffolk A.1, 48.

[7] *Mem.* ii. 294. He is found as precentor between 1220 and 1222, when he witnessed a charter of Abbot Hugh in that capacity along with Prior Richard and Richard (of Newport) the sacrist (B.M. MS. Add. 34689, f. 18ᵛ). He must have taken up office in 1217, when Richard de L'isle the precentor became sacrist (see below).

[8] *Mem.* ii. 294.   [9] *Bury Chronicle*, pp. 8, 12.   [10] *Mem.* ii. 294.

Henry of Lynn; born Norfolk.

Henry Rufus. Old. Perhaps the brother of Roger Rufus? (see below.)

Herbert; subrefectorer by 28 June 1214.

Herbert; prior from 1200[1] until his death, 10 September 1220.[2]

Jocelin; almoner, probably from the late 1180s.[3] Elderly.

John of Diss; a monk of Bury before 1198,[4] a guardian of cellary manors after 24 April 1215. Born Norfolk.

Osbert or Osbern; prior's chaplain by December 1214, perhaps in succession to Master Nicholas (see below).

Peter of Tivetshall; associated with the cellary after 24 April 1215. Born Norfolk.

Peter of Wordwell; born Suffolk.

Philip; appears in a charter of Abbot Samson, c. 1211.[5] Young.

Richard de L'isle;[6] precentor from c. 1186[7] and abbot's chaplain as well c. 1200–11.[8] Later sacrist, 1217–20,[9] prior 1220–2,[10] then abbot of Burton 1222–9, finally abbot of St. Edmunds, 1229–33.[11] Born Ely.

Richard of Newport; subsacrist from at least late 1214, sacrist from 1220.[12] Born Essex or Berks., died c. 1230.[13]

Richard of Stortford or the Bald; young, born Essex or Herts.

Richard Taillehaste. Local?[14]

Robert of Graveley; sacrist after 1206;[15] possibly subsacrist 1200.[16] After 1217 abbot of Thorney,[17] dying in 1236.[18] Born Cambs. or Herts.[19]

Roger Rufus; perhaps the brother of Henry Rufus? (see above.)

Roger of Stanham; born Norfolk.

Solomon.

Thomas the Goat.

W. the lay-brother.

---

[1] *JB*, p. 128.   [2] *Bury Chronicle*, p. 4.

[3] *JB*, p. 68; *Kalendar*, p. 90.   [4] *JB*, p. 115.

[5] *Kalendar*, p. 154.

[6] Named Richard alone in the *Electio*, but as all the others of that name have surnames, by elimination this must be the de L'isle who appears as a Bury monk both before and after the period of the dispute (see below).

[7] *Kalendar*, p. 98, etc.   [8] Ibid., pp. 90, 162, 163, 166.

[9] *Mem.* ii. 293; *Bury Chronicle*, pp. 4–5.

[10] Ibid., p. 4. The *Gesta Sacristarum* (*Mem.* ii. 293) does not mention that he held this office.

[11] *Bury Chronicle*, pp. 7–8.   [12] *Mem.* ii. 293.

[13] Since he was succeeded by Gregory, who 'cum ibidem non diu stetisset' (*Mem.* ii. 294) became prior in 1234 (see above).

[14] Cf. *Kalendar*, pp. 83, 147, for a Henry Taillehaste.

[15] Ibid., p. 90; *Mem.* ii. 293.

[16] *Kalendar*, p. 112.   [17] *Rot. Litt. Claus.*, p. 347.

[18] *Monasticon*, ii. 595.

[19] Probably the former, since Thorney is in Cambs., and this might account for his election to the abbacy there.

W. du Bois. Too common a name to be localized, but possibly from Suffolk.[1]

W. or Robert (if they are not separate people), priest of St. Saviour's hospital; associated with the cellary after 24 April 1215.

Walter Gale; subsacrist by February 1214, until 25 May–28 June; infirmarer after 24 April 1215. Out of office *c.* 1217–20.[2]

William Mothes.

William of Stanhope; pittancer from at least May 1214 until the next year, and also(?) subchamberlain after 28 June 1214. Born Norfolk.

B. *The Defending Party*

Alan of Brooke; born Norfolk.

Master Alan of Walsingham; born Norfolk.

Charles.

Guy; possibly precentor after 1234, in which case literate.[3]

Master Henry of Ely.

Hugh of Hastings; born Suffolk.[4]

Hugh of Northwold; professed 1202,[5] subcellarer before election as abbot. Bishop of Ely 1229–54.[6] Born Norfolk. (See Appendix V.)

Hugh of Thetford; abbot's chaplain *c.* 1220–22.[7] Born Norfolk.

James.

Jocelin of the Altar (*al.* of Brakelond); cellarer 1198–1209,[8] and previously abbot's chaplain, guest-master and subcellarer.[9] Elderly and literate.[10] Born Bury.

John of Lavenham; 'firmarius' from August 1212 until May 1214 at least. Born Suffolk.

John of St. Edmunds; born Bury.

Joseph; abbot's chaplain some time between 1217 and 1220.[11]

Young Maurice.

Master Nicholas of Dunstable; professed not long before 1211.[12] By

---

[1] Cf. *Kalendar*, p. 148, where a Robert de Bosco appears.

[2] Since he was succeeded by Master Nicholas within this period; Bodl. Ch. Suff. A.1, 48 (see below).

[3] B.M. MS. Add. 34689, f. 19ᵛ. 'Scribi fecit' Cambridge Pembroke College MS. 94, and B.M. MS. Roy. 2 E. ix.

[4] A local family of importance, the de Hastings claimed the office of abbey steward by hereditary right by the end of the 12th century; *Kalendar*, pp. l–li.

[5] *Mem.* ii. 10.   [6] *Bury Chronicle*, pp. 7, 19.

[7] He witnesses a charter of Abbot Hugh in this capacity, along with Prior Richard and Richard the sacrist; B.M. MS. Harl. 743, f. 142.

[8] *Kalendar*, pp. 90, 95, 129.   [9] *JB*, pp. 26, 35, 114, 129.

[10] Professed 1173 (ibid., p. 1); wrote the *Cronica* and a lost *Vita S. Roberti*.

[11] He witnesses a charter of Abbot Hugh in this capacity along with Prior Herbert and Richard the sacrist; Bodl. Ch. Suff. A.1, 48.

[12] *Kalendar*, p. 154.

1212 prior's chaplain; infirmarer *c.* 1217–20,[1] and cellarer during the same period.[2] Perhaps abbot's chaplain after 1222.[3] Born Beds.

Nicholas Roman; born Rome?

Nigel.

Young Peter of Lynn; cellarer 1209.[4] Born Norfolk.

Peter of Worthstead; cellarer from 1212; warden of St. Saviour's hospital after 24 April 1215 and infirmarer between 1217 and 1220.[5] Born Norfolk.

R. of Oxford.

Ralph.

Ralph of London.

Ranulf

Richard de Flamvill; born Suffolk.[6]

Richard of Hingham; born Norfolk.

Richard of Saxham; subcellarer by 1214, deposed 16 May; also 'firmarius'. Warden of St. Saviour's hospital after 1220.[7] Still alive after 1234.[8] Born Suffolk.

Robert; chamberlain since *c.* 1206[9] and perhaps still in office after 1222,[10] having been briefly precentor in 1205.[11] Probably third prior *c.* 1217–20,[12] and perhaps subprior after 1234.[13]

---

[1] As infirmarer he witnessed a charter of Abbot Hugh along with Prior Herbert and Richard the sacrist (Cambridge University Library MS. Ff. 2. 33, f. 129).

[2] As cellarer he witnessed a charter along with Prior Herbert and Sacrist Richard; Bodl. Ch. Suff. A.1, 48. Presumably his term as cellarer followed that as infirmarer. He was out of office before *c.* 1220–2, during which time he was succeeded by Henry; Cambridge University Library MS. Add. 6006, f. 51.

[3] A Nicholas certainly witnesses one of Abbot Hugh's charters in this capacity, along with Prior Henry and Richard the sacrist (B.M. MS. Lansdowne 416, f. 80), but this may be Nicholas of Warwick, who became sacrist after 1234 (*Mem.* ii. 294). A chaplaincy was a very junior obedientiary position, generally offered to young monks who had not previously held an office.

[4] *Kalendar*, pp. lii–iii.

[5] In this capacity he witnesses a charter along with Prior Herbert and Sacrist Richard; Bodl. Ch. Suff. A.1, 48.

[6] Robert de Flamvill was abbey steward 1180–2, 1188–98 (*Kalendar*, p. li).

[7] He witnesses a charter of Hugh's reign in this capacity; Bodl. Ch. Suff. A.1, 49.   [8] He witnesses a charter along with Prior Gregory; Bodl. Ch. Suff. A.1, 35.

[9] *Kalendar*, pp. 90, 155.

[10] He witnesses a charter along with Prior Henry, who came into office in that year (*Bury Chronicle*, p. 4; B.M. MS. Add. 34689, ff. 24ᵛ–25). However, a certain Richard held this office between *c.* 1217 and 1220 (Bodl. Ch. Suff. A.1, 48), and Master Thomas of Walsingham *c.* 1220–1222 (see below). There may therefore have been two Roberts holding this office at different times.

[11] *Kalendar*, p. 92.

[12] A Robert witnesses a charter as third prior along with Prior Herbert and Richard the sacrist; Bodl. Ch. Suff. A.1, 48.

[13] A Robert subprior witnesses a charter along with Prior Gregory; Bodl. Ch. Suff. A.1, 35.

Robert of St. Botolph; born Norfolk.

Roger FitzDrew; guest-master after 24 April 1215. Born Suffolk.[1]

Roger of Northwold; refectorer. Born Norfolk.

Simon of Walsingham. Literate, the cousin of Master Thomas of Walsingham (see below), and perhaps elderly.[2] Pittancer during Hugh's reign.[3] Born Norfolk.

Master Thomas of Beccles; third prior; born Suffolk. Out of office *c.* 1217–20.[4]

Master Thomas of Walsingham; ordained 1213. Warden of St. Saviour's hospital before 1220.[5] Chamberlain *c.* 1220–22.[6] Born Norfolk.

William of Diss; a monk of Bury before 1198,[7] abbot's chaplain after *c.* 1206,[8] and sacrist for four days only towards the end of Samson's reign.[9] Still alive after 1215.[10] Literate,[11] born Norfolk.

Young William of Stanhoe; born Norfolk.

William of Thompson; born Norfolk.

John, afterwards abbot of Hulme, cannot be assigned a side in the dispute, as he was elected abbot soon after August 1214, dying later in the same year.[12]

---

[1] Richard FitzDrew, who had several sons, was a local man of means in the 1180s. *Kalendar*, pp. 22, 27, 78, 82; *JB*, p. 45.

[2] He composed an extant poem on St. Faith in which he states his relationship to Thomas; D. Legge, *Anglo-Norman in the Cloister* (Edinburgh, 1950), p. 11. He would have to be of advanced years if he was the 'Simon pictor' who painted the abbot's throne before 1200 (*Kalendar*, pp. lii–iii; *Mem.* ii. 291), but this man was probably a professional.

[3] B.M. MS. Harl. 27, f. 76ᵛ.

[4] He was succeeded during this period by Robert (see above).

[5] In this capacity he witnesses a charter along with Prior Herbert and Sacrist Richard; Bodl. Ch. Suff. A.1, 48. Presumably he was succeeded by Richard of Saxham (see above).

[6] He witnesses a charter in this capacity along with Prior Richard and Richard the sacrist; B.M. MS. Harl. 743, f. 142.

[7] *JB*, p. 138.

[8] *Kalendar*, pp. lii–iii.

[9] *Mem.* ii. 293.

[10] He witnesses a charter of Abbot Hugh, together with Hugh of Hastings; 'Warkton Book', MS. in the collection of the Duke of Buccleugh, p. 5.

[11] 'Scribi fecit' Cambridge Pembroke College MS. 27 and B.M. MS. Roy. 7 C.v. He also wrote a short addendum to Jocelin's Chronicle (*JB*, pp. 138–9).

[12] Knowles, Brooke and London, *Heads of Religious Houses*, pp. 68–9.

APPENDIX IV

The Meeting of the Rebel Barons at St. Edmunds, November 1214

In the introduction it was suggested that Hugh could have been in contact with Stephen Langton and the barons concerning their proposed meeting at St. Edmunds which, as it was *quasi orationis gratia*,[1] probably took place on the feast of St. Edmund, 20 November 1214. But such an authority as Professor Holt is inclined to doubt the importance, possibly the very existence of this famous gathering.[2] Firstly, its purpose seems a mere repetition of that which Wendover gives for the council held at London, 25 August 1213, when Langton supposedly revealed the newly discovered coronation charter of Henry I to the assembled barons.[3] Yet what is inconsistent about the idea of more than one such showing? It could, for instance, have been repeated for the benefit of such barons as could not be present at London. Or a series of exhibitions of the charter might have been proposed, like the showings of a relic, to arouse enthusiasm in the baronial cause. In any case Holt demonstrates convincingly that Wendover's account of the London meeting, which is at variance with all others, is unlikely to be correct. If this is true, then the St. Edmunds gathering seems more conceivable and actually gains in importance. But the contemporary Bury sources, observes Holt, are silent about it. With regard to the *Electio* this is not so surprising since, as we have shown, its author was not writing a general chronicle, but an edifying monograph on a particular subject of local interest. From his undeviating concentration upon the events surrounding Hugh's election not even the most cataclysmic events taking place under his very nose could shake him. Litigation between the abbey and the burghers resulting from the king's onerous demands during the vacancy, a great fire in the vill, and a loan made by the convent to two of John's captains pass unmentioned.[4] After the king's departure from the house on 5 November, in fact, the author summarizes the sittings of the papal inquiry on 14 November and 9 December, omitting any mention of conventual affairs between these three dates. It is perhaps more surprising that no mention is made of the meeting in the *Bury Chronicle*, the first part of which, to 1265,

---

[1] Wendover, ii. 111–2.　　　　　　　　[2] *Magna Carta*, p. 138.
[3] Ibid., pp. 137–8; Wendover, ii. 83–7.　　[4] See above, pp. 6 n. 2, 164 n. 2.

was written by John de Taxter, who became a Bury monk in 1244.[1]
Twice he mentions the baronial rebellion: 'In this year [1215] about
Easter-tide the war between King John and the barons began', and
under the following year, 'The pope excommunicated the barons and
laid an interdict on England in their presence, because they had
rebelled against the king.'[2] The writer of such a passage as the last in
particular evidently regarded the baronial revolt with an unfriendly eye,
and could not, therefore, be expected to record any association of his
abbey with it. Now until the year 1212 at least, and almost certainly
until some time after 1215, Taxter based his account on the *Annales
Sancti Edmundi*, which seem to have been compiled during Hugh's
reign.[3] The statements quoted above, therefore, probably represent the
view of the annalist. If that were so, then we should not expect the
Annales to have mentioned the baronial meeting alongside them, and
consequently Taxter himself could hardly have noticed it. The *Cronica
Buriensis* also uses the *Annales* up to 1212, completing the sentence at
which they break off in the surviving manuscript and continuing in an
annalistic style, no doubt following the same source, up to and including
the year 1215.[4] For his notes on the year 1214, however, the chronicler
transfers from the *Annales* and gives an account of the baronial meeting
from John of Wallingford's chronicle.[5] He need hardly have done this
if he could have drawn on the *Annales* instead. I suggest, therefore, that
the Bury Annals did not mention the baronial meeting, and that this
can be explained in terms of the attitude expressed in the two passages
from the *Bury Chronicle* quoted above, which were probably drawn
from them. This is consistent with the approach of the *Electio*'s author,
who is at pains to demonstrate Hugh's loyalty to the king, who never
explicitly criticizes him, and who says as little as possible about relations
between Hugh's party and the barons, while making it perfectly plain
that they did exist.

Finally, Professor Holt feels that 'Bury was an unlikely venue for
potential rebels whose chief weight still lay in the northern counties'.
I do not think that it was so unlikely; as one of the greatest pilgrim-
shrines in the country, Bury afforded an ideal cover for such a meeting.
Possibly, too, the gathering had religious overtones; surely one of its

---

[1] *Bury Chronicle*, p. xvii.   [2] Ibid., pp. 2–3.
[3] Ibid., p. xviii. The Annals end, incomplete, in the year 1212 in the only
extant MS.; however under 1202 they record that Hugh, obviously the abbot,
took the habit as a Bury monk (*Mem.* iii. 10). This entry, made in the same hand
as the others, could only have been made after 1215. As the compiler did not
think it necessary to add 'abbas' to Hugh's name, the note must have been made
during his abbacy, probably soon after its commencement.
[4] *Mem.* iii. 9–11.
[5] Gransden, 'The *Cronica Buriensis*', p. 79 and n. 2.

purposes was to invoke the aid of St. Edmund, the defender of his men against tyranny.[1] It may be significant in this connection that the rebels sought to give a quasi-religious flavour to their cause. Robert FitzWalter took on the title of 'Marshal of God and His Holy Army'.[2]

But a more positive case for the existence of this meeting can be constructed. Firstly, the *Electio* states that on the vigil of the saint's passion, 1213, 'Archbishop Stephen came to St. Edmunds, led there by devotion and veneration.'[3] Also present were Earl Roger Bigod, later to be one of the leaders of the rebellion, and 'many clerks, laymen, and monks from other houses'.[4] On this feast, second in importance only to that of St. Thomas of Canterbury, the same men would almost certainly be present in the following year. Robert FitzWalter, who held service of one knight within the area of the abbot's jurisdiction, would probably also make the pilgrimage as a matter of course.[5] In other words, all political considerations aside, it would be strange if Langton, Bigod (the saint's hereditary standard-bearer),[6] FitzWalter, and other eminent East Anglians did not meet at Bury on the feast of St. Edmund, 1214. Secondly, Wendover is not the only contemporary writer to mention this meeting. The other is the author of the second part (1199–1220) of the *Chronique de l'Histoire des Ducs de Normandie*.[7] Admittedly, this chronicler did not come to England until late in 1215, but his information is respected as generally reliable.[8] His brief account of the meeting is obviously not dependent on Wendover's, and is carefully worded; the chronicler's information was evidently thin, but his guarded attitude inspires confidence. He gives the council's date as following John's return to England after Bouvines; he does not give its venue, presumably because he did not know it. But he does give a short list of barons present, explicitly noting that some were from the north: Saer de Quency, Gilbert de Clare, Geoffrey de Mandeville, Robert de Ros, Eustace de Vesci, Richard de Percy, William de Mowbray, Roger de Montbegon, and 'many others'. He does not mention the presence of the archbishop, but does give the main decision resolved upon: to make John observe the terms of Henry I's charter. The diffidence with which the list of names is offered suggests that it is no mere invention, but has its basis in the limited information available to the chronicler in England a year or more later. There seems no reason not to accept it,

---

[1] Davis, 'The monks of St. Edmund', p. 228.
[2] *Magna Carta*, p. 139. Cf. Coggeshall, *RS*, p. 171.
[3] See above, p. 21.   [4] Ibid., p. 23.
[5] *JB*, p. 121. Other rebels, Robert de Vere and Simon de Pattishall also held knights' fees within the lands of St. Edmund (ibid., pp. 120–1).
[6] See above, p. 88 n. 1.
[7] Ed. F. Michel (*Société de l'histoire de France*, Paris, 1840), pp. 145–6.
[8] Ibid., pp. l–lv; Painter, p. 286.

in which case not only does it support the existence of the meeting, but also affirms its importance. It was evidently more than a merely local affair, since most of the men named in the *Chronique* are in fact northerners. The implications of this for our understanding of *Magna Carta* cannot be assessed here; the way in which it reflects on the relations between Hugh's followers and the baronial party is examined in the introduction.

APPENDIX V

Hugh of Northwold

A FULL biography of Hugh of Northwold, with an appropriate assessment of his role in contemporary affairs of Church and state, would be
the subject of an extended monograph, and would have to be preceded
by a thorough study of the Bury and Ely cartularies.[1] Here I propose
only to attempt an outline sketch, correcting and supplementing the
account in the *Dictionary of National Biography*.[2]

About the year 1200, Jocelin of Brakelond wrote: '[If I live to see
another vacancy,] it will be my counsel that we should choose one who
is not too good a monk or too good a clerk, nor yet too ignorant or too
weak, lest, if he knew too much, he should be too confident in himself
and his opinions and disdain others, or, if he be too stupid, should be
a reproach to the rest of us. "The middle way is safest." '[3] This might
well have been the criterion by which he and the other six electors fixed
on Hugh of Northwold in 1213.

Little is known of Hugh before his election to the see of Ely in 1229.
His parents were Peter and Emma of Northwold, evidently people of
substance, since they were remembered as generous benefactors to the
abbey.[4] Hugh was not an only child, for although nothing is known of
his brothers or sisters, he had a niece and two nephews. One nephew,
William, and the niece, Lucy, resided in Bury.[5] The other nephew,
Nicholas, is well known, although his relationship to Hugh has not
until now been recognized.[6] He was archdeacon of Ely about the middle

---

[1] I have myself had occasion to examine all of the Bury cartularies, with rather
meagre results; not many of Hugh's charters survive (about 24), as compared
with his immediate successors' and predecessors'.

[2] Ed. S. Lee, xiv (London, 1895), pp. 648–50.   [3] *JB*, p. 15.

[4] They are named in a list of 'sonitus per annum' in Douai Bibliothèque de
la Ville MS. 553 ('Registrum Coquinariae'), f. 6ᵛ.

[5] William 'nephew of Abbot Hugh' witnesses a charter along with Simon of
Walsingham, pittancer; B.M. MS. Harl. 27, f. 76ᵛ. The half-erased opening
line of a letter from 'Lucy of St. Edmunds' to her brother Nicholas archdeacon
of Ely (see below) is found in a Bury library-book, B.M. MS. Roy. 10 B.xii,
f. 25.

[6] The relationship is stated in a late-14th-century note in B.M. MS. Harleian
1005 (H), f. 42: 'Note that Elias of Cowling the chaplain celebrates mass at
the altar of St. Edmund the confessor behind the chapel of St. Robert for the
souls of Hugh of Northwold bishop of Ely and earlier abbot of St. Edmunds,
and of Nicholas bishop of Winchester, nephew of the same Hugh, bishop and

of the century, later becoming bishop of Worcester and Winchester, and chancellor to Henry III.[1] His career is of great interest in relation to Hugh's, firstly, because it suggests that Hugh's family was both able and wealthy; secondly, because Nicholas's later political attitudes, notably his sympathy with the baronial cause under Henry III, bear the stamp of his uncle's influence.

Hugh can hardly have been out of his twenties when he professed as a Bury monk in 1202.[2] This date, and that he subsequently became sub-cellarer,[3] is all that is known of him before his election as abbot. Apart from a brief and conventional eulogy,[4] the writer of the *Electio* does not direct his attention to Hugh's character, and provides the reader with little information about his personality. One can only infer that he was a man courteous but firm; fair, as evidenced by his promotion to obedientiary positions of some of his erstwhile opponents;[5] capable of righteous anger, as in his sharp rebuke to the sacrist.[6] That he was a conscientious and able administrator in the best Bury tradition is suggested by the survey of the abbey property which he ordered in 1215.[7]

The period of his abbacy is, to say the least, obscure. Few records from his reign survive, fewer still are in print.[8] What evidence there is indicates that he conferred a certain measure of prosperity on the house. It is known that a vigorous building programme was carried on,[9] and that he was a generous benefactor to the convent, who singled out his anniversary for the rare honour of a 'magnus sonitus'.[10] He took a small

---

abbot, and for the souls of all benefactors of the church of St. Edmunds, living or departed. For this Bishop Nicholas gave to the high altar of St. Edmunds a beautiful enamelled chalice for use at the daily mass.'

[1] *Dictionary of National Biography*, vi. 762–4. [2] *Mem.* ii. 10.
[3] See above, p. 9 n. 5. [4] See p. 11 n. 5. [5] See pp. 165–7.
[6] See p. 129. [7] See p. 167.
[8] His charters, the more important of which are cited in this work, are scattered thinly through most of the surviving Bury cartularies. All other extant evidences are quoted here.

[9] *Mem.* ii. 293–4. It is not usually realized that a new cloister was begun under Hugh (see below).

[10] Douai Bibliothèque de la Ville MS. 553, f. 8ᵛ; the passage deserves to be translated in full: '*Magnus sonitus* for Abbot Hugh II, later bishop of Ely. He gave the convent a chasuble ornamented with fine gold and precious stones, a cope of particoloured cloth, and 7m. 6s. 8d. for the mending of another. Also eight large dishes and six small ones, and eight silver salt-cellars weighing £16. 12s. for the use of the convent in the refectory. Also he assigned to the convent 60s. annual rent which his predecessors had had from the manor of Ingham, and 50 marks for the commencement of the new cloister. He also gave the convent the first part of a very precious Bible and procured many other good things for us. He is buried honourably at Ely, at the feet of St. Etheldreda. He also returned to the convent £100 which was their's by right, since they had loaned it to him,

part in the affairs and governance of the realm, being created itinerant justice for Norfolk in 1227.[1] Together with the abbot of St. Albans he presided at the first General Chapter of Benedictine monks for Canterbury province, held at Oxford in 1218–19.[2] But it is only as a bishop that he emerges as a first-class administrator and prominent civil servant. About 1230 he adopted a rent-raising policy on his episcopal estates, managing nearly to double some by 'acquiring new and growing franchisal powers which, although exercised on the king's behalf, could be used for private profit.'[3] A careful farmer, he ordered a complete survey of the bishop's manors, and had halls built on many of them to facilitate easy visitation.[4] By astute bargaining he succeeded in doubling his knights' scutage, and augmented the revenues of the see by purchase of manors and advowsons.[5]

Although, as mentioned earlier, Hugh was never merely a king's man, he could not escape the obligations of his high office.[6] His life was a constant round of routine duties performed in the service of both pope and king. To choose but a few examples of many: in 1236 he was sent with the bishop of Hereford to Provence to conduct Eleanor, Henry III's betrothed, to England,[6] and in the following year he was nominated one of the royal ambassadors to the projected conference summoned by the emperor at Vaucouleurs.[7] In 1234 he was appointed a papal judge-delegate and acted on behalf of both his masters in repressing disorders in the university of Cambridge.[8]

His modest interest in education has already been mentioned;[9] but he was more important as a builder, his most enduring monument the fine retro-choir at Ely, begun in 1235 and dedicated with great pomp and splendour seventeen years later.[10] This work, 'whose quality accords with the noble character of the man',[11] marks the transition from the 'relative bareness of the Wells nave, relieved only by the capitals and spandrel foliage, to the rich elaboration of the Westminster transepts'.[12]

as may be seen from the deed of acquittance. Altogether 267 marks plus the chasuble and Bible.'

[1] J. Bentham, *History and Antiquities of the Church of Ely* (2nd edn., Cambridge, 1812), i. 146; *Monasticon*, iii. 105.
[2] W. A. Pantin, *Chapters of the English Black Monks*, Camden 3rd ser. xlv (1931), i. 7, 8.
[3] E. Miller, *The Abbey and Bishopric of Ely* (Cambridge, 1951), p. 277.
[4] Ibid., p. 77.   [5] Bentham, *Ely*, i. 147–8.
[6] Miller, p. 77; see above, pp. xlv–xlvi.
[7] Matthew Paris, *Chron. Maj.* iii. 393.
[8] *Letters Illustrative of the Reign of Henry III, RS*, i. 398–9, 430–2, 552–3, 556.
[9] See above, p. xxxviii.   [10] Bentham, *Ely*, i. 148.
[11] T. D. Atkinson, *Monastic Buildings of Ely* (Cambridge, 1933), p. 5.
[12] L. Stone, *Sculpture in Britain in the Middle Ages* (Harmondsworth, 1955), p. 124.

Essentially a generous and hospitable man, he was the friend of
Langton as later of Grosseteste,[1] and it was this side of his character
which most impressed Matthew Paris: 'In the same way as he showed
his devotion at the spiritual table, that is, the altar, . . . so at the table
for bodily refreshment he showed himself hospitable, profuse, cheerful,
and composed.'[2] Nor did he ever lose his love of the monastic life. After
his promotion to the see of Ely, records Paris, he retained both the habit
and behaviour of a monk,[3] and he reorganized and increased the revenues
of the cathedral priory and two Ely hospitals.[4] Throughout his later life
Hugh remained on friendly terms with his old abbey, giving the
episcopal benediction to abbots Henry of Rushbrook in 1234 and
Edmund of Walpole in 1248.[5] At the foot of the rich, purbeck marble
tomb of the *flos nigrorum monachorum*,[6] where he lies in his own retro-
choir, is carved the history of the martyrdom of St. Edmund.[7]

[1] *Roberti Grosseteste Epistolae, RS,* no. 96.
[2] Matthew Paris, *Chron. Maj., RS,* v. 454–5.
[3] Matthew Paris, *Hist. Angl., RS,* ii. 305.
[4] Bentham, *Ely,* i. 147.
[5] *Bury Chronicle,* pp. 8, 15.
[6] Matthew Paris, *Chron. Maj.* v. 455.
[7] Atkinson, op. cit., p. 31. The lid of the tomb is carved with a nearly life-size
effigy of the bishop in mitre and pontificals, with a crozier and the right hand
raised in blessing. Unfortunately the face has been mutilated. The carving
below his feet depicts the shooting of Edmund with arrows, his decapitation,
and the guarding of his head by a wolf.

INDEX OF QUOTATIONS AND ALLUSIONS

A. THE BIBLE

GENERAL INDEX

A. of Redgrave, Master, 152–3
A. Scot, monk of St. Edmunds, 148–9, 184
Abbo of Fleury, xvii
Adam, 52–3
Adam, cellarer of St. Albans, xiv
Adam, dean of Salisbury, 156 and n. 1, 157
Adam, foster-son of Hugh, monk of St. Edmunds, 30–1, 84–5, 148–9, 184
Adam, infirmarer of St. Edmunds, xxxix, 8 n. 4, 14–15, 30–1, 44–5, 84–5, 140–1; condemns Master Thomas, 40–1; refuses to meet Hugh, 76–7; proctor, 90–1; his treachery, 114–17; takes oath, 148–9; appeals to the pope, 152–3; refuses to accept Hugh's confirmation, 158–9; goes to the king, 162–3; made guardian of manors, 164–5, 166 n. 1; career, 184 and n. 6
Alan of Brooke, monk of St. Edmunds, 86–7, 186
Alan of Wales, monk of St. Edmunds, 84–5, 102–3, 184
Alan of Walsingham, Master, monk of St. Edmunds, xxxvi, xxxix, 86–7, 134–5, 160–3, 186
Albinus, subprior of St. Edmunds, xxxix, 84–5, 136–7, 144–5, 152–3, 160–1, 164–5; elector, 8–9; exercises discipline, 14–17, 44–7, 60–3; orders Hugh's return, 20–1; supports the sacrist, 28–9; hears appeals, 42–3; acts in place of the prior, 64–5, 76–7, 102–3; writes to the prior, 104–5; takes oath, 148–9; career, 184
Albold, abbot of St. Edmunds, xxv n. 3, xxvi
Alexander II, Pope, xxix
Alexander III, Pope, xiii, xxix, xxx
Anjou, 6–7
Annales S. Edmundi, xiii and n. 1, xiv, xxviii, 190 and n. 3
Anselm, St., archbishop of Canterbury, xxvi, 24 n. 3

Anselm, abbot of St. Edmunds, xxv n. 3, xxix, xxxvii n. 7, 10 n. 2
Aquitaine, 6–7
Attleborough, xlii

Babwell, 84 n. 1
Babylon, xviii, 28–9 and n. 5
Baldwin, abbot of St. Edmunds, xxv n. 3, xxvi, xxix
Baldwin, prior of St. Edmunds, xxvi
Barton, 164–5
Battle, Benedictine abbey of, 74–5
— abbots of, *see* Odo
Bedfordshire, xl–xli, xliv, 72 n. 4, 80 n. 4, 109 n. 3, 111 n. 2, 187
Benedict, St., *Rule* of, xvii, 10–11, 14–15, 46–7, 74–5, 136–7
Benedict of Sawston, bishop of Rochester, 166–7 and n. 4
Berkshire, xl, 185
Bernard of Clairvaux, St., 24 n. 3
Bologna, xviii–xx, 28–9 and n. 5, 72 n. 4, 153 n. 3
Bouvines, battle of, 191
Bradfield, 164–5
Burton, Benedictine abbey of, xvi, 185
Bury Chronicle, xiv and n. 3, xxiv, 189–90
Bury St. Edmunds:
— town of, 34 n. 3, 80 n. 4, 83 n. 1, 84 n. 1, 104 n. 2, 112–13, 147 n. 1, 167 n. 6, 186, 189, 193; fire at, xxiii, 169 n. 5; walls of, xlv n. 1; burghers of, 6 n. 2, 76–7; King John at, 117 n. 8, 126–7
— Benedictine abbey of, *passim*, and xx–xxvi, 18–21, 50–1, 178–82, 185, 193 and n. 6, 194; scriptorium at, xiii n. 4; historiography at, xiii–xiv; relations with popes, xxix–xxxi, xxxiii–xxxiv, 74 and n. 1, 75; obedientiaries of, xxxv; relations with kings, xliii–xliv, xlvii; vacancy at, 6 and n. 2, 7; election at, 10 and n. 1, 11, 37 n. 9, 94–5; legate at, 26 and n. 2, 27, 28 n. 2, 30 n. 2,